'SWEET WAIST OF AMERICA'

'SWEET WAIST OF AMERICA'

Journeys Around Guatemala

ANTHONY DANIELS

HUTCHINSON

London Sydney Auckland Johannesburg

Copyright © Anthony Daniels 1990

All rights reserved

This edition first published in 1990 by
Hutchinson

Century Hutchinson Ltd,
20 Vauxhall Bridge Road, London SW1V 2SA

Century Hutchinson Australia (Pty) Ltd,
20 Alfred Street, Milsons Point, Sydney NSW 2061

Century Hutchinson New Zealand Limited
PO Box 40–086, Glenfield, Auckland 10, New Zealand

Century Hutchinson South Africa (Pty) Ltd,
PO Box 337, Begvlei, 2012 South Africa

British Library Cataloguing in Publication Data
Daniels, Anthony, *1949*–
  Sweet Waist of America: journeys around Guatemala
  1. Guatemala. Description & travel
  I. Title
  917.281°;453

ISBN 0–09–173585–8

Typeset by Speedset Ltd, Ellesmere Port
Printed and bound in Great Britain by
Mackays of Chatham PLC, Chatham, Kent

Cuando sonó la trompeta, estuvo
todo preparado en la tierra,
y Jehová repartió el mundo
a Coca-Cola Inc, Anaconda,
Ford Motors, y otras entidades:
la Compañía Frutera Inc
se reservó lo más jugoso,
la costa central de mi tierra,
la dulce cintura de América.

When the trumpet sounded
Everything was prepared on earth,
And Jehovah shared out the world
Between Coca Cola Inc, Anaconda,
Ford Motors, and other entities:
The Fruit Company Inc
Reserved for itself the juiciest,
The central coast of my native land,
The sweet waist of America

Pablo Neruda

ACKNOWLEDGEMENTS

I should like to thank all those in Guatemala who helped me by giving so generously of their time. Many, but not all, are named in the text. I met with only kindness and courtesy all the time I was in Guatemala. Naturally, the views expressed in this book are my own and cannot please everyone. I hope, however, I have not mis-represented anyone and I apologise in advance if I have done so. I should like to express special gratitude to Michael Shawcross, who so generously accommodated me for so long, and to Sra Maria Elena de Ovalle, who listened to me with great patience and forbearance. I should also like to thank my editor, Kate Mosse, for all her sensible advice.

The quotations used in the text are as follows: the epigraph is from the Penguin edition of Pablo Neruda similarly the poem on p8; 'Bird of Life, Bird of Death', Jonathan Maslow, Viking, p11; *Donde enmudecen las conciencias*, Carlos Guzmán Böckler, Secretaria de Educación Pública de Mexico, p12; Introducción a *la historia agraria de Guatemala 1500–1900*, J. C. Cambranes, Serviprensa Centroamerica, p35; the poems of Otto René Castillo, Orbis Press, p38; the poem on p53 is by Sor Juana Ínes de la Cruz; El Autócrata, Carlos Wyld Ospina, p102; *Fire From the Mountain*, Omar Cabezas, Jonathan Cape, p115; Poemas, Ernesto Cardenal, Educa, p124; Guatemala, Amnesty International, p133; *The Order of the Death's Head*, Heinz Höhne, Hamish Hamilton, pp 140 & 181; *La patria del criollo*, Severo Martínez Pelaez, Editorial de la Universidad Autónoma de Puebla, p175; 'Days of the Jungle', Mario Payeras, Monthly Review Press, pp176, 179, 180, 181; Poemas, Ruben Darío, p215; *Brevíssima relación de la destrucción de las Indias*, Bartolomé de las Casas, p227; *The Volcanoes Above Us*, Norman Lewis, Century, p242. All translations, except those of Omar Cabezas and Mario Payeras, are my own.

ONE

Guatemala is a small country, known for volcanoes and cruelty. When I crossed the frontier from Mexico I alternately lifted up my eyes to the hills, and scanned the roadside for corpses. There weren't any, and I felt slightly cheated by the books about Guatemala I had read; such was the reputation of the country that I expected its evil to be immediately manifest. The *Policía de Hacienda*, the Treasury Police, stopped the bus but gave us no trouble. It was not difficult, however, to imagine them being brutal. They wore dark green uniforms of sheeny man-made fibre, bush-whacker hats and cartridge belts with many cartridges missing. They wore mirrored sunglasses and holstered revolvers that rode prominently on their right hips. Even their politeness seemed sarcastic, and when they smiled I saw that their upper teeth were rimmed with thin bands of gold which I thought sinister – for some reason I have never entirely trusted people with gold in their teeth. But in Guatemala I was mistaken for, as I quickly discovered, gold is much favoured by dentists and their clients alike, and many people have gold stars inlaid in their teeth purely for decoration.

I had come to Central America in the second half of 1987 to observe and write about the ravages of war and foreign intervention. I intended to spend my time equally betwen the five republics of the isthmus: from afar they had a unity of culture and history that tended to dissolve on closer inspection. Within two weeks of my arrival in Guatemala, I decidcd that the country deserved more than the perfunctory chapter or two I should have been able to devote to it if I carried out my original plan. By the time I left eight months later, I regarded Guatemala as a second home and was almost a Guate-malan nationalist. This is a not uncommon story: people come for a week or a month and stay a lifetime. Those who cannot stay return time and again, in spite of (or is it because of?) the political turmoil. A North American woman who returned to Guatemala at every possible opportunity was once overheard to denounce very volubly the terrible conditions and tyrannous government of the country.

'Then why are you here?' asked a long-term resident.

'To renew my anger,' she replied.

For all its years of war and incipient revolution, Guatemala remains largely unknown to the outside world, except to a small band of enthusiasts. On the world scale of things it is no doubt insignificant, a country smaller than England with a population less than half that of Mexico City and an economy one five-hundredth the size of that of the United States. Yet, as almost everyone senses the moment he arrives, Guatemala does have a significance far beyond its size. I know of no place on earth where the important questions of life make themselves felt so urgently, not as matters of abstract intellectual interest, but as matters of immediate practical concern. Guatemala is not a country in which easy suburban routine is possible. When the daily news is of kidnappings and abductions, guerrilla warfare and the destruction of whole communities, small talk loses its charms. Everyone in Guatemala, even a member of the notorious upper class with its entrenched privileges, has been through so much that it is rare to find anyone who cannot speak from personal acquaintance of the extremes of human experience. I do not believe in tragic cataclysm as a method of moulding character; yet I have little doubt there is more human nobility, as well as vicious-ness, to be found in Guatemala than in many more fortunate countries. And it is surely the sense of living on the edge of a precipice that attracts some to Guatemala . . .

There are other reasons to come, of course. Though small, Guatemala is infinitely varied in landscape: jungle, mountain and volcano, palm-fringed shore and high plateau. There are Mayan ruins and colonial antiquities. The Indians of Guatemala, who are over half the population, have exotic customs and beliefs, and each Indian community has its brilliant costume of many colours. But almost everyone arrives in this diverse and complex country with strong opinions that are impervious to subsequent experience. When first I arrived in Guatemala City I stayed at the Chalet Suiza, a cheap hotel that catered mostly for travelling bums and solidarity workers. The communal showers smelt of athlete's foot and cheap soap. I paid my money in advance and was warned by the woman at the desk (who had one eye fixed on a flickering television drama) to beware of thieves amongst the guests. An ageing North American rebel, with his greying hair gathered into a pony tail by an elastic band, was complaining loudly in the corridor to anyone who would listen that citizens of the United States and Canada required visas to enter El Salvador. They took at least six weeks to obtain; and the

Salvadoreans demanded a certificate of good conduct from the police of the applicant's last place of residence, an impossible condition for the complainant to fulfil since he had several convictions for possession of drugs.

'If the US is going to prop up these little fascist dictatorships,' he said, 'the least they could do is let us in without all this hassle.'

He received the deep-felt sympathy of the other guests of the Chalet Suiza. It was here that I first encountered a solidarity worker. After a brief holiday in Guatemala, she was on her way back to Nicaragua where she was making reparation for the policies of President Reagan. Her job there was to co-ordinate the work brigades that came down from the States for a month to pick coffee. I asked her whether she didn't think it a little odd that North American professionals and academics should come all that way to do unskilled labour in a country where labour was not in short supply. If I had said that I was in daily communication with the Archangel Gabriel, she could scarcely have looked at me more quizzically. Did I not understand that it was the gesture, not the practical economic effect, that was important here? Perhaps I should have guessed that in a psychotherapeutic culture there is little distinction drawn between doing good and feeling good.

My solidarity worker felt guilty, of course, about being in Guatemala, and guiltier still that she was enjoying it so much after the virtuous austerities of Nicaragua. The consumer goods that were available in Guatemala but not in Nicaragua were, needless to say, mere baubles; baubles, moreover, available to only a minority of Guatemalans, which made her enjoyment of them all the more illicit. But she was, as she herself admitted, the child of her culture and upbringing. Deprived of inessentials in Nicaragua, she felt tension rising within herself until she simply *had* to consume something. I shop, therefore I am. Her tension discharged, she was ready to return to Nicaragua.

But why, I asked, feel guilty about being in Guatemala?

'Because,' she replied, 'it's such a brutal dictatorship.'

I objected that Guatemala now had a democratically elected government, but she said it was only for show; in reality, nothing had changed. She was one of those people who found it easy to distinguish between appearance and reality. As an ex-psychiatrist, I had come to the conclusion that behind appearances lay more appearances, and so on *ad infinitum*. I had given up the quest for ultimate reality a long time ago and even found it hard to conceive of what it might be like when found; how did one know when one had found it? But the solidarity worker had discovered to her own satisfaction the ultimate reality of Guatemala after a stay of only a few days.

Next day I moved into more comfortable quarters, a small family hotel in a relatively quiet side street, occasionally used as a urinal by passers-by. Guatemala is a city from which it is necessary, for those unused to it, to take frequent refuge. The streets in the centre, the *Zona Uno*, are narrow and crowded, arranged on the grid pattern into *Avenidas* and *Calles*, Avenues and Streets; the main shopping thoroughfare, the Sixth Avenue, is overhung from end to end with garish neon signs advertising jeans and hamburgers. Through the narrow streets pass scores of ill-maintained diesel buses, belching black fumes like the smokescreens of old battleships and grinding their engines to sound like the bellow of wounded bulls. The fumes and noise linger; as often as not, a grey-brown pall trapped by the surrounding hills hangs over the city. Through the smog filter the rays of the sun, giving everything an uncomfortable greenhouse warmth. In Guatemala City I was breathless from pollution for the first time in my life. The diesel fumes gave me a headache and when young bloods passed by on motorbikes with the silencers removed to impress girls, I felt an irresistible urge to flee to the comparative quiet of my room. I was told – by way of consolation, I suppose – that Mexico City on a bad day is worse; that birds there, ascending into the smog, drop dead of suffocation. But in Guatemala I doubt they would even start their ascent; though in both places certain people take a perverse pride in the pollution of their environment, as being symptomatic of progress and modernity.

In the hotel, I soon found myself engaged on a delicate act of diplomacy, keeping apart some North American guests of strong but diametrically opposed political views, with all of whom I had, out of a pusillanimous desire to please, thoroughly but separately agreed. The first was a handsome and distinguished-looking man, formerly in the military. He was on his way down to Panama, he said, to meet a lady friend ('women are my weakness'). He had once been stationed in Panama, but was vague and elusive about the details of his military career, from which I concluded that he had been either in intelligence or the corps of caterers. Among other accomplishments, he had developed a mathematical formula which prevented him from losing money on the Stock Exchange (but this was before the Crash, and I did not meet him afterwards). When imparting information that he implied was not available to everyone, he lowered his voice conspiratorially: his confidences were a form of flattery. He had, he said, unimpeachable evidence that all the unrest in Central America was part of a concerted plot by the Soviet Union to seize the Panama Canal, this being a sub-plot in the master plan to encircle the United States. It was therefore essential to make the region safe for democracy by arming to the teeth all the countries that had not already succumbed to subversion. I heartily agreed.

Also at the hotel was a middle-aged couple, president and vice-president of a construction company in New York. They were good liberals: that is to say, they believed that all the problems of Central America were caused by the interference of their own government, and that if only this interference ceased, all would be well. I agreed entirely.

I managed to keep the subject of conversation at the breakfast table non-political. But all the guests held one opinion in common, namely that the power for good or evil of the United States was without limitation, and that the fate of a country like Guatemala was so wholly dependent on the actions of the United States that the behaviour and opinions of Guatemalans were, for all practical purposes, irrelevant. Many times I was to encounter this faith in North American omnipotence: a faith that survived the repeated failure of anyone to foresee what would happen the following day or the day after that.

The liberal North American construction contractors hired a car and offered to take me, by now a fully paid-up fellow liberal, with them to Antigua, the old capital of colonial Guatemala abandoned after the earthquake of 1773. It was an offer I gladly accepted, for I had fixed no itinerary in the belief that to go wherever opportunity presented itself was as good a way to see the country as any other. Before long we lost our way and made a tour of areas of Guatemala City that appear in no tourist guides. In my travels, I had seen worse slums and worse poverty, but they afforded my companions a not unpleasant *frisson* of indignation.

Like most capitals of what is somewhat cavalierly known as the Third World, Guatemala City has grown of late at an accelerated pace. When Aldous Huxley wrote of it in the early Thirties, it was a sleepy town of less than a quarter of a million, which was no more than a tenth of the country's population; but now more than one in four Guatemalans live there, and the population of the city is more than two million. It came as no surprise to me that they were not all

equally well-housed, to say the least; only the strange juxtaposition
of tin and cardboard shacks clinging precariously to the sides of the
steep gulleys that scar the land around the city, and a cemetery for
the rich, with gleaming marble monuments, immaculate lawns and
swept gravel paths, fanned the dying embers of my sensibility.

Towards the city's perimeter, on the road to Antigua, were a
staggering number of fast food restaurants, thrusting ever larger,
ever higher, ever more wasteful neon signs into the sky. This
concentration of North American-style restaurants sparked off a
discussion in our car of something my companions called Cultural
Imperialism, by means of which the United States allegedly imposed
its vulgar and shallow values on weak and defenceless countries like
Guatemala. They thought the subversion of national cultures was
deliberate, part of a co-ordinated scheme (everyone sees plots in
Central America). It was all the worse, they said, because it was done
in the name of an utterly debased, worthless, commercialised and
synthetic culture which scarcely deserved the name.

Again I sensed inverted patriotism. If it were no longer possible to
believe that everything best in the world was American, it was at
least possible to believe that everything worst was; and thus the
United States, which first brought vulgarity into the world, retained
a special mission, albeit an evil one. How pleasant to be always on
the side of the angels, and yet retain one's American passport! For
my part, I said that the success of American culture around the
world was not the result of a plot but of its intrinsic attractiveness to
the great majority of ordinary men and women; and while it might
be galling to intellectuals that people preferred Mickey Mouse ears
to Mozart, it was something we democrats had to learn to accept
with a good grace. Besides which, America's contribution to world
culture was not confined to cheeseburgers and baseball hats. So
animated became our conversation that, with the fast food restaurants behind us, we managed to miss the magnificent landscape that
opened up to us in the twenty-five miles between the new and the old
capitals of Guatemala: the slopes of the volcanoes of Agua, Fuego
and Acatenango that mysteriously seem close enough to touch while
they are still far away.

The dormant volcano of Agua is one of the most beautiful
mountains in the world, a powerful but graceful and almost perfect
cone in whose shadow is the city of Antigua. The sky, the clouds and
the light play an inexhaustible series of variations on its dark green
slopes, so that it is never the same two hours in succession and never

repeats itself, to the unceasing delight of the eye. The climate of the valley of Panchoy in which Antigua lies is equable and mild, the eternal spring of the eternal tourist brochures; the soil is so fertile and generous that the valley has long been thought an Arcadia, a Garden of Eden, except for the devastating earthquakes that from time to time interrupt the paradise years.

Yet Guatemala has a strange way with landscapes. However beautiful they may be, the political and social turmoil that has engulfed the country for so long has an inexorable tendency to complicate one's response to what one sees. In the seventeenth century a Guatemalan landowner and colonial official of the purest Spanish descent, Antonio Fuentes y Guzmán, wrote an immensely long and detailed account of his colonial homeland, the *Recordación Florida*, in the course of which he passionately extolled the fecundity and beauty of Nature in Guatemala, its exquisite landscapes, flora and fauna. But in 1971 a Marxist historian Severo Martínez Pelaez, used the *Recordación* as a touchstone of his own account of the colonial era, *La Patria del Criollo*. According to him, Fuentes y Guzmán's paeans of praise to the wonders of his native land were less the expression of aesthetic appreciation than a tool in the class struggle between *criollos* (Americans of Spanish descent), of whom he was one, and *peninsulares*, Spaniards born in Spain but given the highest posts in colonial administration. If Fuentes y Guzmán could prove that Nature in the Americas was not a degeneration of European Nature (as was frequently maintained), but rather its equal or superior, then – illogically, perhaps – it would bolster his claim that *criollos* were the equals of *peninsulares*, and therefore worthy of the highest positions of state.

At first, I found this extension of the materialist interpretation of history absurdly far-fetched. Had Martínez Pelaez never sat in a courtyard garden of a colonial house in Antigua, the cone of Agua rising above the red tiled roof, the sun and breeze spreading a balmy warmth, the air crystalline, the shrubs brilliantly flowering and a cool fountain playing? Had he never sat under an orange tree in blossom while a jewelled hummingbird hovered gently to suck the nectar for a few tantalisingly brief and tender moments? Had his vision of life become so politicised that appreciation of beauty was for him nothing but a *petit bourgeois* diversion from the reality of the class struggle?

Yet it wasn't long before I too saw the landscape in a different light, at least some of the time. Two weeks after I first read Martínez

Pelaez, I gave a lift to a fireman on his way to work as I drove between Antigua and Guatemala City. I asked him how things were these days in Guatemala, and he said they were better, *gracias a Dios*. In what sense, I asked? Well, one of the duties of firemen in Guatemala was to recover bodies from wherever they might appear, and he had noticed that these days there were far fewer bodies appearing. But in the days of *la violencia* they had been everywhere. He worked in a village on the fringes of the capital, not remarkable in any way for political activity, but even there he had had to collect fifty or so bodies, many with their throats cut or with other signs of violent death. Once he had recovered the body of a man accused of being a guerrilla, buried upright in an ants' nest. Nothing like this was happening now, or at least, not so often.

The fireman spoke without flamboyance or desire to shock, as though everything had been in a day's work. He was, as far as I could tell from our brief acquaintance, entirely normal and happy, untraumatised by his grisly work, and not at all brutalised by it either. Next day, I visited him in his station where he spent the day awaiting calls, which included those to rescue cats stuck up trees. On the walls of the station were municipal testimonials to meritorious service. What he wanted, he said, was to lead a normal life, to live quietly with his family and to give his children a chance of education. With a civilian government in power, his dream might just be possible.

But I wondered whether he would ever see again the beauty of the landscape from which he had recovered headless corpses, whether in fact anything could ever be the same for him again, and I recalled the lines from Pablo Neruda's poem of the Spanish Civil War:

> *Preguntaréis por qué su poesía*
> *no nos habla del sueño, de las hojas,*
> *de los grandes volcanes de su país natal?*

> *Venid a ver la sangre por las calles,*
> *venid a ver*
> *la sangre por las calles,*
> *venid a ver la sangre*
> *por las calles!*

(And you will ask why does his poetry/ not speak to us of dreams, of leaves,/ of the great volcanoes of his native land?/ Come and see the

blood in the streets,/ come and see/ the blood in the streets,/ come
and see the blood/ in the streets!)

Four months later, while I gave a lift to two nurses as I was driving
through El Salvador, I praised the scenery (more volcanoes). They
retorted by pointing to an infamous tree, dead and hollow but still
standing, used as a respository for corpses by kidnappers and killers.
In Central America, therefore, Neruda's lines have a certain
unrhetorical poignancy. Yet still I remembered the hummingbird at
the orange tree in flower. If love of beauty is to be postponed until all
is right with the world, surely we shall create only hell on earth.

TWO

Antigua is a charming city, though its entire *raison d'être* is now tourism. This gives rise to much disparagement among would-be explorers; Antigua, they say, is not 'real' (some aspects of reality being more real than others). It is a criticism not often levelled at Venice, however, which for two centuries has relied on tourists to keep it economically above the waves.

Antigua's charm lies in its location and the fact that it has remained almost wholly colonial. It was the seat of the Captaincy-General of Guatemala (which then included the whole of Central America and the Mexican state of Chiapas as well) until 1773, when a devastating earthquake shook its twenty churches and ten monasteries and convents to ruins, in which romantic state most of them have remained ever since. As Antigua – then called Santiago de los Caballeros de Guatemala – had only just recovered from another earthquake in 1717, it was decided to move the capital elsewhere. This attempt to avoid the wrath of God was not notably successful, since the new capital was just as subject to earthquake; but it was the saving of Antigua, which has suffered hardly at all from the dismal architectural consequences of unbridled demographic growth.

The grid-pattern streets are still cobbled and the city council has wisely restrained the commercial urge to festoon the buildings with exhortations to achieve true happiness through the consumption of soft drinks. Most of the houses are single storey, for obvious reasons, with austerely elegant exteriors, severe and massive, and huge wooden doors to keep the world at bay from the intense privacy within. How different is everything inside! The sober rectitude of the street façade suggests an owner who is a devoted and incorruptible public servant – whose model perhaps is Philip II of Spain. But inside lives the fond father, the hospitable host, the lover of nature. For every house has its courtyard with tended garden, where the only sound is the soothing plash of a fountain. Perfect tranquillity reigns, whatever tumult there may be without the doors; and such is the solace of the courtyard garden that one almost understands the lengths of cruelty to which the Spaniards and *criollos* were prepared to go to enjoy it.

Standing among the houses are the ruined churches and convents, some of them huge and magnificent, others small and intimate. Some are bereft of decoration, others elaborate beyond description; there are plaster saints and apostles out of number, many having lost their heads. Across the Calle Santa Catalina (now more prosaically known as the Fifth Avenue), is the famous arch of the convent of Santa Catalina, by means of which the nuns were enabled to cross the road without meeting the gaze of the profane. Looking from the direction of the yellow baroque church of La Merced, the arch perfectly frames the cone of Agua: a composition that no-one since the invention of the camera has been able to resist.

Not everyone is charmed by Antigua, however. Jonathan Maslow, who visited the city in the early eighties and wrote a much-praised book about Guatemala called *Bird of Life, Bird of Death*, had this to say about it:

> Antigua . . . struck me as a town that had died ages ago, and not just once, but repeatedly. Even after it was dead the first time the earthquakes and the volcanic eruptions, the plagues and the pestilences, kept right on hitting it, so the place had the quality of a stinking, mutilated corpse . . . You could smell the rigor mortis.

Of course, beauty is in the eye of the beholder and the author visited Guatemala at one of the worst times in its history. Yet I cannot help feeling his description owes more to his outlook on the country as a whole and to his determination to find in Guatemala the worst of all possible worlds than to anything he actually saw or smelt in Antigua. For in other respects, the accuracy of his information is not entirely to be relied upon. Calling himself a political ornithologist, he has remarkable powers of observation. For example, he saw smoke emerging from the crater of Agua, which has been dormant for centuries. Perhaps he misidentified it, but this is not an easy thing to do. He stayed in an hotel in Antigua that does not exist, and describes Guatemala as the largest country in Central America (it is smaller by a third than Nicaragua). He expatiates at length and with passion on the 'infamous fourteen families', reputed by him to own Guatemala, 'or those parts of it worth owning', giving a brief history of the families and describing how they intermarried to retain control of the country, until the innocent reader is boiling with rage. Unfortunately, though, the fourteen families are infamous not in Guatemala but in El Salvador – or rather, *were* infamous, since even there things have grown a little more complex. This is a small and easily comprehended error (for are not all Central Americans short men with brilliantined hair and clipped moustaches, neither distinguishable nor worth distinguishing?), but it nevertheless rather lessens the reliance one places on what he says he saw. And he is less than complimentary about the *ladinos*, the Guatemalans of mixed race and predominantly Hispanic culture who are between four-tenths and a half of Guatemala's population. There is a small number of pure Europeans in Guatemala and a smaller number still of blacks. The rest of the population is of Mayan descent, divided into twenty or more groups, who cling tenaciously to their language and customs despite, or perhaps because of, centuries of persecution and ill-usage. Antigua being a city of rich Guatemalans, retired North Americans and *ladino* traders, one can parade the purity of one's political opinions by affecting to despise it. The only Indians in the city are those who come to sell their handicrafts, sitting on the sidewalks in their brilliantly coloured costumes, occasionally to be swept off the streets by policemen zealous for the cleanliness of their city, and for the bribes the Indians pay to be allowed back on to their sales pitches.

The policemen, of course, are *ladinos*, which explains their behaviour. The *ladinos* have had a very bad press ever since they appeared as an intermediate stratum between the Creoles and the Indians. The Creoles feared them as potential competitors: Fuentes y Guzmán described them as shifty, dishonest, uncouth and a menace to peace and good government, a description that has stuck. Envious of their superiors but contemptuous of their inferiors, no doubt they did not always behave well: but what person, let alone entire social stratum ever did? There is now a settled orthodoxy about *ladinos*, who are denied sympathetic understanding by observers of Guatemala. Few are the writers who, in condemning injustice, do not also condemn the *ladinos* who are said to profit by it: condemnations that are often couched in terms that would be unacceptable if they were used of any other racial group:

The *Ladino* is the product of the rape and violation of Indian women, he was organised politically in the service of foreign metropoli, his economy is that of an intermediary, his legislation is foreign (ie a faithful copy of foreign codes), his system of education is imported . . .

The offspring of rape is here condemned for his own conception, and is accounted quite worthless, having no culture of his own and being incapable therefore of creating anything of value.

These words, which have the unmistakable whiff of a Pol Pot, are actually those of an Indian, Pop Caal, quoted with approval by the Guatemalan anthropologist Carlos Guzmán Böckler (not, one suspects from his name, a man of wholly Indian descent). Of course, Pop Caal spoke these words in Spanish and probably learnt his sentiments at university; but this should not be taken to affect their authenticity. Did not Pol Pot study in Paris?

I lodged at first with a *ladino* family in Antigua. The head of the family was a mechanic; his wife Doña Isabel (who was larger than he) kept a small shop opposite the ruins of the elaborate baroque church of San Sebastian. There she sold hard little cakes and rolls, sweetmeats and domestic trifles. They had three children and Doña Isabel's aged parents-in-law also lived with them.

The house was long and narrow, somewhat jerry-built on a single floor, with a passageway giving on to rooms on the left and to a long, narrow courtyard through an arcade of red brick arches on the right. In one of the columns of the arcade was a little alcove that lit up automatically at night, in which there was a head of Christ upon a pillow, blood trickling down His face from the crown of thorns, His auburn hair (real, I think) in startling contrast to the paleness of His complexion. Several times as I crept in late at night trying not to disturb the family, who generally went to bed early, the effigy gave me a slight turn, and, though not Catholic or a believer of any kind, I felt almost constrained to cross myself.

My room was at the far end of the house and a little separated from it. The clay oven in which Doña Isabel baked her bread and cakes was just outside, and in a recess between my room and the rest of the house slept the servant on a camp bed amongst various pieces of household equipment awaiting repair. The garage gave directly onto the sitting room, so that the front end of the powder blue, thoroughly battered family car intruded into it, as though a careless or drunken driver had crashed into the house from the street outside (I never saw the car move and suspected that it had no engine).

I took my meals with Doña Isabel's parents-in-law. They were very old: he was eighty-eight and she was ninety. He was a short gargoyle of a man who had never been tall but was now shrunken to less than five feet tall. He was rotund and of wholly Indian descent, to judge from his nut-brown face; she was slight and white-haired, a pure European. Soon we developed a ritual at mealtimes: when she came to the table, I would draw out her chair for her and she would thank me, addressing me as *joven*, young man, and she would call down the blessings of the Virgin upon me. Then, on sitting down, she would complain almost tearfully that at her age life was a torment, there was nothing she could do except pray that God would soon have mercy on her and let her die. Then she would turn to me and cackle shrewdly. During this recitation, her husband always showed signs of impatience; he dished out her food for her (of which she ate very little) and cut it up as if she were incapable of doing so herself – for she was nearly blind, or so at first I thought.

The old man was only too glad to reminisce about his long life. His grandchildren did not want to hear his stories of the old days: they were more intrigued – hypnotically so – by the North American television cartoons, dubbed into Spanish and beamed from El Salvador for several hours a day. The old man remembered everything, including the revolution of 1920 that overthrew the bizarre and paranoid tyrant, Estrada Cabrera. His part in it had been small, confined to passive presence in the crowd of students and discontented inhabitants of the capital who confronted the hated army that for twenty-two years had sustained the monster in power. The soldiers shot into the crowd, but it was too large for them and they were overwhelmed. The old man's revolutionary ardour had cooled almost at once when he saw mobs dismembering army officers. As for Estrada Cabrera, he had been a man in advance of his time: totalitarian fear was universal during his rule, when father could not trust son, nor son father, because no-one knew who was a spy and who was not. In those days, one did not speak even in a whisper. Some time after the revolution, a friend of his who was the son of an important general (later also to be president) suggested that they should join the army for, with the help of connections, they would be made colonels within six months, with opportunities to amass wealth beyond their dreams. But the old man turned the offer down, for he despised the army.

Earlier, he had been to boarding school with a boy who was later to become one of the most famous presidents of Guatemala, Juan José Arévalo. Arévalo was a pedagogue, philosopher and author of many books, who lived in exile in Argentina during the dictatorship of General Jorge Ubico between 1931 and 1944, returning to Guatemala only after Ubico had been overthrown and he himself had been democratically elected president by an overwhelming majority. His doctrine was called Spiritual Socialism, somewhat misty and mystical, but generally benevolent. His government instituted a series of reforms that was revolutionary for its time and place. While I was in Guatemala, where Arévalo still lives, I never heard any ill of him, in contrast to all the other public figures whom I discussed there.

And what did the old man remember of Arévalo's schooldays? Did the future president show, for example, precocious brilliance or signs of future political eminence? No; Arévalo was a quiet boy who was in no way remarkable, except that he had a terrible guilty secret. What was it, I asked? Well, all the pupils of the school slept in a vast dormitory and Arévalo repeatedly wet his bed. Boys are cruel and his embarrassment amounted to agony. Of Arévalo's schooldays the old man remembered little else: Arévalo was a few classes below him and there was no reason why he should have taken particular note of him. This, then, was the smallest of footnotes to history, of interest only to those who explain great events by reference to the early psychological trauma of the leaders who take part in them.

While the old man reminisced, it was the turn of his wife to display impatience. She became fidgety and agitated, and eventually began to cry. The old man would then have to interrupt his stories and lead her back to the bedroom. At first I thought her impatience was the result of senility, but I was mistaken; her supposed blindness and senility were her way of punishing him for years of marital infidelity.

I was curious as to the old man's profession, and one day he told me had had once been a rich man, owning two large *fincas* (plantations) as well as a house in Guatemala City. Although about to enter his tenth decade, he was still alert and took a lively interest in the world around him. He read the newspapers with passionate interest every morning, intoning the articles out loud to his wife as she sat on the edge of the bed. He forgot nothing of what he read and loved to discuss the latest political developments. A few days after I arrived in Guatemala, there was a nationwide strike of businesses against the government's proposals of modest tax increases, some of which would affect even the rich, something almost unheard of in Guatemala. CACIF, the organisation of Guatemalan businesses, arranged a strike by shops, restaurants and other businesses to try to make the government change its mind. CACIF had organised such strikes before, not without intimidation I was told; and this time compliance, at least in Antigua, was total, except for certain restaurants that pretended to close but had touts on the street ushering potential customers through furtively opened doors. Eating a sandwich that day was like drinking in a speakeasy in the days of Prohibition.

The old man's oldest grandson took a respite from the cartoons to have a heated discussion with him about the proposed tax increases. Old age is conservative, youth radical; but in this instance, the grandson had somehow entirely absorbed the arguments of CACIF, though I never saw him read a newspaper or listen to the news. He argued that in Guatemala any increase in tax revenue would merely feed the corruption of the bureaucracy. Trembling with excitement and enjoyable rage, the old man countered that Guatemala already had the lowest taxes in the world; that powerful developed countries like Germany and France (he included *Inglaterra* out of deference to me) exacted much higher taxes. How was the government to build the roads, hospitals and schools the country needed if it had no money to pay for them?

They shouted at one another, repetition and increased volume taking the place of argument. I wondered whether, should I reach the old man's age, I should still care so deeply about political matters, or whether impending death would make them all seem unimportant.

In Guatemala, advocacy of somewhat increased taxation puts one on the left of the 'respectable' political spectrum. Thus the old man was of the left; and I was surprised therefore to discover that he was a fervent admirer of the dictator Ubico. Since his death in New Orleans a few months after his overthrow, not much has been written in favour of Ubico (though there was more than sufficient in praise of him before). In fact, in printed sources he is presented as a monster: the man who reintroduced forced labour into Guatemala and passed the infamous *ley fuga* (law of flight) which allowed his police to shoot whomever they pleased on the pretext that the victims were running away. Arévalo plays the part of Beauty to Ubico's Beast.

The old man's opinion of Ubico was very different. The dictator was clearly the kind of man who made trains run on time. He was not by nature cruel, he just didn't like opponents. In Ubico's day there was law and order; you could leave your house open, or a suitcase in the street, in the certain knowledge that nothing would be stolen. It was true that wages were low in Ubico's day, but so were prices, and you could eat for three *centavos* of a *quetzal* (the *quetzal* was then at par with the dollar). It was true also that he introduced forced labour, but only for those Indians who were without land or employment. They used to call him *Tata Ubico*, Father Ubico, and they venerated him. He put them to useful work, like building roads. There had been no corruption in the public administration in his time, either, for Ubico detested corruption (though he once allowed the Congress to vote him a 'gift' of $200,000 in recognition of his inestimable services to the *patria*). At the time of his departure from office, there was money in the national treasury, something unprecedented in Guatemala's recent history. Only students and intellectuals hated him: had it been otherwise, he would not have been able to head parades through the city on the national holiday (his birthday) on the magnificently caparisoned horse of which he was so fond. He had needed no bullet-proof vests or windows to protect him.

It was strange how many times I heard praise of Ubico – and not just from rich or privileged people – considering the unanimity of condemnation of him in books. I discounted some of what I heard as the nostalgia of the ageing for a past they remembered as having been peaceful and free of bewildering change. But I heard the other side of the story, too, from a man who grew up in Antigua during the Ubico years. What he told me captured the fractious childishness of absolute power as well as its corruption. Ubico came one day on an official visit to Antigua, and was in a very bad mood because the City Council, in an aristocratic gesture of independence, had not asked him to sign the city's book of distinguished visitors. Furiously angry, the dictator strode across the main square, where a mason happened to be repairing the pedestal of a statue of Rufino Barrios, the liberal president of the nineteenth century whom Ubico much admired and whose distant relation he was. Visiting his anger and frustration on the statue, he kicked the pedestal hard. Then he looked down at his boots and saw they were now covered in a film of dusty lime. Ubico, a stickler for uniforms, was very proud of his boots, which normally shone like mirrors, and their defilement made him angrier still. He lifted up his riding crop, which he carried with him always, and struck the poor mason. Then the police, ever anxious to display their devotion by zealous anticipation of the dictator's wishes, waded into the mason with their rifle butts. This my informant saw with his own eyes. Yet he, too, was not without an axe to grind where Ubico was concerned: of German descent, his family home had been expropriated by the dictator for his personal use during the Second World War when he tried to prove to the Americans his adherence to the cause of democracy by confiscating all German property in Guatemala.

The old man seemed to have lived his life on the fringes of power. He was present at a famous banquet in the twenties when a powerful general was poisoned. He knew Castillo Armas, the president who led the overthrow of President Arbenz; he knew Ýdigoras Fuentes, the president who took over after Castillo Armas was murdered. Ýdigoras was an outlandish figure, hated by many for having been Ubico's chief of secret police. One day during his time as president the presidential palace came under attack from rebel aircraft. He went up on the roof with a machine gun and shouted, 'Here I am, come and get me, you bastards!' Then he waved the gun about and sprayed the heavens at random with bullets. Hearing such stories, one realises that the Latin American literary technique of magical realism is rather less magical than realist.

I thought the old man must have been a prominent lawyer to have known so many presidents. In fact, he was a nightclub owner. Ýdigoras and others were good customers of his and he prospered. But then came the locust years when there was a prolonged curfew for political reasons. Everyone had to be home by nine o'clock. His nightclub went bankrupt, he lost his *fincas* and ended up a poor man. But he recounted his losses – whose causes, I felt, were somewhat more complex than he admitted – with serenity. If an old man is without hope, at least he is without ambition.

Here I could not have been more mistaken.

The old man, despite his eighty-eight years, had his eyes on the servant girl. A neighbour told me he had a record of affairs going back over sixty years (hence his wife's revenge). Undaunted, he made advances to the servant, only to be rebuffed. He offered her money, but still she refused. Finally, he lost his temper and called her lazy, stupid and dishonest, like all Indians. His son asked him to remember his own ancestry; Doña Isabel burst into tears of humiliation. The innocent servant's days in her employ were numbered.

I had always felt sorry for her, though my pity was of no use to her. She was a country girl who had never lived in the town before, and she worked from six in the morning till nine or ten at night for a monthly wage of 70 *quetzales* ($28). An excuse for her dismissal was found soon enough. Doña Isabel left her alone one afternoon in the house and while she was away a thief entered the shop and stole a bottle of compressed gas used for the stove. When Doña Isabel returned she accused the girl of having been in league with the thief, which marked the end of her career in Doña Isabel's house.

'But the real reason for her dismissal,' said the neighbour, 'was the old man's desire.'

Within a week, I too had left Doña Isabel's. I discovered that $150 was missing from my room, and rather than make unfounded accusations or cause further domestic upset, I departed under a pretext. I was sad to go, for everyone (except, of course, whoever took my $150) had been kind to me; I was sad also because a cousin of Doña Isabel's had begun to bring me the novel he was writing for my criticism.

The aspiring novelist worked in an orphanage whose orphans were created by the civil war. It was their plight that impelled him to take up his pen. Some were too young to know even their own names; others remembered all too vividly the deaths of their parents and destruction of their villages.

His novel recounted through the eyes of a child the burning of a village by a gang of armed men. Everyone in the village was killed except the child. The author had never written anything before and read his manuscript tremulously, with the anxiety of a man who is revealing his innermost self. Disclaiming expertise, I said that in my opinion the most searing events should be simply described, for there was no literary effect as powerful as the reader's imagination. He thanked me for my sincere advice, and promised to expunge rhetorical flourish (to which writers of Spanish are particularly prone) from his writing.

My departure from Doña Isabel's meant that I heard no more of his novel, and to my regret I lost the opportunity of contributing slightly to the development of Guatemalan literature.

THREE

I decided to make Antigua my home while I was in Guatemala, the base to which I should return after my explorations of the country. I chose it because it was beautiful, it had one of the best libraries in Guatemala, and because there were good restaurants there. I have never believed in discomfort for its own sake, and I do not see who would have benefited if I had refused to eat well. I particularly enjoyed *El Sereno*, an excellent restaurant in a graceful courtyard, guarded every night by a policeman with a machine gun. *El Sereno* was therefore more than an aesthetic experience; it provided a faint and far from unpleasant tingle of danger.

I went to stay with the García family. They were *ladinos*, neither rich nor poor: they always had enough to eat but not much money to spare. Illness that interrupted their income would have been a disaster for them. The four children were without the toys whose absence might have been considered severe hardship in the North American continent. Far from being wretched, however, the children were happy with what they had, and the courtyard rang with their laughter. It was at once evident that the joy of their parents' life was to spend time with their children, playing and talking and walking with them. Secure in that love, the children needed very little else. Doña Victoria, their mother, was appalled by stories she had heard of neglect of children in Europe and the United States, of children cruelly mistreated or given no moral guidance. So bitter and self-righteous was the denunciation of Guatemala from Europe and the United States that it was rather refreshing to hear criticism in the reverse direction. The general condemnation of *ladinos* has blinded many to their good qualities.

The García family was devout, in the best possible sense. Their religious devotion was entirely compatible with tolerance. Before a meal, they thanked God for his goodness not unctuously but with the quiet sincerity of people who do not take their next meal for granted. They did not seek to convert others to their Catholicism, but neither did they wish others to disturb their religious notions. On one of their windows facing the street they had stuck a little printed notice with a picture of the Virgin and the words: 'We are Catholics, please do not disturb us.' These words were directed at the itinerant Mormons, evangelicals and pentecostals from North America who see in Guatemala a field for a harvest of souls. There are thousands of missionaries in the country, divided into innumerable sects. In the telephone directory (surely not a complete list), I counted 97 different denominations in the white pages, and more than 120 in the yellow pages.

Iglesia Adventista Central – Central Adventist Church
Iglesia Adventista del Séptimo Día – Seventh Day Adventist Church
Iglesia Apostólica de la Fé en Cristo Jesus – Apostolic Church of the Faith in Christ Jesus
Iglesia Asemblea de Díos – Assembly of God Church
Iglesia Bautista Betania – Bethany Baptist Church
Iglestia Bautista de la Zona Central – Baptist Church of the Central Region
Iglesia Bautista Jérico – Jericho Baptist Church
Iglesia Bautista Monte de Olivos – Mount of Olives Baptist Church
Iglesia Berea Misión Cristiana Elim – Christian Mission Church of Elim
Iglesia Bíblica Centroamericana – Biblical Church of Central America
Iglesia Católica – Catholic Church
Iglesia Central del Príncipe de Paz – Central Church of the Prince of Peace
Iglesia Centroamericana Díos es Amor – God is Love Central American Church
Iglesia Cerrito del Carmen – Church of the Little Hill of Carmen
Iglesia Corpus Christi – Corpus Christi Church
Iglesia Cristiana Evangélica la Verdad – The Truth Christian Evangelical Church
Iglesia Cristiana Hebron, Maranata y Verbo – Christian Church of Hebron, Maranata and the Word
etc, etc, etc.

Antigua is the centre of Catholic orthodoxy in a country where Catholicism is otherwise highly syncretic, an amalgam of Catholic ritual and pre-colonial belief. But even in Antigua only a small proportion of the excessive number of churches have been restored to use. Those that have contain the full Hispanic panoply of agonised statuary, bloody Christs crowned with thorns, Christs in robes of purple velvet staggering under the weight of crosses, Christs pale and emaciated in glass coffins, Marys with enormous brown eyes turned heavenwards in ecstasies of compassion.

In the restored church of San Francisco is the holiest shrine of the city (at least in popular estimation). It is the tomb of Pedro de Bethancour, known as Hermano Pedro (Brother Peter). His coffin is contained within an alcove in the wall, protected by a thick iron grille. Supplicants pass by, lingering a few moments to touch the coffin and ask for Hermano Pedro's intercession. Fixed to the walls around the tomb are the testimonials and messages of thanks of successful supplicants, carved in stone and engraved in brass, written on paper in pencil and ink, decorated with flowers and embroidery, framed in wood and silver, with sketches of hospital scenes and snapshots of babies snatched from the jaws of death, photocopies of degree certificates, diplomas, and the freehold deeds of tiny houses. High above, like the trophies of some victorious war, are hung the crutches that have been thrown down, no longer needed, thanks to Hermano Pedro. At first, anyone not brought up in this tradition feels inclined to laugh or sneer; but as one reads the simple votes of thanks – from Guatemalans, Salvadorans, Nicaraguans and even South Americans – one mellows and begins to wonder whether anyone can live completely without irrational hopes and fears. To read of the joy of someone who has obtained a home at last, his testimony written in a child-like hand with child-like spelling, is strangely moving; and when such a man in his letter of thanks to Hermano Pedro calls himself, his family and his home humble, he means it not just in the empirical sense but in the philosophical one too. Humility is a virtue – if it *is* a virtue – that has long fled from northern lands with their rights and freedoms.

It was a curious fact that the number of testimonials of recent date far exceeded those of fifty or sixty years ago (none was older than that). Was it that the cult of Hermano Pedro had become more popular and widespread? That needs had become more desperate? Or simply that as new testimonials appeared, old ones were removed?

At the entrance to San Francisco, on Sundays, one can buy pictures of Hermano Pedro, prayers written by him and hagiographies of him. These make him out to be a holy fool, a type always popular in troubled times (and what times are not troubled?). Hermano Pedro was first proposed for canonisation in 1697, thirty years after his death, but so far he has been only beatified. It is said against him by those who oppose his canonisation that so far there have been only two verifiable miracles attributable to him, while the rules require three. In Guatemala and elsewhere in Central America, however, his devotees are convinced he has already been responsible for many more than three miracles, and delegations of eminent men have been sent with petitions to the Vatican to pursue the matter. Probably, his canonisation is now but a short time away: the Catholic church is a waning power in Guatemala, and the promotion of the brother to a saint would undoubtedly prove a tonic.

Hermano Pedro was born in the Canary Islands which he left for the Americas when he was twenty-one, settling in Guatemala. There he wanted to enter the priesthood, but try as he might he could never master enough Latin. He became instead a Franciscan lay brother, and soon his reputation for saintliness grew. He lived in a cave so small that he had to sleep sitting up. His diet was frugal, to say the least: he was said to fast three hundred days a year and from time to time drank vinegar mixed with bile. When a well-wisher brought him delicious soup to help him recover from an illness, he ordered it to be diluted until it had no flavour. He tended the sick regardless of their social status (*even* Indians, as one biography puts it), and produced miraculous cures of horribly suppurating sores by licking them clean. He was a devoted self-flagellator, managing twenty lashes a day for years on end, and every Easter crawled on his knees past all the Stations of the Cross to the church of El Calvario while bearing the heaviest possible crucifix on his back. He promised every year to write a letter to the Virgin with his own blood as ink. At night, he roamed the city tinkling a little bell and reciting one of his own simple poems:

> *Acordaos hermanos*
> *que una alma tenemos*
> *y si la perdemos*
> *no la recobramos.*

(Remember brothers/ that we have a soul/ and if we lose it/ we shall never recover it.) His nocturnal tintinabulations did not please everyone, but his asceticism fired the popular imagination. When he died, the calluses which had formed on his knees from a lifetime of praying and crawling were sliced up and preserved as miracle-working relics.

Shortly after my arrival in Antigua, I had watched a religious procession from the church of San Francisco that gave an opportunity to the faithful to demonstrate their faith. It was the saint's day, and the procession was headed by a small truck bearing a huge wooden bier on which was an effigy of Saint Francis, surrounded by plastic flowers. The truck moved slowly through the cobbled city streets followed by devotees, who carried also a small and wobbly statue of the Virgin. Among the followers was a glorious brass band playing both out of time and tune, whose very lack of precision gave the music an expressiveness it would otherwise have lacked. But the slow progress through the streets was too much for the truck's engine and steam began to issue copiously from under its hood. Attempts at repair were unsuccessful, and there was nothing for it but for the faithful to push the truck the rest of the way. They did it willingly, storing up their treasure in heaven. The next week there was a procession from the church of la Merced. The principal float this time was carried by volunteers, followed by a strange little tricycle on which was perched a diesel generator to provide power for the fairy lights attached to the Virgin's halo. As the procession returned to the church, a large crowd gathered and many – old ladies mostly – went down on one knee, crossed themselves and kissed the thumbnail of the hand with which they had done it. The sky darkened with black clouds over Agua, though the sun still shone over Fuego and Acatenango, the former with its perpetual plume of smoke. The contrast between light and dark was as sharp as between good and evil in the mind of a Manichaean; and when some boys, bored with the procession, began to shy their baseball at the bust of Fray Bartolome de las Casas, Bishop of Chiapas and Protector of the Indians, atop a short column outside the church, the black heavens, angered by this disrespect, released carmine bolts of lightning into Agua's crater. It was a most impressive performance, just the thing to give belief to the unbeliever or rekindle the faith of a back-slider . . .

Or foster superstition, of course. The evangelical and other sects that have moved into Guatemala – by the boatload, according to some detractors – are hot against unbiblical superstition. I went to visit such a missionary living in Antigua to learn his views. Mr Brady was well known among other expatriates in the city for his general lack of intelligence, his narrowness of mind and bigotry: precisely the traits commonly thought by unbelievers – myself included – to characterise missionaries. His house was on a patch of land cleared of colonial buildings, whether by earthquake or demolition I do not know; but there was no doubt he had built a Mid-Western suburban house in their place. It was a bungalow in a spacious garden, in which were parked a car and a huge station wagon, large enough for several families of poor Guatemalans to live in, the kind of vehicle from which the death squads operated, though in this case it had a sticker on the back window proclaiming the love of Jesus for everyone. I was let in the front door by Mrs Brady, a woman whose style of dress and manner had been scarcely touched by thirty years of residence in Guatemala. She asked me to sit down, called her husband and then went into the kitchen to supervise the servant.

I looked around the room. It was comfortable, and everything had been imported from the United States. There was scarcely anything individual about the contents of the room: it was as though they had appeared by some kind of sociological imperative rather than having been chosen by individual human agency. They reflected not the character of the family but the character of a class; even the family photographic portrait, hair-lacquered and smiling, could have been substituted for thousands, if not millions, of others. There was little in good taste, or even in bad taste; there was simply no taste at all, literal tastelessness. The little plastic plaques upon the walls, with saccharine religious sentiment rendered into doggerel and sur-rounded by mauve and pink flowers, were precisely what was to be expected. There was a small electric organ against the wall, on which to play evangelical dirges, and the bookcase was filled with fundamentalist tracts and missionary memoirs with titles like *Forty Years Among the Heathen*. My predisposition against the missionary grew stronger.

The trouble with meeting people, however, is that they cease to be mere caricatures. This obvious truth became ever more apparent the longer I stayed in Guatemala: people refused to play the roles I allotted to them in my imagination. So when Mr Brady, a tall and powerful man, asked me with kindness what he could do for me, I realised that what I really wanted was for him to say something bigoted and outrageous so I should have an easy target. Naturally, I was unable to tell him this.

The best way, I have found, of getting people to say something silly, short of deceitfully agreeing with their views (a dangerous thing to do with evangelicals, since they will then assume one shares their intimate knowledge of the Bible), is to remain studiously noncommittal. This technique is usually quite sufficient for en-thusiasts and fanatics, since they cannot conceive that anyone who listens to them might not be in sympathy with them. And so I asked the missionary a neutral question about the purpose of his mission.

It was not long after that I was able to ask him slightly more difficult questions that initially might have aroused his suspicions to my motives. Was he not concerned, I asked, that the evangelicals' emphasis on personal salvation would lead to accusations of political conservatism, of tacit support for a despotic *status quo*? In the first place, he replied smoothly, his faith required a more radical change than any demanded by mere political revolution. Jesus asked that people take responsibility for their own lives, while other creeds put the responsibility onto others, 'out there'. His kitchen servant had converted and faced persecution by her husband and former friends for it, proving that conversion was no easy alternative. Becoming a Christian – he used the word in a technical sense, that excluded Catholics – was not a way of avoiding problems; on the contrary, a man who 'accepted Christ' would have to give up the strong drink in which he had previously drowned his sorrows, so that his family might live better, without fear of the domestic violence that so disfigured family life amongst Guatemalan Indians.

In the second place, he said, so many people in Guatemala had now become Christians – again, in the technical sense – that it amounted to the beginnings of a social revolution. To prove his point, he brought me computer print-outs of the numbers of the Saved, district by district. Here, with a precision any demographer might envy, were the numbers of those who had 'accepted Christ' according to the rites of his particular sect. In all, there were about 25,000, mainly in the highlands.

Thirdly, he continued, it was not true that his church approved of holding people in economic subjection. He himself paid people – his gardener, for instance – above the going rate, and his gardener had even refused an offer of employment elsewhere, because his new would-be employer was not such a good man. The gardener had changed from drunken sottishness to complete sobriety, much to his economic advantage, and only Jesus could have effected such a change.

Lastly, he pointed out that his church *was* involved in social affairs: it built schools and clinics, had reafforestation projects, and bought land for redistribution to poor peasants (who had 'accepted Christ'). But he reiterated that progress depended on a change in the heart of each individual, and to prove it he fetched the Bible – fortunately the Authorized Version – and read passages from the Old Testament prophets. From then on, with Bible in hand, he quoted from it in response to whatever I asked. He was one of those men for whom sacred texts answer every question: had he been born in Russia he would have had his Lenin; in Syria, his Koran. His education had been narrow but intense, and I felt a sneaking admiration for the way he could pluck a plausibly relevant text from anywhere in that long book.

I asked why he had come to Guatemala. He said he wanted to spread God's word to those who had never had an opportunity to hear it (a quotation from St Paul). But had not Catholicism been in the country a long time, I asked? Yes, he replied, it had; and he had nothing against the Catholic church, he never preached against it and his relations with it were good. But, alas, the Catholic church had for long set its face against the spread of God's word. Did I not know, for example, that the Catholic church had not only failed to encourage Bible Study, but until recently had actually burned Bibles when in the possession of ordinary folk? But, I persisted, why Guatemala? Were there not many people in his own country who had never heard God's word? Well, went his answer (after another quotation from St Paul), if ten men were to shift a tree trunk, you wouldn't want them all at one end, would you? Thus it was with bringing the world to Jesus.

I could think of nothing in reply. He smiled a kind of QED smile. His wife brought me an orange drink (no stimulants allowed) that had obviously been imported from the States and had lain in the sun on the quayside for some considerable time. The gulf between us was unbridgeable; I simply couldn't conceive of a state of such certainty about the way life ought to be lived that I should, on the strength of it, decamp to a completely alien land to get them to change their immemorial ways.

'And what would you answer,' I asked, 'to someone who said your conversions were the result not of a change of heart, but of awe and envy of the material culture from which you came?'

I had in mind the full-throated ease of his 6.2 litre station wagon, his inexhaustible supply of miracle-working gadgets, and even his enormous physical stature compared with that of Indians and most *ladinos*. He took the question in his stride: he was certain it was the Holy Spirit, not the zinc roofs, that changed the way people lived; though of course it was true that once they let Jesus into their lives, they lived better materially too.

It was time to go. He pressed a couple of pamphlets into my hand, one about the imminent end of the world (which one might have supposed was the pamphlet's form of built-in obsolesence), and a fund-raiser for the folks back home. Credit card contributions were accepted. This pamphlet, which had a photograph of him and his wife with their heads together like lovebirds in a cage, explained that Antigua was the centre of various pagan cults and unbiblical practices. Mr Brady was a good deal less tolerant of Catholicism in print than he had been in speech; and it is my experience that when a man expresses tolerance on one occasion and intolerance on another, it is, alas, the intolerance which is the truer. Nevertheless, he waved goodbye to me with real affability, and wished me God bless. He was not an evil man or a stupid one, nor was he intent on exploitation, as some had alleged. He lived comfortably, but was no sybarite; he was not better off than he would have been at home. Neither was he an agent of cultural imperialism. He was simply a man who, having been born in the high tide of the most powerful material culture the world has ever known, confused – as missionaries have always done – power with truth.

At one point he had guessed I was not much in sympathy with his ideas or religion, for in the middle of our conversation he had volunteered – as though it might win me over – that his theology, unlike the pentecostals', did not require the speaking in tongues as a condition of salvation. It so happened that in the week of our meeting a pair of pentecostal preachers and faith healers from Louisiana had come to Antigua, and were to hold a service in the city's football stadium. Posters had appeared all over town with their photographs, with the words 'Explosion of Health for Guatemala' underneath, and pairs of discarded crutches flying all over the place. Their service was something I did not want to miss.

I went with a North American guest of the family with whom I was staying. Her husband was on his way down from the States, bringing a pick-up truck with him to sell in Guatemala. He had done this once before and made a handsome profit; unfortunately, he had entrusted the proceeds ($5000 in cash) to a casual acquaintance of a few days who was returning to the States from Guatemala. It came as a genuine surprise to both husband and wife that the $5000 failed to appear in their bank statements. They had been counting on the money to continue their odyssey through Latin America. They were prey to innumerable disasters in their business dealings; nevertheless, like latterday Candides, they remained optimistic, and I couldn't decide whether this was admirable or just stupid. They were vegetarian food-faddists of a vaguely mystical turn of mind, believing in Energies and Emanations as though they were everyday facts of experience, like teapots or socks. She was a teacher of yoga and massage, he a chiropractor and herbalist, who used to announce at the table that lentils or carrots were good for your liver or kidneys or pancreas, without the faintest flicker of consciousness of what it might take scientifically to prove such an assertion. He had changed his name from Daniel to Kyrie because he liked the sound of it; his pronouncements on the healing powers of saffron or coriander (if supplemented by selenium or zinc) made me wish to change my name to Dies Irae.

We went, the mystic vegetarian masseuse and I, to the stadium. At the entrance were a few North American missionaries acting as stewards, their black-covered Bibles tucked under their arms as part of their uniform. 'Welcome!' they said in that tone of implacable sweetness that always implies they have turned the other cheek in advance of the first being struck. Missionaries arrived by the station-wagonful, with pale children, picnic baskets and cool boxes full of soft drinks. The Guatemalans, many of them Indians dressed in *traje*, the colourful costumes of their communities, came on foot; cripples arrived by charitable car. Everyone gathered in the one covered stand of the stadium, which faced the volcanoes, except for the cripples who were lined up on the edge of the football pitch, waiting for miracles. The start of the proceedings was nevertheless somewhat delayed by that invisible and intangible force that in Guatemala prevents anything from starting at the advertised time.

The ceremony (or performance) started with hymn-singing, led by a *ladino* whose voice was louder than the checks on his jacket. Jesus had washed him clean a long time ago, though I thought he still had the manner of a crook, or at least of a salesman with a dubious product. There were some prayers and finally the two evangelists from *los Estados Unidos* were introduced. They were a husband and wife team. She was a large lady – big boned, as patients say when they explain their excess weight to their doctors – dressed in a loose, pleated mauve dress and what looked suspiciously like a wig, shiny brown and tightly curled. Her teeth were large, white and false, and her lips were as red as a cardinal's hat. Her husband, by contrast, was a small and unimpressive man, pale and bald, who looked as though he had spent his life serving in a provincial ironmongery store.

They stood on a little dais facing the stand from the football pitch, he under a black umbrella held by an acolyte to prevent the sun from burning his pale pate. She spoke a few words in Spanish, apparently unaware that it was pronounced differently from English, so that

even I winced with linguistic pain. Mercifully, she soon reverted to
English, translated by a small girl at her side whom she could easily
have eaten. What she said was interrupted from time to time by
hallelujahs from the man in the check jacket, as well as the tinkling
of a little bell fixed to the hand-propelled ice cream cart at the bottom
of the stand. She foresaw a splendid shining future for Guatemala,
coming soon when God's word ruled there, a rule for which she
sensed the Guatemalan people thirsted. In the meantime, here was
her husband.

At first he discoursed about the end of the world, but then he got
down to the nitty-gritty. What was necessary for salvation, he said,
was baptism; but no-one could be baptised unless they had first
spoken in tongues. To prove this rather odd conclusion, he quoted a
verse from the Bible, not once but several times, pausing for
translation. I was the only one who smiled; probably the ice cream
salesman would have smiled also, had he been listening. Of course,
continued the evangelist, those who were unused to letting themselves be taken over by the Holy Spirit might at first find speaking in
tongues a little difficult. But really it was quite easy. To prove it, he
gave a demonstration. Suddenly he was transformed from a
respectable if somewhat dull man into a cavorting exhibitionist,
thrusting and jerking like a rock star (except that he was followed
round by the protective black umbrella), declaiming gibberish and
growing ever more excited as he did so. His gibberish did indeed
sound language-like, and perhaps a Chomsky would have detected
grammar in it. But then, as suddenly as he had started, he stopped;
he asked the congregation (or was it an audience?) how many of
them had ever received the gift of tongues. About half raised their
hands, and he invited the others to come down, right out of their
seats, to the football pitch, where he would teach them how to
receive the gift. Before long a throng of people a few hundred strong,
mostly Indian women in *traje*, gathered around him. At first, their
efforts were but murmurs, but under his direction – he waved his
arms about like a demented conductor – they were gradually
whipped up into a state of disinhibition, so that a crescendo of
nonsense rent the air.

Meanwhile, his wife had started a healing service on another part
of the pitch. All those who needed healing were laid on the grass
while they waited to be touched by those who had received the gift of
healing through having been healed themselves. This was what an
Explosion of Health meant: an exponential increase in the number

of healed and healers. And all that was necessry to be healed (apart from the touch) was to believe. That was all very well, I thought as I watched the healers move from prostrate person to prostrate person, touching them lightly on the head, for those who suffered from anxiety attacks, headaches, rashes, pains in the joints, palpitations and the thousand other natural psychosomatic shocks that flesh is heir to. But it was a refined form of cruelty for those with stroke, polio, and cerebral palsy who had been lifted on to the ground from their wheelchairs, over whom the healers lingered and prayed with special intensity. No doubt they meant well, but the idea that faith and faith alone was sufficient to heal any illness was cruel, lazy and stupid; for did it not mean that those who failed to recover were deficient in belief, and therefore blameworthy?

With a sudden upsurge of disgust, I felt obliged to leave. On the way out of the stadium, I expressed my feelings to my companion. I railed against the absurdity of teaching Indians to speak in tongues and the idiocy of the healing ceremony. I took her silence to be agreement. Later I learned through a third party that she had found the whole event in the stadium deeply moving, and had come to the conclusion that something of profound spiritual significance had been enacted there. We had seen precisely the same physical occurrences, yet our interpretation of them was not only different but opposite: a warning, perhaps, to those of us who think we understand at a glance the meaning of what we see.

FOUR

If events in Guatemala of no great importance are ambiguous in their meaning because people interpret them so differently, at least the meaning of the whole history of the country is clear enough, if certain books are to be believed. Indeed, this history is often written as if the entire life of the country over several centuries could be reduced to a few premises of almost Euclidean precision, and hence its future deduced with the certainty of a geometric theorem.

What, then, is the history of Guatemala? It is a morality tale, whose dénouement – the punishment of the wicked and the establishment of happiness – is inevitable but has not yet happened.

The trouble started with the Spanish. The handsome but psychopathic *conquistador*, Pedro de Alvarado, was sent by the conqueror of Mexico, Hernan Cortés, to subdue the lands to the south of Mexico, which he did with efficiency and the utmost ruthlessness. Arcadia was replaced by a system of exploitation that, in essence, still exists. Finding that the newly conquered lands were endowed with little of the precious metal for which the Spaniards so craved (though any mines that were found were worked by slave labour in conditions of indescribable horror), the conquerors soon realised that Guatemala had to become an agricultural colony. The few Spanish settlers took large areas for themselves which, by a variety of expedients, they forced the Indians to work. The Indians were left small plots for their subsistence; thus began the system of labour migration that endures to this day. On the land of the masters was cultivated a succession of commodities that enjoyed a boom in international markets, until superseded by other commodities or other producers. The rich *criollos* lived a life of gracious ease; the Indians one of wretchedness and despair.

Independence came to Guatemala not through struggle – the Spanish were never defeated there – but because, after the loss of Mexico and South America in the 1820s, the retention of Central America, never profitable to Spain, made no sense. Any change after independence was for the worse, for now the tiny local elite was unfettered by the slight control of the Spanish crown. The old captaincy-general split into five republics, each local elite brooking no control from elsewhere.

Then, in the middle of the nineteenth century, a change was forced on Guatemala. With the discovery of chemical aniline dyes in Germany, the principal export crops, indigo and cochineal, lost their value. A substitute, coffee, was found, and this proved so profitable that increasing areas came under its cultivation. The Indians were further dispossessed, and in the process a new landed elite was created, composed of German immigrants and *ladinos* who seized the new economic opportunities (and the land). It was in their interest that the 'liberal' revolution of 1871 happened; yet it was liberal only after an idiosyncratic, Central American fashion. It enacted harsh labour laws that ensured a supply of cheap labour to the plantation owners, improved the infrastructure, establishing roads, railways and telegraphs, and expelled the foreign priests who (then as now) formed the majority of the country's clergy. This 'liberal' regime lasted until the revolution of 1944 – though not without minor revolutions of its own – and included the dictatorships of three autocrats, Rufino Barrios, Estrada Cabrera and Jorge Ubico.

It was in the time of Estrada Cabrera (1898–1920) that the United States came first to exercise its hegemonic power in Guatemala and the rest of Central America. Concessions of land to grow bananas for export were made to what became the United Fruit Company, under terms so favourable that bribery must have been involved. Gradually the company (known as *el Pulpo*, the Octopus) came not only to own far more land than anyone else in the country, but to control the railways, ports, external shipping, electricity generation, telephones and telegraphs of Guatemala. It was said to be responsible for a fifth of Guatemala's national product, yet its holdings in the country were only a small part of its worldwide business. Needless to say, it did not use its great power entirely scrupulously.

In the meantime, a small elite continued to enjoy its traditional privileges, owning what the Octopus did not own. But in 1944, the students, the growing *petit bourgeoisie* of the capital and some disgruntled junior army officers (paid not as much as they thought they were worth) united to overthrow the *ancien régime*. Genuine elections took place for the first time, laws were enacted for the protection of the common people, educational facilities were expanded, rural health posts built and a system of social security set up for urban workers. Most radical of all was the land reform carried out under President Jacobo Arbenz, an army captain involved in the revolution of 1944, and who was elected president after Arévalo in 1950. But the land reform was his downfall, and the downfall of democracy in Guatemala.

Much of the United Fruit Company's land was left uncultivated, supposedly as a reserve against the diseases that frequently affected banana plantations, but in reality – so it was said – to exacerbate the land shortage that forced Guatemalan peasants to seek seasonal work. When the Arbenz government compulsorily purchased most of the unused land for the sum at which the company itself had valued it for tax purposes, it sealed its fate. In taking on United Fruit, the enmity was earnt of the then North American Secretary of State, John Foster Dulles, who was a shareholder in United Fruit and had been the company's chief lawyer. Already inclined to see the influence of communists everywhere, Dulles thought he saw the spectre hovering over Guatemala. His brother, conveniently enough, was head of the Central Intelligence Agency (and also a shareholder in United Fruit). A plot was hatched to overthrow Arbenz: a leader of a putative uprising was found in the figure of Colonel Castillo Armas, then selling encyclopaedias in Honduras; and in 1954 a ragtag army of mercenaries, supported by a few American-piloted fighter-bombers and armed entirely by the United States, invaded from Honduras. The Guatemalan army betrayed the government, Arbenz fled, the brief springtime of Guatemalan democracy ended and the *ancien régime* was restored, leading to an era of military dictators who became ever more ferocious in the suppression of discontent over the grossly inequitable distribution of land in Guatemala. Only revolution can save the day, as it inevitably will.

This, in summary, is the history of Guatemala as presented in practically all modern books – both foreign and Guatemalan – about the country. It is a version so universal that it might be called orthodox, or even official. And for any version of history to have gained such wide currency, there must have been a considerable element of truth in it. Yet when almost everyone agrees in a field where an infinite variety of interpretations is inherently possible, one begins to suspect something more than just coincidence: that the dead hand of fashion is stifling thought or original investigation. And in the orthodox version, at least as written by Guatemalans, there are curious omissions, to say the least.

The most glaring, and at first sight most surprising, of these is the failure to emphasise that in the first hundred years after the Spanish conquest, the population of Guatemala declined by between 80 and

90 per cent. In my naïve way, I thought that such a decline might have had significant effects that resonated through every phase of Guatemalan life – economic, political, intellectual – and that such a catastrophe might have left some permanent trace on the consciousness of the survivors and their descendants. But if so, it is not a matter that has much interested Guatemalan writers of the last decade or two: at best they give the demographic collapse a passing mention, at worst they fail to mention it at all.

Most striking of all in this respect is Martínez Pelaez's *La Patria del Criollo*, a volume of nearly eight hundred pages devoted to the colonial era of Guatemala. The book is famous throughout the country (though it was banned by some of the recent dictators) and has gone through at least eight editions. It is well-written, without disfiguring jargon, and undoubtedly a classic. Despite its length, however, and its copious notation and bibliography, there is scarcely a mention of the demographic collapse. The depopulation was evidently of no great interest to this materialist historian.

Why *did* the population decline so rapidly? An eminent Guatemalan Marxist historian, J. C. Cambranes, hints at the answer and then almost ignores it, as though the question were not really of interest or importance to him. He says that epidemic disease decimated the population, for the Spanish brought with them not only a new religion and way or ordering society, but new diseases to which the native population had no immunity. Instead of alleging, as one might have expected, that the treatment meted out to the Indians would have increased their susceptibility to these diseases, there is a curious passage in which Cambranes says that the predominance of Blood Group O amongst the Indians meant they were unable to form antibodies to the plague bacillus, which therefore decimated them. This is a curious passage because there is no evidence that people of Blood Group O are especially susceptible to plague, or that plague itself was the disease chiefly responsible for the population decline (almost certainly, it was not). Cambranes, otherwise a careful and even pedantic writer, gives the impression that the whole matter is one he would prefer to skate over.

This impression is confirmed on the very next page, when the author mentions the causes of the shortage of labour in colonial Guatemala:

The conquest and first century of Spanish occupation meant the death of millions of American peasants – productive forces – as a result not only of the military actions unleashed by the European invasion but also of maltreatment, mass enslavement, forced labour, famines etc.

The etc includes the epidemics. It is as though the author has been able to assimilate the fact of the epidemics only at the conscious and intellectual level, and that they form no part of his emotional picture of the world.

Why should this be? For some time I pondered the reasons for this odd reluctance to admit the importance of disease in Guatemalan history, a reluctance which grew more evident the more I read. Oversight could not explain it.

I came to the conclusion that Guatemalan intellectuals feel the need to be the saviours of the nation, that they possess what one might call a messiah complex. This arises from the orthodox version of history, which presents four and a half centuries of the past as a story of ever-worsening misery (it is almost impossible to find in modern Guatemalan texts an unequivocal statement that at any time since the conquest have things ever improved in any respect for anybody, except for the tiny elite which grew richer and richer). And because everything has always got worse, and started off from utter degradation, the present must be unutterably dreadful, hence the need for salvation. Fortunately, the means of salvation can be deduced from a few simple propositions:

The people of Gutemala are miserable.
They are miserable because they do not have enough land.
Therefore land redistribution is necessary.
But landowners will never relinquish land.
Therefore a violent revolution is necessary.

And who is to lead the violent revolution? The intellectuals of course.

They disagree among themselves over minor points, such as whether Indian culture should be fostered or exterminated, whether it is a bridge to the future or a chain from the past. But on vital issues they are agreed: that the *essential* nature of their society can be known, and that it is therefore wholly in the power of intellectuals to mould and control it according to their wishes.

Hence a factor like epidemic disease is not welcome in their conception of history, for, while undoubtedly material in nature, it is scarcely explicable by reference to the corporate or individual interests of anyone. And if it were true that such an uncontrolled and unwanted factor once played a big part in history, might not such a factor arise again? And if so, what of the role of intellectuals? Perhaps they are not needed to save their country after all.

The Chiliastic and Manichaean mentality of Guatemalan intellectuals is best seen at the University of San Carlos. This university has greater importance in the life of Guatemala than any university has in the life of more settled and stable countries. San Carlos is guaranteed, by articles of the constitution, not less than 5 per cent of the total national budget, the complete monopoly of university education by the state, and absolute autonomy in the running of its affairs. This autonomy was granted in 1945 to prevent the kind of political interference that happened during Ubico's dictatorship. But autonomy has come to mean rather more than this: no agent of the Guatemalan state may enter the university grounds, except by permission of the university authorities, who are partly chosen by, and certainly in fear of, the students, of whom there are now 50,000.

San Carlos was founded in the seventeenth century, and the original building still stands in Antigua. It is highly baroque, built round a courtyard, its rooms now hung with rather gloomy religious paintings of enormous size. But the new university is in the new capital, a vast assemblage of depressingly functional modern buildings with enchanting names such as S2 and T4, just off the *periférico*, the highway that runs round the city. Concrete does not wear prettily in an atmosphere that chokes with pollution. The campus has been provided with ample grounds, but the grass is neglected and brown, the trees stunted, and the ground strewn with empty soft drink cans.

The buildings themselves are adorned with political slogans, revolutionary iconography, posters and poems. On one wall, for example, is a painting of a radical lawyer who 'was disappeared', as the phrase goes; around him is painted a crowd of angry demonstrators, among them a woman militantly snarling, the painter having captured – perhaps more forcefully than he intended – the fact that as a political passion hatred is stronger than love. And on another mural, in the courtyard of the Faculty of Law, the students have quite unconsciously betrayed the egocentricity of their conception of themselves and their place in history: for on a field a student lies dead – evidently shot by the army – with a book marked *USAC* (*Universidad de San Carlos*) under his lifeless arm, while far in the background, silhouetted and featureless, is a mass of peasants in the 'V' formation of migrating birds, obviously following the student on to revolution. From the look of things, there is not much doubt about the post-revolutionary hierarchy. The painting is entitled *Ideas Do Not Die*.

Most of the buildings are defaced and filthy. Anyone who wants to see what the world would be like when ruled by radical young intellectuals should go to San Carlos. One building, as defaced as all the others, bore this slogan:

COMPAÑERO, CUIDE LA PRESENTACIÓN DE ESTE EDIFICIO
(Comrade, Look After the Appearance of This Building)

I glanced in at a few of the faculty libraries, and the difficulty of being a scholar or engaging in research in such a place suddenly made itself evident to me. Not only were the libraries disorganised and neglected, they were poorly stocked. The learned journals, such as there were, mouldered unbound on the shelves, and many of them were missing or stolen. As for the university bookstore, it did so little business that a notice requesting that the correct change be tendered was posted on the door. It was not permitted to browse among the bookshelves for fear of theft; besides which, there would have been little point in doing so, for in total there were no more than seventy or eighty titles available. There were more assistants by far than customers, and the books in the window gathered dust, their pages yellowing and their covers curling under the combined assault of heat, light and age.

Of all the faculties, that of law has the reputation of being the most fiercely revolutionary. Groups of armed students do not hesitate there to push aside professors as they lecture, in order to deliver fierce political harangues instead. The faculty was deserted when I visited it, as the students were preparing for their annual parade through the streets of the city known as the *Huelga de Dolores*. I was let into the building through a heavily barred iron gate by the porter, who found my desire to see inside distinctly odd, indeed suspicious. It was not, after all, an architectural masterpiece that might interest a tourist; reluctantly, he let me through.

It was shortly before the election of the dean of the faculty, and every available inch – quite literally – was taken up with poster appeals to the student electors to vote for one or other of the candidates, each professing an undying love of humanity and devotion to the cause. Inside and out there was row on row of these posters, giving the impression that no one cared for the aesthetic consequences. The only space on the wall not covered by posters or

political murals was given over to a revolutionary poem by the poet
Otto Rene Castillo, who joined the guerrillas in the early sixties and
was killed in action in 1967:

Un día	One day
los intelectuales	the apolitical
apolíticos	intellectuals
de mi país	of my country
serán interrogados	will be interrogated
por el hombre	by the simple
sencillo	man
de nuestro pueblo.	of our people.
Se les preguntará	They will be asked
sobre lo que hicieron	about what they did
cuando	when
la patria	their nation
se apagaba	was slowly
lentamente,	extinguished,
como una hoguera dulce	like a sweet and gentle fire
pequeña y sola.	all alone.
No serán interrogados	They will not be asked
sobre sus trajes	about their suits
ni sobre sus largas	nor about their long
siestas	siestas
después de la merienda	after luncheon,
tampoco sobre sus estériles	nor about their sterile
combates con la nada	struggles with nothingness
ni sobre su ontológica	nor on their ontological
manera	method
de legar a las monedas.	of bequeathing money.
No se les interrogará	They will not be interrogated
sobre la mitología griega	about Greek mythology
ni sobre el asco	nor about the self-disgust
que sintieron de sí	that they felt inside
cuando alguién en su fondo	when they begin to die
se disponía a morir	a cowardly death.
cobardemente.	
Nada se les preguntará	They will be asked nothing
sobre sus justificaciones	about their absurd
absurdas	justifications,
crecidas a la sombra	grown in the shadow
de una mentira rotunda.	of a total lie.

Ese día vendrán	On that day will come
los hombres sencillos	the simple men,
los que nunca	those for whom there was never
cupieron	room
en los libros y versos	in the books and poems
de los intelectuales apolíticos	of apolitical intellectuals
pero que llegaban todos los	but who daily
días con	delivered
los huevos y las tortillas,	eggs and tortillas,
los que les cosían la ropa,	who made their clothes,
los que manajaban los carros,	who drove their cars
les cuidaban sus perros	who looked after their dogs and
y jardines,	gardens,
y trabajaban para ellos y	and worked for them and they
preguntarán	will ask
Qué hicistéis cuando los	What did you do when
pobres	the poor
sufrían, y se quemaban en ellos	were suffering and
gravemente, la ternura y la	when the tenderness and life in
vida?'	them was deliberately burnt
	out of them?'
Intelectuales apolíticos	Apolitical intellectuals
de mi dulce país,	of my sweet land,
no podréis responder nada.	you will not be able to answer.
Os devorará un buitre de	A vulture of silence
silencio	will devour
las entrañas,	your entrails,
os roerá el alma	your own misery
vuestra propia miseria	your soul will be gnawed
	by your own misery
y callaréis	and you will be silent
Avergonzados de vosotros.	Ashamed of yourselves.

It was a better poem than I had expected, and its sentiments
understandable in the circumstances. But the obsession with politics
I found oppressive and dispiriting. Suppose no-one had engaged in
works of art or speculative thought until the reign of political justice,
should we not still be living in caves? We might be equals in our
skins, but where would our cathedrals be?

All universities have their political activists, of course, and it is right that this should be so; but universities also need their artists, mountaineers, sportsmen, bibliophiles, philatelists, archaeologists and lepidopterists. At San Carlos there appeared to be no cultural life divorced from political sloganeering. True, on the noticeboard of the Faculty of Law was the announcement of a poetry competition, open to all the registered students of 'our beloved faculty'. But the poem (in verse or prose) had to be on the subject of 'protest or denunciation'.

It was not difficult, alas, to imagine the entries to the competition, in which vehemence of declamation was mistaken for purity of heart and literary talent. But there was a phrase in the announcement of the competition that haunted me: 'our beloved faculty'. Why should so bourgeois an institution as a law faculty be beloved of students allegedly concerned to overthrow the state? The answer, I think, is in the length of time it takes the average student to graduate: ten years. There is nothing as oppressive or authoritarian as a time limit in this faculty (which breeds eternal students *à la* Chekhov), and it is unheard of that a student should complete his course in the minimum time specified. Most of the students are not from wealthy families, and therefore have to work part-time while pursuing their studies. So San Carlos, which charges no tuition, encourages adolescents to postpone maturation almost indefinitely, while allowing them to imagine that in doing so they are keeping alight the sacred flame of justice and revolt. It never occurs to the students, who see exploitation everywhere but inwards, that to prolong unnecessarily their attendance at a university which spends 5 per cent of the national budget is grossly exploitative, and has not even the defence of economic productiveness to justify it.

Through a mutual acquaintance whom I think it best not to name, I met a man who had once been Professor of Philosophy at San Carlos, but who retired from his post as soon as he was able. On the walls of his room were portraits of Locke and Hegel, whom he was delighted that I could recognise; they represented the twin poles of western thought, he said. As for his own sympathies, they were with Locke; the professor was a philosopher in the Anglo-Saxon mould, having received his postgraduate training in the United States. He believed in philosophy as analysis, and eschewed flights of metaphysical fancy. This was not an easy furrow to plough in Guatemala where precision of thought, or any form of intellectual discipline, was not much valued, where everyone wanted to apprehend the Whole Truth of Everything directly, intuitively and without effort.

He spoke precise, elegant and clear Spanish, a language that (for cultural rather than linguistic reasons) is more often associated with orotund rhetoric than with clarity. He used Occam's Razor to shave superfluous words; he was not a man to let sounds take precedence over meaning. His rejection of flamboyant expression had given him a serenity (or was it the other way around?) that pervaded his office, which had a calm orderliness that would have secured the contempt of more Bohemian intellectuals.

Racially he was as much Indian as European, a *ladino* by culture. As a youth in Ubico's time, he had attended one of the only four state secondary schools then in existence in Guatemala. Like most institutions of the time, the school was highly militarised. Ubico, a deeply frustrated man with a childless marriage and an inferiority complex as large as the world, sought to impose Prussian order on a country peculiarly refractory to it. The professor spent the anti-Ubico revolutionary years and their counter-revolutionary sequel in the United States, eventually returning to a chair at San Carlos. The atmosphere in the university rapidly became one of political intimidation rather than of free inquiry; unpopular teachers – that is, teachers with unpopular views – had their cars damaged and their lives threatened. The chemical laboratories were used by students for the elaboration of drugs, and the campus became the distribution centre of cocaine for the whole country. Ice cream vans on the campus sold drugs, not ice creams. Two rectors who tried to stop the abuse were murdered, a lesson not lost on their successors.

In the late sixties and early seventies, when there was a guerrilla insurgency in the *oriente* (a region ill-suited to it for both military and social reasons, but within easy reach of the capital by bus), many of the professor's students were weekend guerrillas, leaving the university on Friday and returning on Monday. That insurgency was quickly, though bloodily, defeated. By the late seventies, there was a resurgence, this time in the north-west of the country, where the Indians had centuries of grievance to nurture and the territory was propitious. But the students could not reach the war zone so easily, and their support remained largely theoretical (though the professor noted the sudden increase of student interest in Indian languages just before this second insurgency); but the second guerrilla war, more difficult to win than the first, provoked repression on a quite unprecedented scale. In the midst of this repression, at a time when both students and professors were 'disappeared' at a ferocious rate by death squads outside the campus, while many intellectuals fled the country but the university retained its constitutional autonomy, the professor saw an event from his classroom window that caused many students to leave the university, never to return. In front of a large crowd of students, a man accused of being a police informer was tied up and stoned. Then he was led round the campus and finally burnt to death publicly. Some of the professor's students were so horrified that they fled the university and he never saw them again.

I wondered what could lie behind the seemingly bizarre policy of permitting everything within the university, only to kill staff and students outside. Two explanations, not mutually exclusive, sprung to mind. The government, remembering the part students played in the 1944 revolution, was too afraid of them (now there were 50,000, ten times more than in 1944) to tamper with their autonomy. And to permit youthful revolutionaries an island of freedom in a sea of repression was not only to keep them preoccupied with the shadow-boxing of university politics, but permitted the natural leaders to emerge so that they could be eliminated.

Whatever the truth, the reputation of the university had declined terribly in the last few years. Some said this was because the best professors had either been killed or gone into exile; others, that it was because of the extreme politicisation of life there. But I met no-one who did not agree that standards had fallen precipitously (San Carlos was once one of the finest universities in the Americas), and I met several employers who said that they entirely discounted a diploma awarded by San Carlos. One director of an engineering company told me that he sent recently graduated engineers from San Carlos straight to the carpentry shop as fit for nothing else.

To keep alive the ideal of academic standards and to train the scientists, technicians and others that a modern economy required, a group of wealthy Guatemalans had founded a private university, named after the first bishop of Guatemala, Francisco Marroquín. The contrast between this institution and San Carlos could scarcely have been greater. Still uncompleted, the main university building was a cleverly-designed structure with a pleasing brick façade (not concrete), built on several levels and with restful hanging gardens to avoid the dehumanizing gigantism of much modern architecture. Through rock gardens wound a little stream, the sound of which no doubt exerted a soothing effect on the passions of youth. Could this be Guatemala City?

The students at Francisco Marroquín have to pay, and the fees are beyond all but the well-to-do. The students are well-dressed, fresh-looking and optimistic, in marked contrast to those of San

Carlos, many of whom already have the deep sorrow of perpetual
failure marked on their faces. In Francisco Marroquín, all is order
and concentration on the task at hand and there are computers
everywhere. On the walls there are no political slogans, but on the
noticeboards are announcements of cultural events, research
seminars, postgraduate fellowships in foreign countries, meetings of
learned societies and so forth. The atmosphere is of calm and
unashamed high culture, which I found a relief after the determined
barbarism of San Carlos; but it is also artificial, as indigenous to
Guatemala as the hot-house palms of Kew Gardens are to London.
   .I met the rector at his business premises rather than in the
university (his rectorship being only part-time). We talked in the
boardroom above a busy workshop floor full of large machines
strange to me, but clearly of high capital value. The boardroom table
was long and shiny, strewn with papers, the chairs were expensive,
leather-bound and comfortable. One wall was taken up by a
bookcase containing academic works of economics. I was shown in
by a tall, elegant and confident secretary. The rector sat across the
table from me, a man of the purest European descent, whose gaze
above the half-moon spectacles perched on his nose was gimlet-like,
enough to strike fear into the heart of any student. He spoke English
better than many native speakers, having attended universities in
Canada and the United States. He had a doctorate and was the friend
of many famous economists on both sides of the Atlantic (he at once
gave me a photocopy of an article written by Lord Bauer, in the same
way that missionaries hand out tracts against sin).
   At first he was wary of me. Foreign writers about Guatemala do
not have a very good reputation in the country, at least among people
not of the revolutionary left, for most of the writers about Guatemala
are sympathisers with the guerrillas and simplifiers of the situation.
They portray everyone except guerrillas, Indians and slum-dwellers
in a most unflattering way. I allayed the rector's fears by whole-
hearted agreement with his views.
   He was exasperated by what had happened to San Carlos. When
he and his friends founded the new university, they drew up quite
different rules from those of San Carlos, for example the regulations
concerning tenure for professors.
   'We tell them they have tenure,' said the rector, 'until we find
better professors.'
   He laughed at his joke. In his eye I saw the hard glint of the dismal
science. I asked about academic freedom in the absence of tenure.

'There's complete freedom,' he replied. 'But not to teach nonsense.'

And who, I asked, decided what was nonsense?

'We do, the trustees,' he said – though I shouldn't have been at all surprised if his voice were given more than merely numerical weight.

To give an illustration of the kind of rigour he demanded, he showed me a paper of his, so far unpublished, about the pricing system under socialism.

'The problem with socialism,' he said, 'is that it has never been described.'

His paper stated that in a command economy, the number of mathematical equations necessary to work out prices for even a very reduced number of items was so enormous as to be for all practical purposes impossible. But in fact a modern economy produced millions of different commodities, with a correspondingly exponential increase in the number of necessary equations: an academic way of saying what the old Soviet joke asserted, that there will have to be one capitalist country left after the triumph of world revolution just to find out what things cost. No author, said the rector, had ever described a pricing mechanism without the market.

Returning to the cold comfort of the dismal science, the rector said it was quite wrong of liberals, trade unionists, radicals, communists and others to suppose that legislation or any other government action could in the long run improve the lot of a people. Only the working of ineluctable economic laws could do that. To interfere with free competition was fatal. And it was equally futile to appeal to the compassion of capitalists, for two reasons: first because compassion interfered with the beneficent working of the hidden hand, making businesses less efficient, driving them into bankruptcy, thus reducing the level of employment and therefore driving down wages; and second because capitalists were not compassionate.

I laughed, and found his lack of cant about capitalists – of whom he was one – refreshing. But was it really true that by paying the lowest possible wages one was actually doing everyone a favour, especially when 40 per cent of the people (according to some statistics) were unemployed?

'When I employ a man,' said the rector, 'whether I like it or not I am driving up the rate of wages, infinitesimally, it is true, but if more employers behave as I do, there is an aggregate effect.'

Of course, if other employers do not behave as he, there is no such effect, but there is no remedy for that.

The rector was a highly, even brilliantly intelligent man, and I doubted there were many who could dispute with him in his chosen field. But I had the uncomfortable feeling that, in a mirror image of his opponents, he had reduced life to a few simple propositions from which everything else followed. I was not reassured by his insistence that all students, whether they studied entomology or ancient Greek, should be taught the hard propositions of political economy so that they could fulfil their duties not only as scholars but as citizens. For even if his propositions were true – wholly, indisputably and eternally so – there was more than a hint of ideological indoctrination in his pedagogical notions, again a mirror image of his opponents. As for Marxism, it was taught at his university, but only to be exposed as the farrago of pseudo-scientific nonsense he believed it to be; and no avowed Marxist would ever be allowed to teach there.

'It's been said that in Guatemala we don't respect rights,' he continued. 'But we do respect rights. It's lefts we don't respect.'

In the context of thousands dead or disappeared this joke was not perhaps in the best of taste. At that very time a white truck, a *panel blanco*, was going round the city kidnapping people with alleged left-wing connections, while shortly afterwards their mutilated bodies would appear somewhere on waste land or by the side of the road. Witnesses reported that a group of seven or eight 'heavily armed men' – a euphemism for death squad – would jump out and drag their victim into the truck even in broad daylight, at public places like bus stops. The newspapers reported the movements of the *panel blanco* in considerable detail. Soon the vehicle was made a joke of: any resemblance to the *panel blanco*, said an advertisement for a Mexican gangster movie, was purely coincidental.

I left the rector in his boardroom, impressed by his intellect but frightened by the consistency of his ideas. It is in the nature of intellect, of course, that it should try to impose order on the seeming chaos of everyday experience; but in human affairs, there are far worse failings than inconsistency, and few worse than passion masquerading as disinterest. Besides, what hope was there for compromise in a country where free discussion was impossible even in universities, where universities were regarded as arms depots, havens for drug traffickers, or centres of political indoctrination?

FIVE

Without a doubt, the rector of Francisco Marroquín University belonged to the elite of Guatemala, the elite hated and despised by all those who write of it. In a memorable book of photographs called *Guatemala: Eternal Spring, Eternal Tyranny*, by the North American journalist Jean-Marie Simon, published in 1988, there is a photograph of another member of the elite. He is dressed in black tie while his daughter, in a long white ball gown, is on his arm. The pair are just arriving at, or leaving, a debutantes' ball in Guatemala City and their complacent faces glisten with oily sweat. The picture exactly captures the pointless vulgarity that is supposedly the hallmark of the class to which father and daughter belong. Unlike other elites, the Guatemalan has contributed nothing to the upward sweep of human civilisation and culture, neither as patrons nor as artists. They consume the fruit of other people's labour while indulging in shallow cosmopolitanism (the apparatus that adorns many of their houses to bring them junk television from the north is sometimes called Guatemala's national dish). The caption to Jean-Marie Simon's picture quotes a United States Congressman who gave as his opinion after a brief visit to Guatemala that the elite there was without any redeeming features whatsoever. This opinion sounds reasonable and allows one a pleasant *frisson* of self-righteousness. But then a small voice begins to nag: how many people have you known in your life who were without any redeeming features whatsoever? And can a whole class be without redeeming features if the individuals that comprise it are not?

I was interested in the development of worthlessness as a trait; and when I was invited by a teacher at the *Colegio Americano*, the most exclusive school in Guatemala, to visit the school and talk to her pupils, I jumped at the chance. I expected to find amongst them a premature worldweariness brought on by parents who mistook overindulgence for love and I decided they were spoilt brats before I met them.

The school is in a fashionable suburb of the city, where villas are surrounded, as if by law, by bougainvillea. Of course, the school has its own grounds, and equally to be expected are the thick and strong security gates at the entrance. I was told that the son of the President arrived there every morning, to security measures as ostentatious as (and more expensive than) a fanfare, but this was something I did not see myself and about which I made no further enquiries.

The headmaster was a North American, as were half the teachers. The tuition was half in Spanish, half in English, and all the pupils (80 per cent of whom were Guatemalan) were bilingual. Some of the Guatemalan teachers, I heard, had moments of resentment, because they were paid less than the Americans (though good salaries by Guatemalan standards), and because the pupils were of a class to which they themselves could not remotely aspire. Nevertheless, there were no discipline problems, the school ran smoothly, and order was imposed with a light touch.

I was treated as a distinguished guest, which pleased me because the last time I had visited a headmaster I was not at all distinguished, but a somewhat obnoxious youth. In the meantime, I had transformed myself into a doctor and writer, someone whom a headmaster might safely hold up as an example to be emulated. All the same, if the headmaster of the *Colegio Americano* had suddenly barked an order at me, I should have obeyed it, having been carried back instantaneously to that childhood we never quite leave behind us.

But he was not the kind of man to bark orders. As we strolled through the school, he appeared more an older friend of his pupils than a taskmaster or demigod. And I could not but envy these children growing up in sunshine (I remembered the leaden northern skies of my childhood), with every possible opportunity for physical and intellectual development. They abounded with life, their laughter was open and optimistic, people about to start out on a pleasurable adventure; theirs was youth as it should be.

The headmaster permitted me to take a class of his, so that I could enquire about the ambitions of the next generation of the Guatemalan elite. They were in their final year at school and were preparing for university. All except one intended to go either to Franciso Marroquín or universities in the United States to study, the exception being a girl who wanted to be a vet, the only faculty of veterinary medicine in Guatemala being at San Carlos. But everyone was scathing about the state university. Not only were its standards falling every day, but as alumni of the *Colegio Americano* they would face persecution there. They would be hated for their social origins, regardless of their opinions or behaviour. They would be detested for their clothes alone.

It was not for me to say whether their fears were realistic; but the extremity of their separation from the rest of Guatemalan society was clearly in the making.

Most of the class were girls, of European extraction except for one *mestiza* and a Chinese, and I was taken aback at their choice of career, expecting them to have chosen something culturally ornamental. On the contrary, chemical and electronic engineering were the subjects most favoured by them (according to the nature of the family business), or economics by those whose parents owned a bank. Already bilingual if not trilingual (but not an Indian language among them), by the completion of their university careers they would be members not only of an hereditary elite, but beyond question of a technical and intellectual elite as well. This would make them doubly the object of the envy of those less well-born than themselves. And as if this were not enough, they were both cultured and physically favoured by nature. One among them, a handsome boy, academically brilliant and from an immensely rich family, was junior tennis champion of Central America. To him who hath shall be given . . .

They might at least have compensated for their good fortune by being ill-mannered, bigoted or in some other way unattractive. But to the contrary, they were beautifully mannered, respectful without toadying, and when we moved on to more general and controversial subjects they were able to disagree among themselves without the embitterment that so often disfigures such discussions. The subject of presidents arose, and I mentioned my enthusiasm for the jokes made at the expense of the last president but three, General Romeo Lucas García, a man generally regarded as brutal and stupid, who presided over the worst government Guatemala had ever had, and whose corruption brought the country to the brink of collapse. I said there should be a book published of Lucas García jokes, and a girl who wanted to be an engineer gleefully added to my stock of them.

One day, there is a public competition between three presidents, Ronald Reagan of the United States, Miguel de la Madrid of Mexico, and Romeo Lucas García of Guatemala, to see who can tell the biggest and best lie. Ronald Reagan stands up and says, 'We have no crime in the United States.' There is polite applause. Then Miguel de la Madrid stands up and says, 'The Mexican peso is the strongest currency in the world.' The applause is more enthusiastic. Then Romeo Lucas García stands up and says nothing. The audience grows restless. 'Wait a minute,' he says, 'I'm thinking.' The applause is deafening.

The laughter of the pupils showed they had a healthy disrespect of presidential authority. Then we discussed the social and economic condition of the country. All of them were aware of the injustices, and of their own very privileged position. One girl even wished for a career outside Guatemala not on account of any outrage at the injustices, but because she knew that any success she might enjoy would be attributed by the envious to the influence of her family. Most of the class, however, thought that what was good for their family businesses was good for Guatemala. We talked a little of the statistics, of why on virtually every measure of social welfare Guatemala came next to last in the western hemisphere. Almost everyone said it was because 'we have so many Indians'. They spoke of them not as if they inhabited the same country – which in a sense they did not – but another planet entirely, and as if they were a small and rather quaint minority, rather than the majority. The statistics were very much worse for Indians than for *ladinos*, I agreed, but why was that? Did the blame lie with the Indians or with the *ladinos*, or was the concept of blame in this case too crude? A discussion started, but my forty-five minutes with the children of those without redeeming features was over. I left, wondering when these children would lose their redeeming features.

Alas, there are more children in Guatemala at the wrong end of the spectrum of privilege than at the right end. Among the least privileged of the least privileged are the street children, those who for one reason or another have left home and live entirely on the streets of the capital. In this respect, Guatemala City is by no means the worst of Latin American cities: there are at most a couple of thousand such children there (though the number is growing), while in Bogota or Mexico they are measured in scores or even hundreds of thousands. And Bogota is a very much harsher city.

Perhaps it is a measure of the comfort and complacency of my existence that until I met a North American who worked in Guatemala City for a charity devoted to the welfare of street children I was not even aware of their existence. Of course, I had seen children sleeping in doorways, but insofar as I had not screened them out of my vision completely, I assumed they were simply taking a nap. The American, Mark, gave me literature to read on the subject. It appeared that the problem, though it had long existed, had only just been recognised. Even cities like London and Paris had 20,000 homeless children (a higher proportion than Guatemala City) who lived by scrounging and petty crime. Among the literature he gave me was a medical thesis from the University of San Carlos, which began – not unexpectedly – by asserting that the problem was one of dependent capitalism. The greater proportion of children sleeping rough in New York might have given the author pause, had he shown any awareness of the need for comparative statistics. Even without them, however, his thesis contained interesting facts about 50 children who attended consecutively a shelter for them set up on one of the main thoroughfares of the city: 41 of them had only one parent living; 31 gave maltreatment as the reason for leaving home; 47 had dental caries; 40 of them used, or abused, mind-altering drugs; 39 of them inhaled the fumes of paint thinner and all of them sniffed glue; 39 were malnourished; 31 had scabies; 34 had worms, 23 the large roundworm *Ascaris lumbricoides*; 26 had lice and an equal number athlete's foot. The thesis states in summary:

> These children, whose lives are defined within a world of violence and physical discomfort without future solution, soon turn bitter, cruel and completely anti-social . . . While the causes of the abysmal social differences in this country are not dealt with, more street children will be produced. The solution to this problem lies in structural changes that permit a more integrated development for the great majority who are dispossessed.

Brave words: in Guatemala, people have died for less. The problem of street children only recently having been brought to public attention, I expected Mark to be something of a proselytiser. Those involved in the discovery of previously unsuspected social problems sometimes exaggerate their importance to the point of obsession. Often the social worker needs the problem more than the problem needs the social worker. But Mark was not like this. He seemed, on the contrary, admirably normal; he was happily married, lived in a comfortable but unostentatious house, and was clean-cut in the American way. He made no claims to be redeeming the world, but simply had compassion for the children amongst whom he worked, a quality not always shared by those who labour for good causes. Two or three evenings a week he went out on to the streets to meet the children, and on one of those evenings I went with him.

We met in the Pan American Hotel, a pre-war institution with a splendid lounge-lobby with Guatemalan murals, through which rushed waiters in Mayan dress carrying trays of drinks on their shoulders. We ate a meal at a fast-food restaurant called *Piccadilly* on the Sixth Avenue and then went out at nine o'clock to patrol the streets. Before long we found two boys, one twelve years old and the other younger, half-asleep in the doorway of a shop. Had I not been searching, I should have overlooked them, or worse still, not seen them at all. They greeted Mark as an old friend, someone they could trust in a hostile world. The older of them rolled up a trouser leg to show a three-day-old suppurating burn which was caused by another street kid (child seems inappropriate here) who, as a joke, poured paint thinner over his leg and set it alight. While Mark and he discussed it, the younger child suddenly flung his arms round Mark's neck and hugged him. It was a gesture that meant much. Later in the evening we returned to the two children and Mark brought them some chocolate gâteau with cream and cherries, which they devoured eagerly, licking the paper on which it came. Mark never gave the children gifts when they asked for them, but sometimes gave them spontaneously. As for his choice of cake as a gift, I thought it perfectly appropriate; for it was what the children might have chosen for themselves (rather than something more nutritious), and was therefore quite uncensorious.

We walked down the Ninth Avenue, towards the *plaza* in front of the railway station. On either side of the avenue were bars and garish restaurants, whose neon signs cast eerie, coloured shadows on to the street. It seemed like a descent into a chiaroscuro hell, with lost souls moving from darkness into pink glare and back again into darkness. From the bars came the thumping base of disposable disco music, imparting a slight vibration to the ground. This was where the street children of Guatemala City 'worked', sometimes as pickpockets and sometimes as beggars, graduating to hustlers. In the doorway of one bar sat a plump youth of about seventeen in a once-white tracksuit. He greeted Mark warmly. He had been one of the first street children Mark had known, and now he was a kind of *capo* of pickpockets, all of whom paid him a share of their earnings, which was why he was fat and contented. He ruled by a combination of natural seniority and physical terror, but he was affable towards us. Sharing the doorway with him was a youth of the same age, though he looked much older, who was raggedly dressed. With the sallowest complexion this side of death I had ever seen, his eyes were as glazed as a waxwork's, his movements were drunkenly incoordinated and his grin had all the joy of death triumphant. He said practically nothing, and that little was slurred beyond interpretation; from time to time he withdrew a little bottle from his trousers – more holes than cloth – that was corked with a rag, which he then held to his nose and mouth. He inhaled the fumes, a form of self-administered rag-and-bottle anaesthesia. It is said that the chronic inhalation of paint thinner fumes does no irreversible damage to the brain, but looking at the crushed and emaciated figure before me, collapsed like a puppet with its strings cut, it was hard to believe it.

On the other side of the avenue, outside the kind of bar in which it is *de rigeur* to spit on the floor, pick fights and boast drunkenly, we met two young women who had been street children but were now in business on their own account. One of them already had a child, but neither of them – to my surprise – was a prostitute. Instead, they led customers in the bar to suppose that they were, spiked their drinks (presumably with a quick-acting barbiturate), and then robbed them of everything they possessed. This provided them with a decent living: at least, the baby was well-provided for. Recently the most famous footballer in Guatemala had fallen victim to their trick, to the great glee of the press. As for the two girls (they were both under twenty), they spoke of their work matter-of-factly, as a postman or bank clerk might speak of theirs. How could I condemn them? Instead, I glimpsed the inadequacy, the sterility of my either/or moral categories.

> *O quién es más de culpar,*
> *el que peca por la paga*
> *o el que paga por pecar?*

We walked on to the square in front of the railway station. The bar there is reputedly the model for the bar called *Mi Apuesta*, My Bet, in Norman Lewis's fine novel of Guatemala, *The Volcanoes Above Us*. An incident was said to have occurred there in which a man challenged his drinking companion to kill the next man who walked into the bar, betting him he wouldn't dare. Well, he did dare, and afterwards the bar was admiringly known as My Bet. Probably apocryphal: but several people told me that in the bad days of the violence you could walk into a bar and someone would ask whether there was anybody you wanted killed. Providing it wasn't anyone special, like a general or a cabinet minister, the cost was 25 or 50 *quetzales* (the *quetzal* was then equal to the dollar).

The square was almost in darkness, the lights of the avenue casting long shadows. Along one side of the square were a few food stalls, run by fat peasant women who seemed to sweat the grease in which their wares were cooked. It was here that many of the street children gathered; they were younger than those in the avenue, and all of them were drunk on fumes of paint thinner. They staggered among the stalls, occasionally delivering incoordinated kung fu kicks to one another, but not speaking. Mark said there was something odd about this night, they were wary even of him. Perhaps they expected something to happen tonight, or perhaps they were affected by the fatal shooting a couple of nights before of a man in the square. It was, after all, their living room, and no one likes a murder in their living room. Just then, two policemen began to walk across the square, guns prominent, a strange royal blue tassel hanging from their truncheons, as though truncheons were instruments of joy or pleasure. The children stopped to eye them closely, but soon resumed whatever they were doing: like zebras watching lions, they knew when their enemies were hunting. The policemen continued across the square, not noticing the children. Mark said that Guatemalan police, by comparison with Columbian, were the soul of kindness and understanding. Theirs was a very dangerous job, they were underpaid, ill-trained and mostly un-educated, yet in his experience many did their best. Some were sadistic but not all, and Mark had even persuaded a few of them to deal with the street kids sympathetically rather than violently. Two now devoted their spare time to unpaid social work among the kids, hardly confirming thereby the stereotype we have of Latin American policemen.

As we stood talking and observing in the square, a vehicle backed towards us, a heavy metallic clanking sound emerging from the back. It was a *panel blanco*, a white van of precisely the kind that had recently been 'disappearing' people. Mark and I looked at one another; the clanking was clearly the sound of prisoners fighting to get out. Had the *panel blanco* come to the square to deposit bodies or find new victims? Had it come for us, and if so should we yield without a struggle or fight? Whatever happened there would be no reliable witnesses, and after an initial report in *La Prensa Libre*, *El Gráfico* and *La Hora*, Guatemala's three newspapers, we should never be heard of again.

But the van left, without having either deposited a corpse or kidnapped a victim. Mark and I returned to the children, who were now all inhaling the fumes of paint thinner. It was the cheapest of intoxicants available in Guatemala; a law had been passed to prohibit its sale to minors but the law was a dead letter. The youngest of the children bought fumes from their elders, paying double if they had to hire a rag as well. All around us was a scene that might have inspired Dante, yet it would have been unsafe to assume that these children were uniformly miserable. Forced from home by cruelty or neglect, they were also attracted to life on the streets by romance, where each day survived was further proof of toughness and skill, and there were no adults to come between a child and his inclinations. Where there was money, there were ice creams and cinemas *ad libitum*, and no schoolmasters to waste time on arithmetic. There were several institutions in the city that offered something 'better' to these children, like regular meals and a real bed, usually in exchange for a little discipline and routine, which many could not accept. I visited such a refuge on the Seventh Avenue, near to the pink baroque post office; not more than a third of the children that entered its programme progressed to a settled existence. The children came and went, taking advantage of the medical facilities (doctors and dentists gave their time free), and sleeping there during the day. A social worker, a Guatemalan lady with a kindly face and a limp which I hastily assumed was the source of her compassion, explained to me clearly and in detail the refugee's programme of redemption. I asked whether the children were unhappy.

'No,' she replied. 'They're not unhappy. We're the ones who are unhappy.'

We, the respectable of the earth, we who are not only unhappy but fearful. These children are for the moment only pickpockets and petty thieves; later, those who do not reach the lower levels of true employment will devote themselves to prostitution, serious crime and – who knows – to political rabble rousing. As Mark and I returned to his car, he greeted a seventeen-year-old black who had once been a street child but was now dressed in a freshly-laundered shirt of sky-blue and white stripes, dazzling white trousers and lizard skin shoes, his wrists and neck adorned with gold bracelets and chains, a pretty girl on each arm. Mark did not know where his money came from, but it was from nowhere very savoury.

We continued past McDonald's where every night at midnight the homeless gather to descend on the garbage which the staff put out for collection next day (though even the homeless have their dignity – they wait until the staff have gone home before falling on the remains of Big Macs to avoid the humiliation of being seen). Our route to Mark's clean and quiet home took us through a street in which transvestites gather, hoping for custom but fearing a raid by the puritanical army, whose soldiers imprison, rape and even kill them.

All that I saw in Guatemala City exists to a greater or lesser extent in every city in the world, including my own. But I had to travel thousands of miles to see it.

SIX

Returning to Antigua after forays in Guatemala City, all was peace and prosperity. Nevertheless, a few strange things continued to happen there. For example, one morning a lady who ran a small store near to where I lived, from whom I had bought ballpoint pens, was arrested. She was a close relation of the last military president of Guatemala, General Mejía Victores (popularly known as *Sapo*, Toad, on account of his good looks), and had kept ten kidnapped children imprisoned in her house, for later shipment to the United States for sale to childless couples. The story was printed in the newspapers and broadcast over the radio, but by the time I left Guatemala several months later, nothing further had been heard of the woman, her business or the children. This was a pattern repeated many times: the report of a crime and an arrest, an initial flurry of interest and then a profound silence. In this instance, perhaps her contacts helped her: but even when less well-connected accused are brought to court, according to Lord Colville, the Special Rapporteur for Guatemala of the United Nations Commission on Human Rights, 98 per cent of them are acquitted, either for lack of evidence, on a legal technicality or because of intimidation of witnesses. If this is so, no one has anything to lose by committing a crime, and the wonder therefore is not that so many, but that so few crimes are committed in Guatemala.

Though Antigua is a conservative town, where improper dress causes offence and where those with wealth to conserve tend to congregate, it did not escape the years of violence entirely unscathed. The priest of the church of San Francisco was murdered in 1983 for reasons that are still unclear and four bodies appeared one morning in the early eighties in the vestibule of the church of *La Merced* (Mercy). It was during this period of history that the police called on a wealthy North American resident at his beautiful colonial home and took him to the Antigua branch of Lloyds Bank, where he was 'encouraged' to withdraw precisely the sum held in his account and hand it over to the guardians of the law, following which he decided to leave the land of Eternal Spring. And I often ate at a restaurant whose owner had received a peremptory demand by telephone for 10,000 *quetzales* in cash (or else), and who fled at once to the United States, from which she had never returned, still not knowing whether the demand came from the guerrillas, the police, the army or just ordinary criminals taking advantage of the general atmosphere of terror.

The level of security was much improved. Nevertheless, peace in Guatemala is fragile. A doctor in Antigua known for his low charges and good treatment of the poor, who lived and worked a few minutes from where I stayed, received a call one evening to the effect that an urgent case was on its way to him. Would he attend it? He said that of course he would. The urgent case arrived and promptly put a gun to the doctor's head. He was a member of the *Fuerzas Armadas Rebeldes*, the Rebel Armed Forces or FAR, one of the guerrilla groups still operating in Guatemala, principally in the jungles of the Peten. The gunman demanded the doctor's anaesthetics. He explained that he had none, being only a general practitioner. The gunman then demanded his antibiotics. These the doctor handed over. The unfortunate man had been the object of the guerrillas' attentions once before, when they held him up and stole his car (an odd choice of vehicle since it was decrepit and unreliable). Was the doctor particularly abominated by the guerrillas? If so, why? He was an unpolitical man, by all accounts, devoted to his patients. There must have beeen many richer and more fashionable doctors, with practices entirely among the elite, whom the FAR could have chosen to rob. Perhaps it was his very benevolence that attracted the FAR's anger, for the existence of such a man makes stoking the fires of revolution all the more difficult.

Ever an habitué of bookshops, I met in Antigua a British bookseller there, Mike Shawcross, who proved a good friend and an invaluable source of contacts. Mike was from the north of England who, having started out in his youth to emigrate to Australia, had stopped first in Canada, then Mexico and finally in Guatemala, where he ran a small bookstore and secondhand book service, providing libraries all round the world with books and documents about Guatemala. He also ran his own relief programme to the Ixil Indians in the highlands, who had suffered more than any other group in the recent civil war. Mike had a reputation in certain circles, particularly amongst those who unilaterally and from afar declared themselves in solidarity with the oppressed, as a man of the extreme right, with links to the army, the CIA and even the death squads. This was nonsense; he simply did not subscribe to the received view of his adopted country as a battleground for the forces of good and evil, with evil having won for four and three quarter centuries, but with good about to triumph once and for all, providing it could muster enough violence to do so. This was not to say that he himself was a trimmer, a man who, endowed with a vision of the complexity of things, was incapable like Hamlet of action. On the contrary, as a typical angular northerner, he pursued what he thought was right with a kind of obstinate, terrier-like determination. I do not think that death or the threat of death (which he had at times received) would deter him from a course of action upon which he had decided. A small example of his uncompromising allegiance to his own lights was his refusal to sell in his bookshop certain contemporary books about Guatemala, even though he could have sold them at considerable profit in large numbers to English-speaking tourists. They contained errors about the country: not just mistakes, but distortions, in his view. Of Maslow's *Bird of Life, Bird of Death* it is unnecessary to speak further (except to say that Victor Perera, the author of a very fine memoir of his Guatemalan childhood called *Rites*, said that it took him a long time to read Maslow's book, not because it was difficult or densely written, but because he kept throwing it at the wall). This book was so far beyond redemption that it would never, under any circumstances, darken Mike's shelves; but another well-known work, Patrick Marnham's *So Far From God*, came under a different category of interdiction. Mike wrote to Penguin, the publisher of the paperback edition, to say that he was willing to stock and sell it, on condition that an erratum slip was inserted to correct a bad mistake with regard to the Guatemalan part of Marnham's Central American journey. I wondered what the mistake could be that produced so stern a reaction.

In 1983, the Mexican newspaper, *Uno Más Uno*, published an account of a horrible massacre in the village of Paraxtut, in the department of Huehuetenango. The story was taken up by a variety of publications and widely disseminated around the world. According to the story, an army detachment entered the nearby village of Chuil and ordered 350 men of Chuil's Civil Patrol (a kind or rural militia set up by the army during the civil war, membership of which was more or less compulsory) to march to Paraxtut, where the captain of the army detachment told them they would have to prove their masculinity to him.

'Do you have balls?' he asked the assembled civil patrollers.

'Yes,' they replied.

'Then touch them!' the captain commanded. 'Make sure you have them! In a minute, you will prove to me that you are real men!'

Meanwhile, the residents of Paraxtut were gathered together and divided into men, women and children. The men of the Chuil civil patrol were then told to touch their balls again and, under threat of death, to kill the men of Paraxtut. This they did. Then the women of Paraxtut were subdivided into young and old, and again under threat of death the men of Chuil were told to kill the older women. The younger women were shared among the soldiers, who spent the night raping them. In the morning the civil patrol was told to kill the women, except for two who were especially attractive. One was taken away on the captain's instructions, the other begged the captain as a favour to kill her. Complying with her request, he shot her.

According to the account that appeared in the Philadelphia journal, *The Other Side*, this woman said to the captain in Kekchi (through an interpreter), 'Please ask the captain to shoot me twice as a gift'. The captain laughed, shot her twice and, before shooting her a third time, ripped off her clothes. The informant, who was from the Chuil patrol, said: 'The feeling we had was very deep . . . We killed many people. As many as three hundred. Maybe more . . . O God, what sadness to have killed our own people!'

This story found its way into the *New York Review of Books*, where the chairman of Americas Watch, an organisation devoted to monitoring abuses of human rights in the western hemisphere, wrote that the information about the massacre came from a Catholic priest and a churchwoman who had it from a member of the Chuil civil patrol.

But the worst thing about this massacre, according to Mike Shawcross, was that it never took place. For as soon as he heard about the story, he went to Paraxtut to verify it. The village was still intact, fully inhabited, and though there had been many incidents in the environs during the preceding months, in which the army had indeed killed scores of people, the massacre as described was pure invention. Eventually, Americas Watch agreed that it had never taken place, though the letter of retraction to the *New York Review of Books* managed to convey the impression that in most respects, save only the unimportant detail as to whether the described events actually happened, the original report had been correct.

The fictional nature of the Paraxtut massacre raises some disturbing questions. Some might say that these hardly matter, since massacres not very dissimilar to the fictional one have indubitably happened in Guatemala. (Mike Shawcross was himself instrumental in verifying one of the worst of these, at the Finca San Francisco.) The fact that such a story could reasonably be believed of Guatemala was significant in itself. Yet the fabrication of the story was not an error, or a case of mistaken identity: the insistence on circumstantial detail proves it. The fabrication was quite deliberate, and it was fed to sources round the world. Why, when there was no shortage of genuine horror stories, and to what end?

Patrick Marnham's book mentions the Paraxtut massacre, and was published some time after Mike had proved that it was apocryphal. The paperback edition carried no correction, and that was why Mike demanded an erratum slip before he would sell it. His demand went unanswered, and so the book remained unsold by him: an awful warning to those of us who write of Guatemala.

Mike was a stern rationalist, a man who could not abide the absurdities – as he saw them – of religion. At the first sign of a religious procession or festival, he would dive for cover into his house, pleading pressure of work. During Holy Week in Antigua, when hundreds of thousands of pilgrims enter the city, he becomes a virtual hermit, keeping indoors to avoid the incessant processions; and when we were travelling together in the north of the country and entered the village of Todos Santos as its inhabitants were preparing for their annual *fiesta* by rehearsing – in a state of total inebriation – the *Baile de la Conquista*, the Dance of the Conquest, he felt he could not stay to watch. The people who were devoting their energies for many days to this dance of slow, hypnotic rhythms of flute and drums, and who spent large sums hiring the colourful costumes and gaudy masks with the sky-blue eyes and golden curls of con- quistadors (Alvarado was known as *Tontiuh*, Sun, by the Cakchikels), should have been constructing latrines or school benches, in Mike's rationalist estimation. He reminded me of no one so much as of Charles Bradlaugh, the nineteenth century humanist, the first avowed atheist to be elected to the House of Commons, who was repeatedly prevented from taking his seat because he refused to swear the oath on the Bible. At meetings of the rationalist faithful, he would stride on to the stage, take out his pocket watch and challenge God to strike him dead in sixty seconds.

Needless to say, this sternness of Mike's was quite compatible with great generosity. For several months, after I returned to Guatemala from a brief tour through the other Central American countries, he put me up without complaint in his home, a fabled caravanserai for all travellers in Guatemala.

SEVEN

When Kyrie, the chiropractor from Wisconsin, arrived in Guatemala with his pickup, I bought it from him. We were both happy: he made a profit of $1000 merely by driving it through Mexico and Texas, despite the $200 bribe he paid at the Mexican border and to policemen at regular intervals throughout Mexico; and I was happy because I no longer had to rely on the uncomfortable and overcrowded, if colourful, buses to transport me to remote corners.

Permission to import the truck required three weeks of paperwork at various government offices and the Bank of Guatemala, which I gladly deputed at a fee to an agent. The process could not be speeded by the payment of what I tactfully termed 'special taxes'; it seemed the process had a momentum of its own, slow but inexorable and honest, which I found simultaneously surprising, admirable and frustrating.

At the end of the three weeks, the bureaucratic process was not yet exhausted. There were still *placas* (number plates) and *tarjeta de circulación* (a road licence) to obtain, by personal application at a police station – or so I was told. It would take at most an hour or two, said my optimistic informant. So where better to apply, I thought, than at the central police station of the entire country, at the elaborate mock-Renaissance palace before which stood a gilded bust of Don Rufino Barrios, the founder of the *Policía Nacional*? From time to time on my visits to Guatemala City I had seen important officers ushered swiftly into the side entrance, their cars with an escort of motorbike outriders disappearing into the bowels of the massive building while traffic outside was held up; and as I entered the building, I glanced up at the highest windows, to check there were no prisoners undergoing defenestration therefrom.

At the door, I asked a policeman with a stubby automatic rifle where I should go. He told me without hesitation that the office I required was on the first floor. I was just about to climb the flight of stairs when it occurred to me to re-inquire of the policemen guarding them. With precisely the same confidence, he told me that the office I required was on the ground floor. He pointed to the line I should

join. I asked the man in front of me in the line the same question, and
he said I needed the Ministry of Finances. By now, I was a little
confused, and so I took a straw poll of passers-by. The majority
(just) were in favour of the Ministry, and it was there that I directed
my steps.

The Ministry is a modern, eighteen-storey tower block of brown
plate glass on the edge of the *Zona Uno*, in a precinct of important
government offices. There is a constant stream of people in and out,
dwarfed by the building and as obliviously purposeful as leaf-cutter
ants. At the base of the building, lined up on the kerb of a nearby
street, are stalls with portable typewriters and typists who wait for
people to come from the ministry with forms that may be filled only
by typewriter. As one approaches the ministry, one sees that some of
the plate glass is cracked, that it is dirty, and that behind it are
draped dusty net curtains that have long remained undisturbed by
human hand.

The scenes inside took me by surprise. There were thousands of
applicants in the Ministry of Finances, in long lines that snaked
round concrete pillars, and in seething, heaving crowds. Behind the
shabby counters were the clerks, moving as though with glue on the
soles of their shoes as the multitudes pressed forward. Such is the
centralisation of the administration in Guatemala that people have to
come from all over to pay their taxes, those without bank accounts
and cheque books cancelling their debts in cash. Once more, I asked
where I should go and was told the third floor. This was reached not
by the lift, which was for the use only of people going to floors
higher up, but by a bare concrete stairwell built as a fire escape. One
of the double doors at the entrance to the stairwell had been
thoughtfully bolted, so that the constant streams of people upwards
and downwards engaged in a never-ending tussle at the door to go
through. As for the stairwell itself, it was like a scene from a film by
Cecil B. De Mille, with helot extras trudging up and down playing
slaves building a pyramid. There were so many people in that
confined space that the temperature rose with humid body heat: this
is hell, I thought, not yet having glimpsed the third floor.

I joined a line there, the longest one. More than a hundred people
were applying for their *placas*. The man in front of me turned and
asked me helpfully whether I had all the documents I needed. I
replied that I had so many documents that I supposed I had. This
assumption turned out to be unwarranted. The man in front of me
quickly demonstrated that I lacked at least one requisite form,

which he told me was obtainable only on the first floor. Moreover, this form had to be filled in by typescript, and then I had to present it somewhere else for fiscal stamps to be affixed and then . . . A short young man introduced himself to me, saying he was a *tramitador*, that is to say, a person who did *trámites*, official business, for people like me. His wife, a *tramitadora*, was with him, a dumpy, round young woman in a tight white dress, white high-heeled patent leather shoes and cherry-red lipstick. Between them, he said, they could probably – though not certainly – arrange my *placas* today. Otherwise . . . I needed little persuasion that left to my own devices I should spend eons in the ministry. (Later I heard the story of a Guatemalan who spent two days there just trying to obtain the correct form, a story I should not have believed had I not seen the ministry for myself.)

I handed my documents to the *tramitador* and went to sit in a nearby café while he did the work. It would take between two and three hours, he said, if all went well. His wife would appear from time to time with new documents for me to sign, and to reassure me that progress was being made. I could see that her husband was not slacking, quite the reverse: I caught a glimpse of him through the brown glass *running* up some stairs between the seventh and eighth floor, racing against bureaucratic time. Two and a half hours later, his wife joined me: her part of the business was over and he was approaching the delicate stage of the negotiations, upon which depended the quick granting or otherwise of my *placas*. I had entrusted her husband not only with the legal title to my vehicle, but a sum of money equal to four months of the legal minimum wage, and I was beginning to feel nervous. In addition to the taxes was a relatively small sum for lubricating purposes.

I sat with the *tramitadora* for more than an hour. She explained that there were hundreds of *tramitadores* who worked at this and every other ministry, acting as pilots through the rocky reefs of Guatemalan bureaucracy. They were officially licensed, having taken examinations in official procedure. The life of a *tramitador*, of course, was far from easy. She and her husband lived an hour and a half from work, which started at eight each morning. Some days they would fail to find a client, others they would have more clients – many of whom were illiterate – than they could satisfy. Because they were away from home so much of the day, they had to pay someone to look after their children. Sometimes they were so busy – like today with my *placas* – that they had no time for lunch. And at the end of the week, they could barely make ends meet. They did not earn enough to save money.

I asked whether they knew everyone in the ministry, and she said yes, from the minister down. I asked whether any of them was honest. She replied that she and her husband had worked there for many years, and that if any official was honest, they had never met him.

Shortly before the ministry closed for the day her husband ran out holding my *placas*, breathless but triumphant. I was so relieved to have them that I gave him more money than he asked for. My emotions that day had been very mixed: horror at the crowds, frustration at the delay, but finally elation and a sense of achievement so intense that I began to wonder whether the seemingly senseless obstruction had a purpose after all; and just as theologians construct excuses for an all-powerful but morally perfect God who nevertheless allows evil to exist, so I constructed an argument in favour of bureaucratic inefficiency. For if my *placas* had been granted at once, without a struggle, what joy would they have given me?

I now had the freedom of the road. Having been confined to the discipline of slow and grinding buses, I felt an irresistible urge to travel widely in the Central American isthmus. I wanted to see the other countries to make a comparison: he little knows of Guatemala who only Guatemala knows. And so I took the road east, the *Panamericano*, with the intention of stopping in the town of Esquipulas for the great religious celebration of 15 January. This proved impossible, for pilgrims from all over Central America, but especially from El Salvador, had poured into the little town so that every room of every inn and lodging house was taken not just by an occupant, but by a family at least. The sanitary resources of the town were therefore considerably stretched, and I found a place to stay in Chiquimula, forty minutes away.

I had first heard of Chiquimula when I saw a book in a bookshop with the intriguing title of *Chiquimula in History* but when I arrived there it did not look like a town with a history, only a continual languorous present. Provincial and undistinguished to the last paving stone, it had an indefinable charm, as do (for me) all such *ladino* towns. Zacapa, not far distant but hotter and dustier, was the same: a town for petty intrigue, infidelity and vendetta to relieve long tropical boredom. Possessed of an improbable statue of Rufino Barrios presented by a grateful chief of police, and a bust of Miguel

Angel Asturias that makes Guatemala's only Nobel Prize winner look like a large golden toad, one feels that the town awaits its chronicler and poet, that one day all those siestas and quarrels will result in a great work of literature, but that in the meantime . . . it is time to go to sleep.

The receptionist at my hotel spent the whole day perfecting her make-up: it is necessary in a town like Chiquimula to have an absorbing interest. She was obsessional; if she had been a writer, she would never have gone beyond the first paragraph. I took my meals in a restaurant across the road in a large covered courtyard which, in addition to being a restaurant, was a family living room, a garage workshop and quite possibly a brothel as well. But it was Chiquimula cemetery that I loved, with the wise words of one Dr Fernando J. Diaz C. inscribed above the entrance: 'Through this door all hatreds are cancelled and all quarrels forgotten.'

I like graveyards in general, and Guatemalan graveyards are particularly attractive. Every little *pueblo* has its cemetery, the plain block-like tombs gaily painted pink, yellow, white, purple, sky-blue or mauve. They are well cared for and not at all dismal. In the large towns, such as Chiquimula, there are also large family vaults with cherubim, seraphim and angels blowing trumpets.

On 1 November, All Saints' Day, I had been in the little town of Salamá, some sixty miles distant from the capital. All Saints' Day is every cemetery's day of glory, the day on which Catholic Guatemalans go with their families to the tombs of their dead relatives and spend the day there. Flowers are taken: real flowers, beautiful but ephemeral, or plastic ones, gaudy but permanent. A few days beforehand, the family refreshes the tomb with a coat of paint and renews the inscription. On the day itself, everyone picnics over grandmama, eating a dish called *fiambre* – rice and twenty different kinds of cold meat – which is prepared only for this day. Even in death, of course, there are class distinctions, no matter that old quarrels are forgotten. Near the entrance to Salamá graveyard, where the local gentry lie buried in imposing vaults, I saw coiffured European ladies in fine silk dresses lay elaborate wreaths for their departed, many of whose names had passed from generation to generation from before independence, taking their titles such as General, Colonel, Doctor and *Licenciado* with them into the grave. A little further into the cemetery, where the tombs were plainer but boasted at least a brass plaque, a local schoolteacher and poet lay buried, who died prematurely and much lamented, though his flowers, planted in an empty tin of *Nido*, a brand of powdered milk, were but a simple bunch. Deeper still into the cemetery, and at its far edges, were the graves of the poor, mere mounds of earth planted with a wooden or iron cross without a name. But those below were not forgotten: the mounds had been scattered with fresh pine needles (such as Indians spread on churchfloors), and the crosses were draped with coloured paper or polythene, each widow or widower remembering which was the grave of their partner. No grave was totally neglected on All Saints' Day, and even the graves of the dead without descendants were newly painted or strewn with a flower or two.

People from northern latitudes often find the customs of All Saints' Day morbid. I found them not only charming, but moving and wise. It seemed to me that death as the inevitable end of life was accepted better in Guatemala than in our own culture, where everything possible is done to disguise the fact of death until the last moment, when it comes as a terrible shock. And surely it is some consolation to the dying to know that at least once a year they will be remembered.

Nothing could illustrate better the contrast in our attitudes to death than the behaviour of the North American lady with whom I visited Salamá cemetery on All Saints' Day. It happened that she was a member of the American Association of Graveyard Studies, which has a membership of 300, and as such I supposed she would be interested in the activities in the graveyard on this of all days. On the contrary, she regarded them as a hindrance to the proper study of gravestones as purely physical artifacts. I was rather embarrassed when, wishing to take a photograph of a particular tomb, she asked the family who had decorated it in remembrance to remove their flowers so that the tomb should appear in her photograph in its 'natural' state. She preferred her cemeteries dead in every possible sense, so that they were strange and alien places on the edge of town, with no connection to the world of the living. Thus death remained a taboo for her, despite her studies; she belonged to a culture in which death was warded off by facelifts, vitamin tablets, the magical avoidance of ubiquitous substances and even the freezing of corpses at $-270°$. Which was the wiser attitude?

From Chiquimula I commuted to Esquipulas, a town long famous as a centre of pilgrimage, but which won new fame when the five presidents of Central America signed an agreement there in 1987 to bring peace to the region. To commemorate this historic occasion, a monument had been raised near the market, a metal map of Central America made to appear like a bird in flight, set atop some slender pillars. The monument was held in as much reverence as the agreement, that is to say it was somewhat neglected, and though by no means old – less than two years, in fact – the monument had been successfully incorporated into the prevailing disorder of the market, its plinth stuck with posters and stained by streams of urine. Around it pilgrims, too poor or too late to find lodgings, camped among the squashed detritus of the market.

But it is the huge eighteenth-century white-stucco basilica that dominates the town, that dazzles the visitor as he catches a glimpse of the town for the first time from the road leading down into the valley in which it is built. The town serves the basilica, not the other way round. It dominates the entire landscape: the eye cannot escape it. And this was no doubt intended by its architect, for it houses the most famous miracle-working statue in all Central America, the *Cristo Negro*, the Black Christ, of Esquipulas. It was carved in Antigua by the Portuguese sculptor Quirio Catano in 1594, and moved to Esquipulas a year later. The statue is a black crucifix, and 15 January is its day of days.

Apart from the basilica, the town is undistinguished architecturally, as though any attempt at distinction elsewhere would be *lèse-majesté*. The town consists largely of boarding houses, hotels, cheap restaurants and gift shops selling the kind of lurid plastic statues which only popular devotional religion can call forth: pictures from the Last Supper that seen from another angle turn into Depositions from the Cross; plaster saints and Virgins with blood-red hearts; Christs crowned bloodily with thorns; angels with cardboard wings; and, above all, reproductions of the Black Christ itself. And outside the grounds of the basilica are salesmen of balloons, cheap toys, pork crackling, ice creams and the like. Apart from the church, the town has the atmosphere more of a fairground than a holy place. One Englishman I met called it a religious Brighton, though Blackpool might have been nearer the mark. But the fairground has a distinctly medieval flavour as well. On one of the street corners stood a man next to a box two feet wide, tall and deep, set on a stand like a stage for a Punch and Judy show. It was covered in green velveteen with yellow trimmings. The man beside the box used a megaphone to draw a crowd and then opened the doors at the front of the box to reveal the head of a boy supported by a chin strap. It appeared he needed the strap to support his head, for his body must have been

horribly deformed or shrivelled (beyond my powers of conjecture)
to fit in what remained of the box. Having revealed the boy's head,
the man with the megaphone shut the doors again and asked people
in the crowd for two *quetzales*, in return for which the boy would
deliver their fortune by means of a written message. There was no
shortage of takers for this unrepeatable offer, and when the doors
were opened again the boy – who looked as bored and fed up as it is
possible for a boy to look – held between his teeth an envelope in
which was a printed prophecy for the person who had paid. I did not
know whether to laugh or cry, whether this was the most abject
cruelty or a laudable and enterprising way of turning disadvantage to
advantage. And if it were cruelty:

> *O quién es más de culpar,*
> *el que peca por la paga*
> *o el que paga por pecar?*

Whoever was to blame, the boy without a body worked very hard:
for he and his master were still there delivering their prophecies
eight hours later.

And at the entrance to the grounds of the basilica was a collection
of beggars with deformities such as I had never seen, though I am a
doctor and by no means untravelled. Here were people whose view
of life was that of the biblical creatures that creep upon the earth,
their stick-like limbs and twisted spines not allowing them to rise
above ground level. Perhaps they grew expert at telling the character
of normal people by the shape of their ankles. Among them was a fat
lady who sat propped up against some railings, her legs before her
with the worst suppurating sores I have ever seen, uncovered for the
better stimulation of compassion in passers-by. So appalling were
her sores, so overflowing with green pus and liquefying tissue, that
she was the most successful of the beggars; yet – here my doctor's
vision recovered from initial revulsion – I knew she was the least
worthy, in the sense that her condition was remediable by relatively
simple measures. I had the slightly subversive thought that perhaps
she would not have welcomed a cure, insofar as her sores were, in a
manner of speaking, her working capital.

Nearby was another beggar, though I doubt he knew that he was
one. He was microcephalic, his head tiny, and his face such as
Stephen Spielberg might have devised. His torso was in proportion
with his head, but his legs without muscles were jack-knifed under

him, and he moved by a kind of rowing action with his fists upon the ground. But he did not move far from the spot at which he had been placed, where alms were solicited by a plastic cup set before him. From time to time he started a rocking movement forward and back, which accelerated until, just as it seemed he must rock himself over, it stopped as suddenly as it had started. Or sometimes his head would shake from side to side, faster and faster, as though he were disagreeing ever more vehemenntly with some proposition that only he could hear. Once I saw his mother (or owner?), an Indian woman in an apron, come to gather the proceeds from the cup. He recognised her as she swooped down on it, and he lunged forward to try to touch her. She backed away horrified, as though his touch were instantly leprous, and hurriedly emptied the cup of moneyy, setting it empty before him again. Then she left him, and he started to utter strange strangled cries, whether of rage or thwarted affection it was impossible to tell. Later that day I saw him still at his post, now wrapped in a shawl. Where, I wondered, do we keep our microcephalics? Do we keep them out of sight as we keep death out of sight?

Winding through the park in front of the basilica was a line of devotees of the Black Christ. It was several miles long: to reach the statue in the apse must have taken hours of standing. There were no signs of impatience, however, indeed the faces were notably serene. Meanwhile, professional photographers with placards bearing examples of their art took snaps of families on the steps up to the basilica, the women from Oaxaca in Mexico wearing special floral dresses and broad-brimmed hats from which dangled plastic fruit and flowers, while the men generally held a replica of the Black Christ. To the south side of the basilica stood further queues of people, ranged along lines painted on the ground, waiting for the fathers from the monastery to issue forth and bless the religious kitsch they had bought. The fathers marched out in a group, each with a plastic bucket of holy water and a sponge on the end of a handle. They worked their way up and down the lines of faithful, sprinkling the people and their purchases as they went. The older fathers sprinkled the holy water with *cariño*, affection and tenderness, but the younger ones – imbued with a new theology, perhaps, and impatient of such superstitious nonsense – did it as a chore, splashing the water about as if it were a game of water polo, and obviously keen to get it over with. Even the most faithful had to duck to avoid a soaking. But those fortunate enough to be blessed by older fathers held up their religious trophies imploringly, so that they might receive a few sacred drops from the sponge and thus acquire protective powers. No doubt religion is the opium of the people, the sigh of the oppressed, the heart of a heartless world; but what in the brave new world soon to be created will give to these simple people the solace that I saw on their faces when their kitsch had been blessed? Or will social arrangements be then so perfect that there will be no need of solace?

Inside the basilica, the atmosphere was very different. It was dark even in the day, illuminated by candles that the Indians had lit and arranged in rows on the floor (there were no pews). The light of candles is conducive to mystery, and the quiet fervour of the congregation, who stood or sat behind their candles, was obvious even to a sceptic. The air was thick with the smoke of *copal* incense and the murmured prayers of those who turned their eyes adoringly on the Black Christ behind the altar. In the aisles, between the pillars and against the walls, there were many confessionals, all manned by priests and each with a little queue of sinners. As for the Black Christ itself, I had expected something much larger; of its artistic merits I can say nothing because I did not come close enough to it. For the faithful who caressed it lovingly it was *la Sagrada Ýmagen del Señor Crucificado de Esquipulas* (The Holy Image of the Crucified Lord of Esquipulas), as an inscription on an old bridge over a squalid drain in the town put it; and so it would have been quite wrong to approach it as a mere tourist in search of aesthetic experience.

The devotions of the faithful were not entirely confined to the basilica. On a hill overlooking the town is the church of El Calvario, with the Stations of the Cross on the path up to it. An entire family, Indian in dress and appearance, crawled up the hill on its knees, pausing at each of the Stations for the father to lead a prayer and read a passage of the New Testament. Somewhat incongruously, he was interrupted by the explosion of rockets lit round the basilica, that left little puffs of white smoke high in the air. (The Guatemalans love rockets and light them on every possible occasion, leading the unwary to suppose that a coup has broken out.)

As the evening lengthened, dark clouds banked behind the basilica, but shafts of sunlight still fell on the white building, picking it out as if it enjoyed the blessing of heaven itself. The lamps on the stalls outside the basilica began to glitter in the increasing gloom; and from the great church groups of pilgrims emerged, stepping backwards in unison down the stairs, singing a hymm of praise to the *Señor* of Esquipulas. Their faces glowed with fulfilment.

It was time to leave Esquipulas: many pilgrims were already doing so, in cars and buses festooned with coloured streamers to proclaim where they had been. But leaving the town, I noticed a red-striped circus tent, and as the performance was about to begin, I bought a ticket. It was a sad little travelling circus, with an audience of not more than ten, and with only eight performers who doubled as trapeze artists and ticket collectors. The music was loud in proportion to the emptiness of the tent, and there were no lions, tigers or elephants as the crudely painted pictures outside had led one naively to suppose, but only three small poodles who ran long distances (all things considered) on their hind legs and jumped through a few hoops. As for the clowns, there can be few more dispiriting jobs in the world than trying to make ten people laugh in a tent that could comfortably hold a thousand. I stayed till the end, so as not to hurt their feelings.

EIGHT

It is only ten miles from Esquipulas to the border of El Salvador. Before leaving from Europe, I had seen the film *Salvador* and therefore expected to find (as had the protagonists of the film, who were changed by the experience) a landscape of smoking ruins and charred bodies, silent except for occasional bazooka fire and deserted except for hard-faced extortionist soldiers. In the event, everything seemed normal. Of course, I was asked for a document which I did not possess, and thought this was a prelude to extortion; but the document was genuinely required by the law, and the officials, without hint of payment, agreed to waive the requirement in my case.

I employed a *tramitador* aged twelve, despite a sign prohibiting his existence, to guide me quickly through the six offices where I had to have my papers stamped. For his help, he demanded three *colones* (60 cents). When I returned to my truck I found a young man waiting for me to ask for a lift to Metapán, the nearest town, where I intended to stay the night. He spoke Spanish in the Salvadorean way, which is as though through mouthfuls of hot potato (the vowels are elided and the consonants omitted). It turns a poetic language into an ugly slur and is said to use so many archaisms that Spaniards laugh.

The young man was returning to Metapán having spent two weeks in Esquipulas, not as a pilgrim but as a bricklayer seeking work. The proceeds of his ten days of labour were precisely seven *colones* ($1.40), after the deduction of living expenses, exit and entry taxes. This explained why he did not want to take the bus, cheap as it was.

He invited me to lunch at his home. He said his family was poor, but always welcomed strangers. And so I drove him home to his village, a couple of kilometres from Metapán down a dusty pebble-strewn track. His house and garden were surrounded by a thicket fence, but the house was little more than a dark mud hut, old and cracked, with a thatched lean-to for a kitchen. The furniture was as simple as could be, and the hut as a whole was not very different from those I had seen in Africa. Industrial society made itself felt only through the telegraph and electricity poles nearby (there was no electricity in the hut), and by items such as metal knives, plastic bowls and buckets, and by the clothes on the nylon washing line. Chickens were kept in the pre-industrial way, as were pigs: they found what sustenance they could on the ground around them.

Jaime's parents were out, but his grandparents were at home. They were more than seventy years old and had moved into these cramped and far from luxurious quarters from their own house two years before, when the army entered their village, killed thirty people in it and burnt it down. They fled to the only other place they knew.

I should never have guessed their sadness from the way they received me. Their house was mine, they said, though it was humble and not such as I was used to. But I was welcome to stay as long as I wanted. The old man, his grandson and I sat round a little table in the shade of a tree while the old lady prepared lunch. The old man talked of the land and of the drought that was presently affecting it. The land the family owned was four miles from where they lived, over some parched hills, not a walk I should have relished after a day hand-hoeing in the heat. The harvest of maize and beans – the monotonously staple foods of Central America – would be poor this year. The only advantage of a poor harvest was that it meant less sacks to carry . . .

Immediately before lunch was served, Jaime said he wanted to buy some soft drinks in my honour. In vain I pleaded with him not to bother on my account, that water from their well was quite sufficient. (It would have been ungracious to add that I abominated those sickly-sweet chemical compounds.) We drove off to the local store, a kilometre further down the road, which was an adobe kiosk stocking a few bottles of bright green, red and orange drinks all at ambient temperature, the bottles sticky as though the excess sugar had seeped through the glass. Jaime's arrival in a motor vehicle was a moment of triumph for him, something to be talked about in the village. He wanted to pay for the drinks with the last of his money from Esquipulas, but I insisted on paying; and when we returned home with the bottles the old man's eyes lit with pleasure, and I felt ashamed of my haughty disdain of such drinks.

The meal was of rice and chicken, served on cracked enamel plates. I was given by far the largest portion of chicken; the grandson had half of mine and the old people only rice and a little of the juice in which the bird had been stewed. Protest was out of the question. I had met this dignified peasant generosity and courtesy in many parts of the world – a kindliness that led romantic intellectuals to suppose that, once in power, peasants would retain their many virtues.

On learning I was a doctor, the old man told me that for more than a year he had been suffering from a deafness and constant ringing in one ear. I said it might be wax, and having noticed a government clinic in Metapán, suggested that he went there so that a doctor might look. 'Ah *señor*,' he said, 'they treat only the rich who can pay. They do not treat poor people like us.'

Could what he said have been true, or was he under some kind of misapprehension caused by a lifetime of enforced humility? It is easy for people who assume that if they are ill they will be adequately treated to forget – or not to imagine – what it must be like to enjoy no such guarantee. The old man's story was not the greatest tragedy I had heard, nor even the greatest tragedy of his life: but small things often give insight into larger ones, because the larger ones are otherwise beyond comprehension. The idea that a man could remain deaf for years for lack of sufficient money to have his ears syringed would be enough to turn one revolutionary: more effectively so, in fact, than abstruse flights of political economy.

After lunch, they said that a cousin of theirs, a beautiful girl, was celebrating her twenty-first birthday in a village eight kilometres away. They asked whether I should like to go, in the clear hope that I would. To the old people such a journey was an adventure, an unexpected treat; and I was astonished to see the agility with which the seventy-year-old lady climbed into the back of my truck (she had refused to sit in the front from modesty or shyness). Our journey took us through cattle-ranching land where beef for export – so the irresistible argument runs – is produced for the profit of a few at the expense of the peasants and poor city-dwellers, who eat only tortillas and beans. For myself, I thought it unlikely that this particular barren land could produce many beans or much maize, at least without irrigation, but I am not an agronomist.

The cousin's house was slightly more elaborate than Jaime's, but still modest enough. All the other relatives at the party were women, more of them widows than one might have expected from their ages; but it was not the time to ask after the causes of their widowhood. We sat on a small verandah eating pieces of cake as dry as the landscape and drinking Coca-Cola (the local equivalent of champagne) until the girl whose birthday we were celebrating emerged fully-fledged from the house. She was dark and pretty, and she wore a satin dress of shimmering kingfisher blue with a white lace sash, and with blue satin shoes to match the dress. The effect was startling, indeed stunning: that blue, that attention to detail, amidst the dusty drabness. And who was it for? There were no eligible young men around, only widows. Was it the Salvadorean version of dressing for dinner in the jungle?

Jaime asked me whether I should like to marry her. I took this to mean: did I not consider her very pretty? But when I turned to look at him, I saw that he meant it quite literally, that he meant would I marry her and take her away from here? It was not the last time I was asked such a question in El Salvador.

The party seemed to drag on. Perhaps my presence inhibited it. A man was said to be bringing beer, but he didn't arrive. The shadows lengthened; finally I returned to my hotel in Metapán. Book in hand, I sought a restaurant. The town – it was Saturday night – was ill-lit and torpid, except for shouts of drunken laughter and incipient brawls emerging from the bar which was also the town brothel. Again I had the feeling that this was the kind of place from which literature might one day spring, forgetting that it had required an eternity of overfed stupor in myriad provincial towns to produce one Chekhov. And what would Chekhov have made, I wondered, of the little cinema showing *Rambo* (whether I, II, III or IV I cannot recall), purveying mass-murder to the mass-murdered.

It seems that many people cannot have enough of violence. In the restaurant where I ate the fried chicken that is standard fare in cheap restaurants throughout Central America, there was a couple poring over a weekly magazine of crime, astrology and supernatural wonders. They chewed abstractedly over a photograph of a mutilated corpse, brutally murdered and retrieved from a well. Cheap weeklies such as these, printed on poor quality paper, are popular throughout Latin America and rejoice unrestrainedly in gore. The Guatemalan version is called *Extra*, costs twenty centavos, and has the highest circulation of any magazine in the country. Its contents may be judged from the headlines of an edition taken at random:

MANIAC NEGRO WANTS TO KILL PROSTITUTES
PARISHIONER KILLS BARMAID
MIRACULOUS CURES BY NATUROPATH IN GUATEMALA
FACE DESTROYED BY SLASHES

VICTIM OF EARTHQUAKE LEAVES GRAVE
AFTER TWELVE YEARS
POLITICIANS BECOME IMPORTANT

Somehow, photographers from *Extra* always contrive to be present when a corpse leaves its grave after twelve years, or a murdered mother of six is excavated from under a kitchen floor. I wanted to meet the editor, but whenever we had an appointment he had to rush off to the scene of some newly discovered horror. I told myself I wanted to meet him because he must be very well-informed about Guatemalan society, but actually it was the same common-or-garden prurience that made everyone buy his disgusting journal.

The night was warm and the hotel's little rooms, hot and cramped, gave on to a small courtyard. Here people sat until it was time to sleep. I chatted to a young man who had, in the words of an advertisement for a night school in Metapán, 'triumphed in life'. ('Triumph in Life' – it said – 'Learn English.') He had not learnt English, but had certainly triumphed. He was born into a poor peasant family and spent only a year at school. Then his father sent him to work in the fields. At the age of twelve, he had a 'lucky' break: a neighbouring landowner offered him the use of some land providing that he gave the landowner half of his harvest. And so, having worked most of the day in his father's fields, he spent the evenings working his own fields. After five years of this, he had accumulated enough money to pay a courier of illegal immigrants into the United States his fee to smuggle him across the Río Grande ($400). Fortunately, he was not caught, and he made his way from Texas to New York where a cousin of his found him a job as a dishwasher in a Greek restaurant. For three years he worked twelve hours a day, seven days a week, fifty-two weeks a year, for Greek bosses who paid him half the legal minimum wage. Then, having saved enough to start his own business, he returned to El Salvador and bought a truck. It had always been his intention to return, and in the meantime he had learned a little Greek and English (not much) and also to read. In his spare time he had studied the Bible and come to the conclusion that the United States was the Sodom and Gomorrah of today, biblically destined for destruction. The epidemic of AIDS proved it. He wanted his children, when he had them, to grow up in an atmosphere of *tranquilidad*, calm.

Of all the astonishing aspects of his story, this was perhaps the most astonishing: that he considered El Salvador *tranquilo*. I said so.

He replied that he had lived all but three years of his life in El Salvador, and in that time he had seen only two bodies by the side of the road. Of course, he knew people who had seen many more, but he had seen only two. New York was worse. And now he had a trucking business, from which he earned as much in a day as a university-trained clerk in San Salvador earned in a month, which he regarded as a God-given reward for the hard work of his youth. Having become an evangelical, his God was a God of just rewards and punishments: atheists got AIDS, Godfearers got trucks. For El Salvador he wanted only peace.

He spoke without bitterness of the harshness of his early years. He was modest about his achievements, and his ambitions were domestic. It was not too much to call his struggle heroic. But his case was far from unique: the Salvadoreans are known throughout Central America and beyond to be hardworking, well organised and ambitious (Los Angeles is now the second Salvadorean city). It is only in their own country, for geographical and historical reasons, that they cannot succeed.

I left Metapán the next morning and drove to the capital, San Salvador. On the way, I was waved down by a group of soldiers at the side of the road. They asked politely whether I would give them a short lift. A newcomer to Salvador, I was unsure whether it was politic to refuse: after all, I had the transport but they had the guns. Therefore I agreed. They piled into the back of my truck which was soon bristling with weaponry, including a mortar, pointing in all directions. Far from finding this protection reassuring, I found it disturbing. A guerrilla in the scrubby hills on either side of the road would hardly understand (or care) that I was but a visitor, an innocent abroad. Probably, he would conclude I was a firm ally of the Salvadorean Army and attempt to blow us all up. Only later, talking to an old Salvador hand, did I learn that it was now possible to refuse lifts to soldiers, as it was to guerrillas; indeed, it was imperative to do so, if one wished to avoid becoming a military target. I told myself I had been generous, but actually I had been cowardly.

El Salvador is the size of Wales; its capital, therefore, is not distant from any part of it, and the road from Metapán was uncrowded. Once the soldiers alighted, my truck went faster. When I reached the capital, I realised the soldiers had taken a small souvenir of their journey with them – a white plastic bag containing the very thing I could least afford to lose, my notebook. It also contained a book I was translating and the first forty pages of my translation. I thought at first of returning to complain to the soldiers' commander; but then I thought of the difficulty of explaining to him why a mere tourist should be taking such copious and important notes. I resolved to rely instead on my memory, and wondered whether it was possible the soldiers had done me a favour after all by clearing my mind of extraneous detail.

I entered San Salvador from the north. I passed through many coffee plantations, whose neat rows of dark green bushes, shaded from the fierce sunlight by overarching trees, were pleasing to the eye, though not to historians or economists who attribute much of the country's present condition to the spread of precisely such plantations in the nineteenth century. For when coffee became profitable, the 'liberals' throughout Central America decided that communal forms of landholding, or small private plots, were anachronistic and held back the development of the country. By purchase, force and fraud the land soon passed into a few hands – the infamous fourteen families in the case of El Salvador. These families were soon more at home in Paris or New York than in provincial El Salvador, but they spread their tentacles into every phase of Salvadorean economic life. The dominance of a restricted number of families had continued down to the present day, it was said, though they had had to ally themselves with the army and share some of the spoils with it to maintain order; for Salvador's population increases faster than almost any other in the world, and being an agrarian country with little land, this makes the situation for the majority ever more precarious.

Desperation, however, rarely makes itself immediately apparent. Entering San Salvador, one passes through affluent suburbs far larger than those necessary to house fourteen families, however extended. The houses were aflame more with bougainvillea than arson. These suburbs are overlooked by the volcano of San Salvador, on whose green slopes – so it was rumoured at the time of my arrival – guerrillas were massing for an offensive. However, to pay too much credence to rumours in San Salvador is to die a thousand deaths (though to pay them no credence at all might one day be to die just one death). The supermarkets and boutiques of the Beethoven Shopping Centre were well-stocked, the cinemas were showing the latest films, the people were well-dressed, the young looked over-confident. Everything was normal, except for the automatic-toting guards at the entrances to the supermarkets and the written requests to customers to leave their guns outside. Even the playgrounds with yellow plastic dinosaurs and pink giraffes outside the hamburger restaurants (one chain going under the charming and cultured name of *Biggest* and another advertising itself as *Hogar del Whopper*, Home of Whopper) had to be protected by men with scars on their faces carrying Uzis, for the children who played there were kidnap material. At night there was often gunfire from the direction of the volcano, and sometimes the city was plunged into darkness as the power lines were sabotaged yet again.

I decided to stay nearer the centre of the city, in an area that was once Belle Époque, built in the golden age of the elite when mass uprisings and guerrilla warfare were unheard of. The mansions had fallen into disrepair, or were shaken into it by the 1986 earthquake, and the elite had long since decamped to the modernity of the northern suburbs, North America having replaced France as the metropolitan model to emulate. But dilapidation has its charms and compensations, amongst which is economy: I stayed in a small hotel that was cheap and convenient to the city centre. Staying in the hotel were two Gujuratis who lived in England. They were trying to buy a form of unrefined brown sugar that their compatriots in England craved. The quantities involved would have been considerable, but they spoke no Spanish and the Salvadoreans displayed no interest. By now a Guatemalan patriot, I advised them to try Guatemala, and gave them some addresses that might be useful. To my surprise, next morning they were gone.

Having deposited my luggage in the hotel, I set out at once in the direction of the metropolitan cathedral of San Salvador. I was struck by the presence everywhere of graffiti, all of it in support of the guerrillas and their organisations. Not only had walls crumbled through earthquakes and neglect, but what remained of them was covered in slogans, giving to San Salvador the atmosphere of a besieged city about to fall. The markets around the cathedral and the neo-classical *Palacio Nacional* – under reconstruction after the earthquake, but already heavily inscribed with guerrilla slogans – had about them a febrile animation. Everyone seemed to believe this might be the last market day before the triumph of the Revolution; and since, as everyone knows, the first consequence of revolution is a shortage of underwear, it was necessary to stock up for the following fifty years.

I entered the huge cathedral. It was being rebuilt in reinforced concrete. I wondered whether the walls would be richly decorated or left totalitarian grey because the church had more urgent calls on its money than decoration. The congregation was large, but there was no organ to fill the vast spaces under the dome with swelling sound. Instead, there was a band behind the altar playing guitars and maracas, whose democratic but tinny sound was soon lost in the air above. The Catholic church had learned something from the evangelicals.

The archbishop was taking mass. He was surrounded by a seething crowd of camera- and sound-effects men, pointing video cameras, trailing microphone wires and focusing arc lights. Photographers with flashlights climbed up on to the altar rails for a better view, and seemed unconscious of the religious nature of the occasion; or if they knew, they did not care. The videos bore the initials CBS, ABC, NBC. At first I thought someone must have tipped them off that the archbishop was about to be assassinated (as his predecessor had been). But my neighbour in the crowd informed me that they were there because Dr Ruben Zamora, an exiled leader of the opposition, had returned briefly to Salvador to test the water, and he was among the congregation. There was a stir among the gentlemen of the press as a neatly suited man with a well-trimmed beard in his late thirties stepped forward to receive the blood and body of Christ. They struggled for position as the cameras rolled and the lights flashed. Then, quite suddenly, the tension was over and the people with cameras, who moments before looked as though they would gladly have killed each other for a better position, laughed affably together, packed up their things and prepared to leave the cathedral. Dr Zamora returned to his pew, where he was surrounded by a group of clean-cut human rights workers who went everywhere with him, and were a kind of bodyguard. Among them was a Catholic priest. A television arc light turned on him as he prayed, and with admirable spiritual concentration (though beads of sweat began to form on his brow) he appeared to pray all the harder.

When I emerged from the cool gloom of the concrete cathedral into the humid sunshine outside, some banners demanding an end to violations of human rights were draped over the railings and I heard a North American lady wail at another with a camera.

'Can't you fit me in with a banner *and* some earthquake damage?'

From the cathedral church I went to a shop that called itself the Cathedral of Books. The range of works available surprised me; many were highly critical of the government, some of them written by members of the Farabundo Martí Liberation Front. I wondered whether the government employed a variant of the tactics used by previous Guatemalan governments with regard to the university and university students: they allowed the publication and sale of such books, but killed anyone found reading them. I took the risk anyway, and bought many of them, including a history of El Salvador by Roque Dalton, the country's most famous poet, a communist who was murdered by his erstwhile comrades over a doctrinal disagreement. I also bought volumes of liberation theology: where Dalton spoke of Final Victory they spoke of Total Liberation, and I felt vaguely irritated that such nonsensical ideas were not only current but actually motivated people.

Worse still were the piles for sale of *Mi Lucha* (*Mein Kampf*) by Adolfo Hitler; *The Protocols of the Elders of Zion*, translated into Spanish and printed in Mexico; a fat indigenous Mexican volume on the world Jewish conspiracy; and a translation of Henry Ford's ravings on the subject. Appropriately enough, they were near the Occult section, by far the largest in the shop where my eye was caught by *Cafemancia*, or the Ancient Science of Foretelling the Future by Coffee Grounds. The book had a cover with a large blowsy gypsy woman who wore enormous earrings and stared at an empty coffee cup set before her like a crystal ball. I do not know whether Salvadoreans are especially drawn to the occult and the quack; but they once had a president, General Maximiliano Hernández Martínez, who trained himself to look at the sun without filters and who put bottles of coloured water on the palace roof because he believed they acquired medicinal properties once they had absorbed the sun's rays. A theosophist, he believed it was a worse crime to kill an ant than a man because an ant had no eternal soul. Not surprisingly, perhaps, he was in charge of the *Matanza* of 1931, when between ten and thirty thousand Salvadoreans were killed by the army and the remaining Indian culture of Salvador was extirpated utterly. He would have found much to interest him in the Cathedral of Books.

I had been given the name of a North American freelance photographer who lived and worked in Salvador and I called him up. We agreed to meet for breakfast in the Camino Real, the swank new hotel of the capital where all the journalists congregated. They used to gather at the Sheraton, but two American land reform advisers were gunned down in the coffee shop there and the fashion had changed after the construction of the newer, more luxurious hotel. As for the Sheraton, I went there one day for lunch, hoping to see the

Salvadorean elite at play. Only a few came. They sat round the pool while a thatched bar dispensed drinks with pieces of fruit and tropical flowers attached to the rim of the glasses. For the amusement of their children, two clowns with foam rubber feet and polystyrene noses wandered from family to family; but the children, prematurely sophisticated, gave them hardly a glance. I wondered who the people were in the clowns' costumes. Students perhaps? And if they were, was the disdain of the children hardening their revolutionary resolve?

I met the freelance photographer as arranged next morning. Dr Zamora was staying at the hotel and I nearly tripped over him. He looked thoroughly bourgeois, not a revolutionary at all. Almost everyone else in the hotel was a correspondent for a large North American or European newspaper: the permanent crisis in Salvador had at least done them some good. By comparison with these battle- and bar-hardened correspondents, I felt very much an innocent. My photographer was a man of about forty with a grizzled beard which somehow conveyed that he had been through and seen everything, which he had.

'Ungo's arriving today,' he said as he pushed some of the buffet breakfast into his mouth. It was clear he was a man who lived on his nerves, who never slowed down for a moment.

'Yes,' I replied sagely, wondering who or what Ungo was. Having passed myself off as some kind of journalist, I was supposed to know.

Guillermo Ungo (I learned later) was another leader of the opposition returning to El Salvador to test the water. He had once been an associate of José Napoleón Duarte ('Leatherlungs' as he was known to the correspondents on account of his ability to talk endlessly and emphatically without ever getting to the point), and had even been his vice-presidential candidate in the 1972 elections. They were defrauded of victory and the two men had subsequently fallen out.

The photographer looked around him nervously at the other people eating breakfast. He was worried they might be on to something he didn't know about.

'Have you heard any rumours?' he asked, leaning forward and whispering.

I hadn't, but it was a golden opportunity to start one. Once I was on a plane from London to Delhi that was diverted to Karachi because of fog. I said there had been a coup in Delhi and there were tanks on the runway there. By the time the rumour returned to me, thousands had been killed.

'No,' I replied.

'Something's going on,' he said. He was like a wild animal that senses a predator is near.

I found myself eating as nervously as he, stuffing chunks of watermelon into my mouth with scrambled eggs, mushrooms and coffee. Evidently, to be a real journalist – which I had never yet been – one needed strong tastebuds.

After a period of trying to sniff out the latest rumour, he turned his attention to me for a short time – though never completely. He had what I discovered was the correspondent's characteristic way of looking at an unimportant interlocutor, with one eye on him and the other scanning the horizon to see if there was anyone more important there. I told him what I was doing in Salvador, without being quite sure myself. He, on the other hand, was eking a living – quite a good one when El Salvador was fashionable, or 'sexy' as he put it, in the North American media. He took photographs of ambushes, massacres, helicopter attacks, explosions and other such events. El Salvador was terrible and he loved it. The comparative calm of the capital bored him. He liked nothing better than to be caught in crossfire in a minefield. In fact, he needed danger as a junkie needs his drug. Without it, withdrawal symptoms set in: lethargy, drinking, depression, and then the whole futility of existence came crashing in on him. I think he must have been brought up in a quiet Mid-Western suburb.

Suddenly he had to leave. He had things to do, unlike me: I envied him. We would meet later, one evening he said.

Some words of it remained in my memory.

'If you don't hate American imperialism now,' he said, 'you will after you've been to El Salvador.'

Maybe he was right, but I thought it strange he did not connect his own behaviour in the cathedral – he had been one of the mob photographing Dr Zamora – with American imperialism. For him, the right of the American people to see his pictures (or not to see them, if something more dramatic cropped up) overrode the right of the Archbishop of El Salvador and his congregation to conduct a mass with reasonable decorum. Arrogance, of course, has more than one face.

I decided to confront the representatives of American imperialism directly, in their lair. I called the embassy and asked for an appointment to meet the press officer. How about tomorrow at two? They couldn't have been more helpful.

My photographer had told me that it would not be necessary to specify to the taxi driver which embassy. *La Embajada*, the Embassy, was all that was necessary to say. Nevertheless, I added, *estadounidense*, of the United States, for appearances' sake.

The concrete wall around the embassy was of tank-repellent and car-bomb-proof thickness. The building itself was surrounded by strange netting that somebody told me was to protect it against rocket fire. None of this, however, had prevented the outer walls from being daubed with blood-red slogans, under the very eye of the marine guard in his bullet-proof tinted-glass sentry-box set high in the concrete wall. 'Here,' declared a slogan, 'is where they plan the massacres of the people.' At one time the embassy paid for the removal of the slogans, but they always reappeared overnight, and now they were just left where they were. There were no volunteers in the embassy, apparently, for the post of Sisyphus.

I entered the embassy through a series of security gates, a label was attached to my collar and the press officer came to greet me. He led me back into his office. The embassy, with its seven hundred diplomats, attachés and aid workers seemed as isolated in atmosphere from the country around it as an astronaut's capsule is from outer space. One sensed immediately that the truth about El Salvador, whatever it was, could neither enter nor emerge from here, not because of conspiracy or even incompetence, but simply because the air conditioning, the comfortable chairs, the American flags, the camaraderie, the iced-water machines everywhere and the open plan offices precluded it.

'Well, Tony,' said the press officer as we sat down, 'what can I do for you?'

His manner was so affable, pleasing and informal, and his tone so eminently reasonable, that I felt myself sucked at once into his view of the world. I wondered whether his charm was natural, or whether it had been taught at some fiendishly sophisticated State Department course for press officers. At any rate, it was irresistible. He ensnared me further with expressions like 'As you and I both know . . .' and 'Let's face it. . .' It would have taken a stronger man than I to contradict him, especially as he had a picture of his family behind him, with such healthy, happy children and so loving a wife. All in all, he persuaded me that everything was progressing satisfactorily in El Salvador, well yes, between you and me there was still a little fighting but the army had 'gotten its act together' and wasn't killing people at random any more, it was more professional thanks to 'training imput', so the country was all more or less under government control; well yes, there was a lot of corruption viewed from our angle, but from a Latin American standpoint it was about average, certainly there were worse places in Latin America for corruption, in Central America even; and I wouldn't like to tell you, Tony, that there wasn't any corruption because, let's face it, you wouldn't believe me anyway, but had I ever been to Mexico, those policemen over there were something else . . .

The only question I asked that gave him even a millisecond of discomfort was why, if everything was now so firmly under control, the embassy had rocket-repellent netting around it.

The answer, of course, was that even with the guerrillas on the retreat – close to defeat, in fact – one couldn't be too careful. Actually, Tony, this was the most dangerous time: facing defeat, the guerrillas might out of desperation resort to pure advertising gimmicks, like blowing up the US embassy.

The marine who let me out of the embassy compound hoped I would have a nice day. And in the evening the wife of the British chargé d'affaires kindly invited me to a party she was giving at her home for the schoolteachers of the British School of San Salvador. Before going to the party, I found a florist who seemed especially strong on wreaths, but I managed to persuade her that I needed something more cheerful. She came up with a bouquet of waxy tropical flowers stuck into a round pot that looked like a typical nineteenth-century anarchist's bomb. I rushed back to my car with it. In the meantime a Peugeot 504 had parked next to me. Normally I should not have noticed this, but the Peugeot had an extraordinary feature: a smoky-dark windscreen with a clear band across it at the level of the driver's and passenger's heads, a band that contained roundels of darkened glass where the heads would be. Was this so that assassins would not recognise them, or so that as assassins they would not be recognised, or perhaps for both reasons? Whatever the explanation, I thought it best to put some distance between the Peugeot and myself.

The chargé lived in a comfortable suburb, but the streets were dark and poorly lit. They were also almost deserted, and when I came across a peasant woman, obviously a servant, and asked her the way, she was too terrified to speak and hurried away without doing so. But I found the house. There were bright lights flooding the garden and a guard with an automatic weapon at the gate. He took my flowers for the chargé's wife, tipped them upside down and gave them a good shake to remove the grenades and Lugers. Convinced there were none, he let me in.

The schoolteachers were standing about on the lawn, drinks in hand. I was introduced to the headmaster and his wife. Before long the headmaster was extolling life in El Salvador. This was scarcely surprising, since previously he had been a headmaster in Hackney. Not only was El Salvador considerably safer than Hackney, but there were bougainvilleas in his garden. All this loose talk of danger was nonsense: it (by which I presumed he meant death) could happen anywhere. In Hackney, for example, one of this teachers narrowly escaped death by a stone from a pupil's catapult. Of course, the British school was an elite establishment – in fact, it was the best school in El Salvador, if not in Central America – so one would hardly expect the same discipline problems as in a slum comprehensive in London. The only slight difficulties encountered in Salvador but not in London were with the almost daily telephone calls to tell the headmaster that a bomb had been placed in the school. He ignored these warnings, which usually came – he suspected – from pupils who had not done their homework and hoped to postpone the moment of reckoning by creating a panic. There was also a problem with the parents of children who failed the entrance examination: they came with bribes and were bewildered when they were refused and their children still not given a place. It was beyond their experience and comprehension that bribes should not produce the effect desired, and it angered them. Apart from this, however, there were no problems. The headmaster would be happy to spend many years in El Salvador, the electricity blackouts notwithstanding. As for his wife, she was also content to stay, for her memories of Hackney did not entice her to return.

The next evening, I met the photographer again. He lived in a flat with the BBC correspondent and another from a famous North American news magazine who was of Salvadorean descent but whose family had long ago emigrated to the States. Both of them were in a panic about transmitting their stories to their respective editors by a certain deadline, stories which might or might not be used. In fact, they lived in a permanent state of anxiety, chasing the next story. The constant fear of missing something, and their inability to step back from the day-to-day events, made their jobs less enviable than I had supposed them to be. My lack of any but the vaguest deadlines, my freedom to write of anything I chose, was luxury indeed.

She was alarmed that, after something of a lull, bodies were beginning to appear again by the sides of roads. This was not only a bad thing in itself; it also meant she would be called out more often to remote places at inconvenient times to see what she had seen a hundred times before. And there were disturbing signs in the city as well. A Salvadorean employee of the American embassy had been murdered recently; this happened only a day or two after a gun attack on an embassy limousine, though it was bullet-proof and no one was hurt. The rumours that a guerrilla offensive was on its way grew ever stronger.

A young North American who worked for a large financial journal as its Mexican and Central American correspondent arrived at the flat and we went out to dinner at one of the best restaurants in San Salvador. He had just returned from an interview with one of Salvador's richest men, the scion of a landowning family, an industrialist and banker. He lived permanently surrounded by bodyguards; there were arms wherever he went; and he carried a gun with him to bed. This was now accepted as a normal part of a rich man's life in Salvador, as normal as a patient with angina carrying a bottle of glyceryl trinitrate with him in case of attack. And though an outsider might wonder whether the light was worth the candle, it had not yet occurred to any members of the elite to divest themselves of some of their wealth for the sake of a quiet life. To give an inch in this respect was – in the circumstances that they or their forebears had to a large extent created – to give a mile. Unlike other Central American elites, the Salvadorean elite had developed no aristocratic charm; it was graceless, vulgar, ostentatious and callous. We were all agreed on this as we sat down at our immaculately laid table, while the waiters hovered in the background with just the right blend of deference and unobtrusiveness.

The restaurant was dimly lit, there were a lot of potted plants, a courtyard and a fountain. It was another of those institutions that had benefited from the civil war, for without the civil war there would have been no correspondents, and without correspondents very few customers. At the next table was a well-known television reporter from one of the big networks who had been making a film about Salvador and was about to fly off to somewhere else terrible. The other tables were taken by the best newspapers in the United States and Canada. So many reporters, so much ignorance to overcome back home: surveys are forever demonstrating that the

majority of people in the United States think the communists are in
power in El Salvador, that Fidel Castro is a cardinal, that Nicaragua
is a close ally of their country. If writers and journalists were ever
inclined to modesty, this would make them modest. In the
meantime, as I ate something excellent, I envied them their expense
accounts.

There were cynics who said that neither side in the war wanted to
win any more than they wanted to lose, for, once the war was over,
United States aid of $700 million a year, from which both sides
profited, would cease. Financially speaking, a stalemate was the best
result. It seemed to me inherently unlikely that the present
stalemate was more than an unstable equilibrium between two
forces brought about without anyone willing it; but people for whom
the world was but a vast conspiracy (not a few, with intellectuals
prominent among them) told me that the commanders of both sides
had come to a solemn agreement not to defeat each other. And my
photographer told me that if ever peace came to El Salvador, he
would have to move on: the orange explosion of a shell against the
green of a hill was an addictive sight, one without which he could not
live.

I didn't usually eat in such elegant surroundings. Near my hotel
was a vegetarian restaurant run by a middle-class lady with a
German husband. It was open only for lunch and around the walls
were advertisements for meditation classes, herbal healers, and so
forth. It was not far from the military hospital, whose crumbling
walls were covered with exhortations to 'honest' soldiers and officers
to desert. The restaurant did not lack for customers, and during
lunchtime one had the illusion of being in a normal place, where
people's main concern was blood pressure rather than politics.
Another time, when in a hurry, I went to a branch of Biggest, a
hamburger chain, where the gilded youth of Salvador tried to look as
Californian as possible; I ordered a Biggest, which was very big
indeed, the kind of hamburger that a person who weighs eight
hundred pounds might consider a snack. But mostly I ate in a
restaurant owned by a Chinese family, in an area of the city I was told
it was fatal to enter after dark. The head of the family sat by the cash
register counting the takings, as if reassuring himself that in the
event of the city falling, he had enough money to start up again
elsewhere. Of course, the moment the city fell, the Salvadorean
currency, the *colón*, the columbus, would be worthless, but for the
moment it could be exchanged for dollars (and vice versa) just

outside the main post office, where touts with large bundles of notes fell on anyone who looked like a potential customer. For the moment, the black market rate of exchange was only 15 per cent above the official rate, evidence no doubt of the huge number of dollars flowing into the country to sustain the war effort. Everyone was agreed that in all other respects Salvador was now bankrupt.

After five days, I left the capital for a short excursion up to the north of the country, into one of the war zones. The chargé kindly informed me which of the roads were mined (according to his latest information), and which I should therefore avoid. Land mines were the single largest cause of injury to soldiers of the Salvadorean army: it was said that one in sixteen combat troops were injured by them each year, and certainly the government made use in their propaganda of the propensity of mines to maim, though I met no one who suggested the FMLN used mines deliberately against civilians, even if civilians were often the victims. The chargé told me it was possible I should be turned back on the northern highway by soldiers, and, as for going beyond the town of Chalatenango, I should need a pass from the military, which it was unlikely they would grant since I was not an accredited correspondent and I had no other plausible reason for going.

I set out. The road soon led through sugar plantations – mile on mile of cane fields. The monotony made one think Salvador was a large country, rather than a sixth of the size of an average state in the United States. Huge trucks laden with cane trundled along the road, strewing cane behind them for the next vehicle to squash which gave off a sour, fermenting smell. The words of an economist to whom I had spoken ran through my head like a refrain: sugar is a fool's crop. It was harmful to the land, needed only seasonal labour, was grown in a hundred other countries and the price was low. But once you started to grow it there was no turning back. It was disastrous to put scarce land to such a use, especially when there was widespread malnutrition. Some thought the solution was to divide up the land to create a class of prosperous peasant proprietors who would provide a market for mass-produced articles from the city; others that it lay in collectivisation and state-directed investment. For myself, I foresaw only difficulties whatever was done: the population was doubling every twenty-five years, and Salvador was already as crowded as Holland. Insofar as there was a solution, it was in mass emigration to the United States, a conclusion to which hundreds of thousands of Salvadoreans had come.

At every bridge over every stream there were pillboxes for the soldiers who guarded them against sabotage. They did not stop me, and the chargé had told me that in this area the guerrillas were decent, sporting fellows who did not attack civilians at random, unlike those in the north-east of the country who were led by a notoriously bloodthirsty psychopath. Thus my journey was without event, except that ten miles before Chalatenango I gave a lift to a hitchhiker who turned out to be a priest in mufti, as priests in Central America almost always are these days. He said he was hoping to go to the village of Flores, where his brother lived, but he was not hopeful of obtaining the necessary permission from the military. If he did, I could go with him.

He also suggested that while in Chalatenango I stay in the *casa parroquial*, the parish house. This was near the church in the central square. On one side of the square was the municipal building, now occupied by the military headquarters for the whole department. Enormous military trucks painted dark olive, with black churning wheels and gears that ground without mercy, went to and fro, loaded with raw-faced recruits in steel helmets. Nearby were stalls where soldiers bought small items of comfort and luxury to supplement their rations, and where they met girls from the town. Not a few of the soldiers were on crutches, or with a leg in plaster, or had a limp or an artificial limb. Cruel and brutal the army might have been, even cowardly, but it was not true its soldiers had paid no price.

The parish house was large and bare. In it had lived four North American nuns and Catholic lay workers who were raped and killed as they returned from leave by Salvadorean soldiers; their deaths had caused – under public pressure – a brief reappraisal of United States policy towards El Salvador, so that it seemed for a time that the fate of the country hinged on the discovery and punishment of the murderers. There were photos of the four martyrs on the walls of the house, together with stylised doves and other symbols of peace. But in ghoulish confirmation of Andy Warhol's famous dictum, that everyone in the twentieth century is destined to be famous for fifteen minutes, the four were forgotten, at least in official circles.

An atmosphere of quiet purpose reigned in the house. Everyone was conscious of doing, and of being, good, and spoke with the not entirely unselfconscious sweetness I associated more with evangelicals than Catholics. I met a visiting Spanish nun who had spent fourteen years in Guatemala before moving to Salvador. She had heard of and seen many terrible things in Guatemala, atrocities committed by the army. I mentioned that the guerrillas of the *Ejército Guerrillero de los Pobres*, the Guerrilla Army of the Poor, had committed some atrocities of its own, that it was not a purely benevolent organisation. At once she grew vehement; the guerrillas *never* committed atrocities. I said I knew of one village where they killed at least twenty people.

'They were Military Commissioners,' she said. Military Commissioners are civilian spies for the army, sometimes volunteers, often not.

'No,' I replied, 'they were ordinary peasants.'

She stared at the wall beyond me. She had not heard me.

'Yes,' she continued, 'the guerrillas have been trying to get rid of the Military Commissioners for a long time.'

Against such an entrenched point of view I had learned that it was pointless to argue. She needed the guerrillas to be immaculate as she needed everything that existed and had hitherto existed to be wretched and miserable. It suited her eschatology, her need for overarching purpose.

There was also a North American father from Honduras visiting the house. At first he was barely civil, as though his preferential option for the poor was enhanced by brusqueness towards the rich (as he conceived me to be). He wore the slightly shabby casual clothes that were the new uniform of the religious. Had priests and the religious in Central America grown so ashamed of the past of their church that they wished to be dissociated from it? He and I slept in the same bare room with hard beds and a dim light. There he told me he was a believer in the Theology of Liberation, and was working for the Total Liberation of Man. I was too tired to ask of what that consisted; whether it meant, perhaps, that Man would no longer ever feel sleepy.

I went with the Salvadorean priest to whom I had given a lift to the army headquarters to ask for a *salvoconducto*, a safe conduct, to the village of Flores, only a few miles from Chalatenango, but in an area often held by the guerrillas. As we entered, we met an officer with an artificial leg, and asked him for the document. To my surprise, he did not ask us to identify ourselves or state a reason for going, he asked only our names and gave orders to a soldier to prepare the document for us. He asked us in the meantime to take a seat in the waiting room near the entrance. There a fattish peasant woman was waiting for an officer who, when he arrived, was almost courtly in his manner. He complied with the woman's request, whatever it was, and when she thanked him he bowed and said, '*Para servirle*', 'at your service.' Meanwhile, the courtyard outside was being swabbed down by soldiers and there was much standing to attention, stamping of feet and saluting. It was not quite as I had expected: all demoralisation, apathy and rudeness.

The priest and I went next morning first to an encampment for refugees who had returned recently to Salvador from Honduras. There were a few hundred of them in an arid valley through which ran a redeeming stream. The men and some of the boys were removing water from the stream in tin cans to irrigate the communal vegetable garden. It was hot work, but social and therefore bearable. The government, they said, had done nothing to help them: on the other hand, it had done nothing to hinder them either, which was an improvement. The houses of the settlement were makeshift, of wood and corrugated zinc, of thatch and cardboard, but the people appeared resilient and determined to make a life for themselves once more. The villages from which they came had been destroyed by the army, they had lost many friends and relatives, yet still they wanted to build anew. Of course they had little choice, but I had seen this astonishing peasant stoicism before – in Tanzania, for instance, where a large proportion of the population was forcibly and brutally removed and herded into new villages where the governing party could keep a closer eye on it, all at the whim of a man the world accounted a saint because he was a fluent and plausible public speaker. Indeed, there seems almost an inverse relationship between the virtue of a government and the virtue of a people: the less admirable the government, the more admirable the people.

We moved on from the camp, along a road that the chargé had said was mined. Local information had told us it was not: still, I drove with caution, as though caution could have made any difference. Before long, the road was impassable in any case and we had to walk the last few kilometres. (Although it was a war zone, I persuaded myself that my unattended truck was somehow inviolable. The mind is a flexible instrument.) It was a strange, eerie landscape that we walked through. It would have been arid anyway, but for several hundred yards on either side of the road the ground was charred black, right up the slopes of the hills. For the first time in my life, I saw what a scorched earth policy meant: it meant a scorched earth. Not a bird sang, not a leaf stirred. The silence was more than the mere absence of sound. And from time to time, we came across an abandoned house, the walls still standing but the upper edges of them charred with carbon where the roof had been burnt. Around the houses grew a few stalks of maize, not cultivated but wild, growing where grains had fallen. There was no detritus in the houses to indicate recent occupation. We spoke little as we walked. Our words were feeble things in that immensity of silence.

We reached Flores after an hour and a half. Somehow it had escaped the conflagration. There was an oasis of green around it and the village's whitewashed church shone across the valley. Everything was normal as we entered and it could have been any of a thousand such villages. The unevenly cobbled main street ran between small stores which were no more than a glass chest and a wooden counter at the entrance to a living room. People stood about talking, young men stretched languidly in the shade of mango trees to sleep after a midday beer. And scattered along the street were young men and women, dressed in military trousers, with water bottles attached to canvas belts, and T-shirts, holding automatic weapons at the ready. They were guerrillas of the FMLN, who had returned to the village after the army had passed through. The priest told me not to be frightened: these were good young people.

We approached a young couple who looked not merely smart but elegant in their fatigues. From the way they carried themselves I should have guessed they were not from the lower strata of society: their movements had the easy grace of those born to command. They passed the time of day with us and their accents proved them educated. They offered us cigarettes and asked whether we had seen the army on the way to Flores. We told them no, which was the truth. Had I seen a patrol, I should undoubtedly have told them, though I am no believer in revolutions. I was reminded of Dostoyevsky who, even though he was as far removed from the revolutionary camp as it was possible to be, said he would not inform the police if he knew of a conspiracy to place a bomb in the Winter Palace.

There were many questions I should have liked to ask the couple, both personal and political. There was no time, however, for they were on patrol. Their relations with the villagers were obviously cordial; no one shrank from them as they might from people given to sudden atrocity. I wanted to ask them how they had become involved with the guerrillas, what impelled them, and how they saw the new, liberated El Salvador? How would they deal with the displeasure at their victory of the United States, which was not only the source of most of El Salvador's imports but, more importantly, the destination of most of its exports? Did they believe the Soviet Union would step into the breach? And how would they avoid the catastrophic drop in agricultural production that usually follows radical land reform?

The couple turned to go. They walked hand in hand up a side street and into the hills. It was all rather romantic, like the happy end of a movie. I am sure they were thoroughly contented, people who had found meaning and fulfilment early in life.

But a guerrilla war is not all happy endings, with lovers going into the hills holding hands. Three days before my arrival in Flores, the BBC correspondent had been there. The village then as now was occupied by soldiers of the FMLN, but they were mainly boys aged about fourteen. An army patrol arrived and a small battle ensued. Two young guerrillas tried to escape from the square in front of the church. One of them got away but the other (perhaps even less than fourteen) was cornered and saw that he could not escape. He threw down his gun, put up his arms and shouted, 'Don't shoot!' With the BBC correspondent watching from the shelter of the church, the pursuing soldiers gunned him down.

It was a cowardly act, a brutal and unnecessary one, and from the purely military point of view a stupid one also. Might the boy not have proved a valuable source of intelligence? As propaganda, the killing of a young lad who had surrendered in full view of a foreign correspondent could hardly have been worse. But I have never been a conscript, dragooned into an army and made to fight a war I did not understand, sent on patrol day after day in a landscape in which any gully, any tree, any cave or rock might hide the agent of my death. Such an experience would perhaps alter my *Weltanschauung* a little. To be a target whatever one's private opinions is hardly an incentive to develop one's faculty of reason. And while the killing of boys who have thrown down their weapons is reprehensible, is the arming of them in the first place entirely praiseworthy?

We went to visit the priest's eldest brother, an ordinary peasant whom the priest had not visited for many years for lack of opportunity. The brother lived in a simple two-roomed house with a verandah of hardened earth. It was down a lane through which an open sewer ran, the delight of piglets, which had been churned into black malodorous mud. On the verandah was a baby's cot – a cardboard carton in which a baby lay, into which it had volumi-nously defecated. As we sat and chatted, I felt ashamed – effete, out of touch with our animal nature – for finding the baby's excrement so offensive and distracting. Fortunately, the mother, who looked too old to have given birth so recently, scooped the carton clean.

The priest's brother supported the guerrillas, at least passively. Why should he support the government? What had it ever done for the likes of him? There were no schools, no clinics, no roads, no drains even. The guerrillas would give them all these things when they came to power, the situation couldn't be worse than it was now, besides the guerrillas had never massacred anyone. What he said was so cogent, and so obviously the result of bitter personal experience, that I felt it would have been callow to counter it with my bookish outlook. Yet if the history of the twentieth century proved anything, it proved that however bad things were, human ingenuity could usually find a way to make them worse. This was not a message for a man who had already lived a hard life. Besides, he would have taken me for an associate of the enemy; most of the foreigners who came to Flores believed in the guerrillas as much as he.

We ate a meal of rice and beans, and then went visiting in the village. Everywhere we were courteously, even affectionately received. There were many *abrazos*, embraces, and relations seemed harmonious to a degree unknown among us. Their suffering had created solidarity. Or perhaps peasant life had always been like that. At any rate, I thought it strange that such ferocity in the civil war should coexist with such personal gentleness.

Having completed our visits, we set out for my truck. Two boys from Flores and an older man accompanied us, the two boys taking it in turns to carry a sack of grain sent as a gift from Flores to the parish house in Chalatenango. Though evening was approaching, it was still hot and the boys sweated profusely, but they treated the carrying of the sack as a game. The older man insisted on carrying the small bag I had with me, and would not hear of refusal. We walked together behind the others and fell to chatting.

He had lived all his life in Flores. The worst years – those of the early Eighties – were now over, though no one could say they would never return. (In many ways, Salvador's recent history paralleled Guatemala's: the dictator Maximiliano Hernández Martínez came to power in 1931, as did Jorge Ubico, and he fell from power in 1944, as did Ubico. The worst years of repression were the same in Salvador and in Guatemala. But still they were very different countries.) My companion told me as we walked how the army had improved of late: now if we met a patrol it would inspect our papers, ask a few questions and continue on its way, when not many years ago it would have shot us dead on sight. Further along the track we came to a corner where the guerrillas had ambushed an army convoy (the road was better then) and killed eighty-one soldiers, for the loss of none of their own. I saw no remaining evidence of this event, but he assured me the place was celebrated for it.

And what, I asked, did he think of *los muchachos*, the boys, as the guerrillas were known? Well, he knew they were brave, highly disciplined, well-meaning and so forth, in fact vastly superior morally and personally to the army of the government; but yet he did not want them to win, unlike most of the people of Flores. He feared the economic consequences of their victory, the shortages that would follow, the reaction of the United States. For a man who said he never left Flores, he was remarkably sophisticated.

Arriving back in Chalatenango, the electricity supply had been blown up yet again, not only there but in the neighbouring towns as well. Telecommunications had been disrupted too, and there had been an explosion in the nearby small town of Dulce Nombre de María (Sweet Name of Mary). When night fell, the only light in the town was that of candles, except for the floodlights in the army headquarters (which naturally had its own generator). The rest of the town was densely dark, with a few weak and guttering lights at the windows. I went in search of a meal and found a bar illuminated by a single candle. The owner was cursing the guerrillas for having interrupted the electricity supply once more. What benefit was it to poor people like her, she wanted to know. The guerrillas were supposed to be helping the poor. Luckily, the beer was still cold. Soon we were laughing about her son, who wanted to spend his whole life watching television and gave no thought to his future. He did no work at school, finding enthusiasm only for football. I said he sounded perfectly normal to me, and then I gave him a dire warning – the privilege of my advanced years – of the consequences for the rest of his life of laziness at school. Now it was his turn to laugh – silly old fool, he thought. It was odd to be discussing ordinary family affairs in the middle of a blackout caused by a revolution. It was reassuring too, a way of denying to ourselves that anything more serious could happen in the night, like an attack on the town or more explosions.

The sun rose next morning, shining indifferently on our large and small concerns. Nothing untoward had happened in the night and I set out to return to the capital. The graveyard was on the edge of town, and I stopped to seek the graves of the four murdered North

Americans. It is difficult to credit now but the placing of cemeteries under secular rather than ecclesiastical control was one of the platforms of nineteenth-century Central American liberalism, a platform passionately defended and attacked. I found three of the graves for which I was looking, simple and unadorned. There seemed an excess of people buried in 1981 and 1982.

Soon after returning to San Salvador I set out for the east of the country, where the psychopathic guerrillas were. Of course I wasn't going to the *really* bad areas – I like my danger to be a mild rather than an overwhelming experience – but still I was passing through areas where harm was not unknown to happen. I was confident of emerging safely, however: we are all immortal until we die, and I had headphones on which to play Schubert songs. Surely no one would kill me while I was listening to Schubert?

I took a road to the south and then east, parallel to the Pacific coast. I had not expected such a melancholy landscape. For many miles the fields and houses were abandoned. The concrete roads had fallen into disrepair and were almost without traffic, and no effort had been made to repair them. For mile after mile every telegraph pole had been chopped in two, the stumps blackened by fire, the wires on the ground, tangled and twisted. Every so often there was a service station, or what had once been one: the pumps were gone, the forecourt empty, the windows of the office smashed or cracked, the doors off their hinges. The Salvadoreans are famous for their industry, but even with peace it would take years, decades, before this land was restored to what it had once been. It took genius to invent and industry to spread the telegraph and telephone; it took an axe or a match to destroy them.

I turned to the north, towards the town of San Miguel, and drove along the *Panamericano*. Here there was traffic and construction activity, both of which were frequently interrupted by the guer-rillas. Good roads benefit the army, of course, but also the people; they increase trade and spread prosperity. The economic effect of a good road can be quite startling: in Guatemala, the end of the paved road is the beginning of greater poverty. I wondered whether in Salvador the glorious future would be worth the interrupted journeys? By degrees, the landscape became one of majestic beauty, of volcanoes (some of them smoking) against the pastel shades of the evening sky.

I stayed a night in San Miguel, a town once briefly occupied by the guerrillas but now restored to normal, at least on the surface.

Someone had had enough confidence in the future to build a modern hotel there. Dining in the restaurant with a few Salvadorean bourgeois, one had again to remind oneself that this was no ordinary country, but one that had threatened continuously to fall apart for the past eight years. Even in a crisis, however, people have to live, shop, make love, drink beer, catch buses. It is newspapers and television that persuade us that life can for long be catastrophe and nothing else.

I spent my last night in a little town with the pretty name of Santa Rosa de Lima. It was something of a diversion, along a road that was reported as dangerous. I went not because the town was architecturally interesting – it wasn't – but because the *South American Handbook*, that most excellent of guides, said there was a restaurant there that served exquisite crab soup and anyone in Santa Rosa would direct you to the restaurant. The Soup was to Santa Rosa what the Embassy had been to San Salvador. As in nearly everything else, the *Handbook* was right: I was directed to the restaurant, which was four tables in the front of the owner's house, and the Soup was delicious. I forgot to ask where the crabs came from – Santa Rosa de Lima is a long way from the sea – but I drank too much beer, and the question seemed unimportant.

This was how one of my abiding memories of El Salvador, a country in which 50,000 people have died during the last eight years of civil war (equivalent in percentage to 500,000 deaths in Britain or 2,3000,000 in the United States), came to be of crab soup.

NINE

Near the border with Honduras, I picked up a Mexican hitchhiker. He had a slight speech impediment and a harelip which had been repaired. He was on his way to Nicaragua. I asked him what he did for a living, and he said he was a doctor.

'I'm a doctor too,' I explained.

I felt at once a certain professional solidarity with him, almost as if we were co-conspirators. But something that was half-voice, half-itch, located near my occipital lobe just inside my skull, kept worrying at the question of why, if he were a fully qualified doctor, was he hitching lifts? Perhaps he had just qualified, I told myself, and had not yet found work.

There were no problems on the Salvadorean side of the border, and at first I thought our passage into Honduras would present no difficulties either. But a Honduran soldier began poking about in my luggage. He soon found my bag of books which, regardless of contents, was suspicious enough (great readers are dangerous). He removed the bag for closer inspection with a colleague of his who sat in a stone blockhouse by the roadside; a fierce wind whistled through the slits in the walls. The Mexican doctor, Carlos, and I watched as the two soldiers took the books out of the bag, piled them high on the table and then subjected them to military literary criticism. It was the criticism of torturers.

They took the books and bent the spines and covers. They thought this would give them a clearer view of the pages. Their hands were dirty and they also put their thumb-prints on the text, like illiterates signing affidavits. Their view of literature was simple: if a book contained the word communist, Cuba or Havana it was subversive. The concept of knowing your enemy was alien to them. One by one they inspected the books, some of whose titles alone were sufficient to condemn them to confiscation. They placed the volumes they had inspected in two piles: permitted and prohibited. Two biographies of Archbishop Romero (the Archbishop of El Salvador who was murdered) were forfeit, as was an anthology of his writings. I had naïvely supposed that, because the two countries

shared the same political outlook, whatever was published in one
was acceptable in the other. I had forgotten that a hostility existed
between the two nations that went far deeper than any similarity of
governments, a hostility that lived in the hearts of the people and
was no mere contrivance to divert their attention from something
else. And the Honduran military was likely to be more embittered
still, since it had not covered itself in glory on the only occasion it
had ever been called upon to fight anyone other than civilians,
namely during the conflict with El Salvador in 1969 that the rest of
the world knows as the Soccer War (but which was slightly less
ridiculous than that disparaging name would suggest). If the
Honduran military could not revenge itself on the Salvadorean
military that defeated it, at least it could confiscate Salvadorean
books.

I had to come to the rescue of *El Autócrata*, the Autocrat, a book
published in 1929 by Carlos Wyld Ospina, not easily found. The
soldiers treated it as though it were a prisoner accused of a terrible
crime, such as laughing at the army. I protested. The book, I said,
was rare: please handle it carefully. They made a show of not taking
any notice, but they were more careful afterwards. I treasured the
book because it tells a wonderful story about President Rufino
Barrios, *el Reformador*, the Reformer, whose statue appears all over
Guatemala:

> On finding himself alone, don Rufino took the programme of the
> revolution . . . and all the promises made to the people, folded
> them in four and sat on them.

I intervened also on behalf of a book of writings and speeches by
President Arévalo which the soldiers were about to confiscate
because it had been printed in Havana. One of the soldiers had
discovered this with a smile of triumph. He had known all along I
was a dangerous character.

I pointed to the date of publication of the book: 1953. The
significance of this was lost on the soldiers, and I explained that it
was six years before the revolution, when Batista was still in power.
The soldiers looked at one another as though unwilling to concede
the point. Castro had retroactively contaminated for them four and a
half centuries of everything Cuban. But, still suspicious, they
slammed the book down on the permitted pile.

Their failure in this case made them only more determined in others. *Así piensan los Salvadoreños urbanos, This Is What Urban Salvadorans Think*, was a slim volume composed of opinion polls taken by Salvadorean academics from the inhabitants of San Salvador concerning their attitudes towards the government, the guerrillas and so forth. The people of the capital did not think much of their government on the whole, but they thought – by a majority too overwhelming to be artificial – that the guerrillas were more to blame for the continuation of the war than the government. The soldiers looked at the pie diagrams, the histograms, the tables and mathematical formulae, and decided they were subversive. The thoughts of urban Salvadoreans were prohibited.

Gradually they censored their way through the books and found twelve that endangered the security of the state. Towards the end, one of the soldiers began to examine my passport with minute attention. It was thick and dusty and faded, my constant companion during thousands of miles of travel through unlikely lands. The eye of the soldier fell at once on a rather modest, illegible green stamp.

'Where's that from?' he asked.

'Mozambique,' I replied.

There was no point in denying it, since a few pages further on there was a large and explicit visa – the People's Republic of Mozambique – complete with sickles and sheaves of wheat and other things now never seen in that country.

'Isn't Mozambique communist?' he asked.

'Yes,' I replied. Had I denied it, he wouldn't have believed me and his suspicions would only have increased. 'But this,' I continued, pointing to another stamp on the same page, 'is from Paraguay. Paraguay is not a communist country: it is very anti-communist, in fact.'

I wondered whether having the stamps of Mozambique and Paraguay on the same page of my passport made me a social democrat.

'I'll have to ask the *jefe* what to do,' said the soldier, rising from his chair.

Normally, this nonsense would have angered me. I would have flushed, behaved badly, thrown my arms about and shouted. But I was writing occasional articles for the *Spectator*, and the soldiers were handing me a subject on a plate. How could I be cross with them therefore? I half-hoped the *jefe* would say, 'Lock him up for a few days.' What a splendid article it would make! The knowledge that one is going to write about an experience helps to make it bearable, distancing one from it even if it involves suffering.

The soldier returned. The *jefe* had said I cound enter Honduras, but only on condition that I went directly to the Nicaraguan border, five hours' drive. Furthermore, I should have to go under armed escort, for which I would have to pay myself. The alternative was to return to El Salvador, so I agreed. In any case, I thought it might be fun.

I received my stamps and papers from various offices. I was not treated as if anyone really believed I was dangerous. Perhaps all along I had been missing a cue to pay a bribe. As the *jefe* handed back my passport he asked:

'Do you want to change any money?'

I said it seemed I was not staying long enough in Honduras to need any. His face fell: he had not thought of the business consequences of his decision.

Outside the office there were many money changers, each with bundles of notes from all the Central American republics. They offered Honduran *lempiras* for Guatemalan *quetzales*, Nicaraguan *córdobas* for Belizean dollars, Costa Rican *colones* for Salvadorean ones; and of course, anything for US dollars. As we were soon to enter Nicaragua, I thought it best to have a few *córdobas*, and in a trice I was a millionaire: forty thousand to the dollar. I was assured I should not find such a rate in Nicaragua itself, as the money changers handed me thick wads of new notes, printed by Thomas de la Rue and Co. in London, bearing engraved portraits of revolutionary heroes heavily overprinted in black ink, changing the denomination from 20 to 20,000 *córdobas*.

Our armed escort sauntered over. Carlos wanted to put him in the flat bed of the truck, but he refused to go, saying that his orders were to stay in the cabin. Then Carlos whispered to me that it didn't matter, we could talk freely once we were in Nicaragua. And so we started out, three in the cabin, with the escort's gun pointing straight at my head, not as a threat, but because of lack of space. Unfortunately, I couldn't think of the Spanish for safety catch. The escort was a taciturn man of very few words, and we had gone only a few hundred metres when he went to sleep with his jaw hanging open.

The road followed the Gulf of Fonseca across which – according to the Americans – the Nicaraguans smuggled arms to the Salvadorean rebels. The landscape was fawn-coloured, folded into mountains that shaded into an indigo haze in the distance, with an austere, water-colourist's beauty. Hernan Cortés gave the best description of such a landscape when asked what Mexico was like. He crumpled a piece of parchment and said, 'There'. The south of Honduras is like that.

It is also underpopulated. Water here is more precious than land. There were herds of hardy zebu cattle, but little else. The main economic activity seemed to be roadblocks. It was deemed essential by those who manned them that all vehicles stopped immediately before the 'Halt' sign. To draw up parallel with the sign was an act of rebellion. The soldiers had developed a swagger, the self-importance of men dressed in a little brief authority.

I had encountered such soldiers in Salvador, when a bus in which I was travelling was stopped at a checkpoint. The passengers were told to alight and stand in two rows, male and female, by the roadside while the *teniente* inspected identity documents. He selected a pretty young woman for interrogation as a means of demonstrating his masculinity.

'Where are you from?'

'Salvador.'

'What part of Salvador?'

'The capital.'

'What part of the capital? The capital is a big city.'

'Miraflores.'

'What do you do there?'

'I am a student.'

'Where?'

'At the university.'

'What do you study?'

'Architecture.'

But the Salvadorean soldiers conveyed not half the menace of the Honduran. They had boots for kicking the abdomens of pregnant women. They did not pass the time of day, they did not speak. It was as if speech itself were subversive.

We had to hurry because the border between Honduras and Nicaragua closed at five in the afternoon (we were making for the only entry point still functioning), and we had little time to spare. Nevertheless, we stopped at a roadside restaurant for a meal, the only time the escort woke. Was my offer of a meal for him pusillanimity or ordinary human decency? Dangerous character as I was, he accepted my offer with alacrity. We ate quickly, and on the way back to the truck he spoke the only words of the whole journey: 'That was good.'

For a time, he appeared to be thinking deeply, and I thought he might even thank me (I had paid for the Mexican as well). But sleep supervened before he could utter the words, if such was ever his intention.

We reached the border with five minutes to spare. The Hondurans are not normally, I should imagine, an energetic people, but our appearance so near to closing time galvanised them, and they completed the complex paperwork at near fever pitch. We said goodbye and drove into Nicaragua.

TEN

'Now we can talk,' said Carlos.

He didn't just mean we were free of our escort and caution was therefore no longer necessary. He meant that, being in Nicaragua, we were now truly free men, as nowhere else. It was then that he revealed to me that his rucksack was full of Cuban literature; with a great pride he showed me his laminated identity card from a Moscow Youth Festival. He was going to Managua to meet some friends he made in Moscow; perhaps he would find work as a doctor there.

To travel through El Salvador and Honduras with Cuban literature and a Moscow identity card required fortitude, to say the least; of the danger to which he had subjected me I did not speak. Had he been searched in either of those countries, it is doubtful I should have been able convincingly to dissociate myself from him. He assumed that we were of identical political outlook (after all, I was going to Nicaragua) and that I should willingly have been tortured to death for the sake of an edition of *Granma*. I said nothing to disabuse him of this strange idea.

The first few yards of the new Nicaragua were not encouraging. The original border post was, as is usually the case, just over the border; but now it was in ruins. Some said it was attacked by Contras, others by vandals, yet others by the Sandinistas themselves, trying to arouse international sympathy. And the first few miles of the country were bleak indeed, with abandoned houses and fields on either side of the road.

After a ten minute drive, we reached the new border post. It consisted of a creosoted wooden building on a raised platform, a row of adobe huts and offices, a peasant's house with a large black pig and several rough wooden chairs on the verandah, and a faded eau-de-nil caravan clearly of East European manufacture with a slogan painted in red on the side to the effect that the Ministry of the Interior, to which the caravan belonged, was working for the happiness of all the people. A couple of soldiers in drab olive uniforms with large buttons stood around aimlessly. Unlike the other soldiers of the region, they wore no insignia, no colourful badges. They told us the border was shut until the morning. As we had nowhere to stay, they told us we could sleep in the wooden building. Later, when it was dark, they brought us an oil lamp which cast a flickering yellow gloom with a radius of about a foot.

The Mexican extolled the friendliness of the Nicaraguan officials, their fraternal manner. I was not so enraptured: they were not rude, but neither were they friendly: indifferent, I thought.

'What a contrast with Honduras,' said Carlos. 'Take this lamp, for example . . .'

It was nothing extraordinary, this lamp; one couldn't read by its light, and even the moths weren't much attracted to it; neither did genies escape from it to fulfil our every wish. But for the Mexican it was deeply symbolic. I failed to dampen his enthusiasm by telling him that I had heard foreigners were required to exchange $60 in cash at the official rate before being allowed to enter Nicaragua: a problem for him, as he had only $12 with him. Instead, he told me that relations between Mexico and Nicaragua were very close (he entwined his fingers); both countries were opposed to US imperialism; and both had had their revolutions. What was $60 compared to revolutionary solidarity?

Privately, I thought it might be quite a lot, but I kept my counsel. We ate a supper of cold rice, cold beans and cold fried pork skin at the peasant's house. I paid. I wondered what it was about me that all over the world, wherever I went, people assumed without question that I was paying for the meal. Then we were joined by some Germans who lived in California, who were also stranded at the border overnight. They had a large camper van from which they produced a bottle of warm *spatlese* which they shared with us. They were driving down to Costa Rica to see some friends and were protesting loudly about these damn commie bastards as though the border post were the Gulag. Luckily, Carlos spoke not a word of English and did not ask me to translate, otherwise he might have spat out the wine and there would have been a scene.

We rose at six, but the border didn't open till eight. I went to the nearby river to wash and found soldiers doing the same. The German-Americans were still outraged and vowed never to return to Nicaragua (except, of course, on their return journey). The first office to open was the bank, one of the rooms in the wooden building. Outside was a notice informing customers that the official exchange rate was 70 *córdobas* to the dollar, but the tourist rate was 21,000. A lady with dramatically scarlet fingernails, but otherwise drab and resentful, changed my $60, and for the second time I became a *córdoba* millionaire.

Then I went to the Ministry of the Interior caravan. There was a small window with steps leading up to it, behind which was a thick and fusty lace curtain. A hand emerged from the curtain to take the proferred passport. Then a voice from inside – to which one could not put a face, however much one peered – asked a few questions. It reminded me a little of the arrangements for commercial blood donation in Greece, where one puts one's arm through a curtain and an unknown quantity of blood is removed.

By now, the German-Americans were even more outraged. Not only had they each been forced to change $60 for their day's journey through Nicaragua, but they were also obliged to pay a further $20 each for transit visas. Thus their two days in Nicaragua on the way to and from Costa Rica would cost them $320. The final straw was the demand that the visas be paid for in cash, not travellers' cheques. Of course, the German-Americans had both cash and travellers' cheques, but it was the principle of the matter . . . They objected strenuously to subsidizing the communist war effort: next time they would fly.

I received a tourist visa of three months' duration which, in contrast to the transit visa, was free.

Meanwhile, Carlos was having difficulty with one of the soldiers who had so fraternally provided us with the lamp the night before. The soldier was insisting that the Mexican change $60 before entering Nicaragua.

'*Sesenta dólares*,' he said with a face of rock.

'But Nicaragua and Mexico,' explained Carlos, 'are allies.'

He went on to talk of revolutionary history and solidarity, of the defeat of imperialism, of his friends in Managua who would put him up and how he therefore wouldn't be a charge on the state, how he might even find work there as a doctor and hence become an asset to the new Nicaragua.

From time to time, as a kind of descant, the soldier said: '*Sesenta dólares*.'

Growing more desperate, the Mexican played his trump card: he pulled the Cuban literature from his rucksack and his Moscow youth festival card from his pocket. Could there be better proof of his good faith?

'*Sesenta dólares*,' said the soldier.

He pleaded some more. He had thrown everything up, he had

made sacrifices to come to Nicaragua, beacon of hope to all Latin
America. It was his goal, his Mecca, his life's ambition . . .

'*Sesenta dólares.*'

Surely the soldier could contact the Mexican ambassador in
Managua? He was certain the ambassador would vouch for him. The
soldier shook his head and repeated the only two words he appeared
to know.

The Mexican doctor, almost in tears, turned to me. Could I lend
him the money? I had given him a lift, bought him lunch and dinner,
paid his Honduran entry and exit taxes: enough was enough.
Besides – my prejudices came into play – I thought he ought to learn
a lesson, namely that rhetoric is not always to be taken at face value.
If I 'lent' him the money, he would at once forget that there had been
any unfraternal difficulties at the border.

'I have almost no money with me,' I lied.

'How much can you lend me?' asked Carlos.

'Ten dollars, perhaps,' I said.

The soldier grew tired of the charade. He demanded that the
Mexican either change $60 or return to Honduras. The soldier asked
me whether I would drive the Mexican back to the border, and I
agreed. Disconsolately, but still asking me to lend him the money,
Carlos climbed into my truck. The soldier came with us to make sure
he really did leave the country.

It was surely ironic that I, who wrote for a conservative magazine,
should have been deported from Honduras while he, a camp
follower of revolutions, should have been deported from Nicaragua.
But if he noticed the irony, he didn't enjoy it; and as he trudged
miserably into Honduras – who knew to what fate? – I began to think
I had behaved badly, that probably he would have paid the money
back in Managua, and in any case its loss would not have been a
tragedy, I should hardly have missed it. Yet if I had given it him, I
should have despised myself for weakness, for having failed to refuse
only out of craven avoidance of his pleading.

I was now free to continue my journey, but only to the nearest
town, Somoto, to shuffle more paper in the customs warehouse (it is
the love of forms, not the love of one's neighbour, that will one day
unite Mankind). Somoto was a dusty little town and the warehouse
had not yet opened, so I ate breakfast at a roadside café opposite the
bus station, where a hopeful crowd had gathered on the rumour of a
bus to Managua. Nicaragua's transport services had become
irregular, infrequent and intolerably overcrowded because of the

war against the Contras or – according to political taste, mere evidence being powerless to decide the matter – because of socialist maladministration. As for my breakfast, it was pork skin again, and I began to wonder whether there was a special breed of animal here that was skin and nothing else (in Czechoslovakia, they breed pure gristle). Coffee came stiff with sugar and lukewarm. There were many young children selling newspapers, and I bought *Barricada*, a government newspaper, and *La Prensa*, the opposition newspaper which the government, in fulfilment of the Esquipulas agreement, had somewhat reluctantly allowed to republish. The former reported the opening of yet more new clinics and the latest resolutions of women's groups, while the latter reported only shortages caused by Sandinista incompetence.

I decided to drive to León, about a hundred miles away, one of the two great provincial cities that for many years battled it out for control of the country (the other was Granada – finally Managua was chosen as capital because it was equidistant from them). On the way I gave a lift to an old peasant, over seventy, who was looking for work. He at once began to complain: the old days were bad, but not as bad as this. At least under Somoza you could find food to buy but now . . . He was glad he was near the end of his days so that he would not live to see what became of it all.

He was on his way to the town of Estelí. It was a convenient place to stop for lunch and the old peasant required little persuasion to join me. It was boiled pork skin with beans, this time in a lean-to restaurant presided over by a vast peasant lady with grease for sweat and with more black gaps in her mouth than teeth. Her size indicated a too enthusiastic consumption of her own wares. The old man ate as though it were his first meal for days and he expected it also to be his last; he couldn't wait to swallow before stuffing more food into his mouth. The meal seemed cheap enough, until one considered salaries: lunch cost four days' average wages. How, then, was the restaurant full? Workmen ate in silence from tables that bore the traces of a thousand previous meals. It was obvious that workers' salaries were only a small part of their income.

Returning to my truck, I found I had a puncture. I removed the spare to find that it, too, was flat. By chance, I had parked next to a *vulcanizador*, a repairer of tyres, who worked in a shack. He was sitting among his equipment and I thought he would be glad of business, especially from someone he could overcharge. I was wrong.

'I can't do anything,' he said, with no hint of regret.

'Why not?' I asked, looking hard at the sign which proclaimed him a repairer of tyres.

'Power cut,' he said.

'Why? What has happened?'

'*Saber*,' he said. Who knows?

'When will it be restored?' I asked.

'*Saber*.'

'Does it happen often?'

'All the time.'

'At what time does the power usually return?'

'Sometimes in the evening, sometimes the next day. *Saber*.'

The prospect of spending hours, or even days, by or in my truck waiting for the power to return opened up before me, and I realized how fine a line divided my equanimity from despair.

I decided I had better make the most of it, and walked to the centre of the town. It was a hot and dusty place, now famous principally for the desperate battle fought there in the civil war between the revolutionaries and the National Guard. The buildings were pock-marked by bullets, as they were all over the country. Many of the walls were painted with the number seven in black and red, the Sandinista colours, indicating the number of years since the overthrow of Somoza. On the way to the main square I passed a Toyota dealer and had the brilliant idea of buying a new tyre, possibly two.

There had once been a showroom, but it was now completely empty, like the unused ballroom of a Russian country mansion. There was an historical finality about its emptiness, as though this too were a triumph of the revolution. Behind a counter were some shelves for spare parts, with just enough merchandise to keep alive the flicker of a Toyota owner's hope that he might find there what he needed. In an adjacent yard I glimpsed a few tyres and my hopes soared: perhaps I shouldn't have to stay long in Estelí after all. But the only person on the premises told me to come back after lunch, adding that he promised nothing.

I resumed my walk through the town. The sun beat down and cast no shadows; it was siesta time and the grid-iron pattern streets were nearly deserted. Yet even so it was possible to tell they lacked the vulgar vigour of commercial life. Commerce is despised by intellectuals, and to call something commercial is practically to condemn it as trivial and worthless. But remove commerce from the streets, as in Estelí, and you are left with something more dead than Pompeii.

Such shops as there were had little to sell, and all of it was covered in dust. I went into a restaurant and café. It was large, with about thirty tables. At the far end were four waitresses. There were no customers.

'Is there coffee?' I asked.

'No.'

'Tea?' I ventured with a sinking heart.

'No.'

'Anything?' I continued, for the sake of completeness.

'No.'

I wanted to ask the point of their employment. But it wasn't the first time I had experienced the phenomenon. In Mozambique, the cafés of the capital had been open in the physical sense, but they too served nothing, not even water for lack of glasses (and possibly of water as well), though they had a full complement of waiters. Even stranger was John Orr & Co., a large department store. For eleven years since independence it had remained open, with assistants ready to help, standing behind glass display cases that had been empty for a decade.

I resumed my walk. There was an ice cream parlour with a cracked window and two assistants. There were no customers there either, but still I entered.

'Is there any ice cream?' I asked.

They looked at me as though this were a silly question.

'Of course. This is an ice cream parlour.'

'What flavours do you have?' I asked.

'Orange.'

'Anything else?'

'No.'

'Then I'll have orange.'

I wondered why, when it was so hot and nothing else seemed available, the parlour was not crowded. The first lick of the ice cream made everything clear.

It was orange in colour all right, but had nothing to do with the fruit of that name. It looked and tasted like frozen largactil suspension, the medicine given to lunatics when they spit out their pills and hide them at the bottom of their beds. How was it possible to produce anything so disgusting? It must have taken years of research.

I threw it away. I found the main square, windswept and bleak. A

Soviet war film was billed at the cinema which was not yet open and appeared very neglected. There was also a large church, built in the 1950s. I went in. The 1950s were not a good time for architecture anywhere in the world. A storm had broken the stained glass above the altar and a group of men were trying to manoeuvre a large scaffolding frame on wheels up the altar steps so that they could repair the window. They asked me to help, which I did. The altar was decorated with large, ugly plastic flowers whose gaudy colours had faded, though this had not made them any the less unattractive. In fact, it was quite beyond the powers of decoration to redeem the work of the architect, an enthusiast more of Le Corbusier than Christ, and even the stained glass was no worse broken than whole. Still, the Nicaraguans are a devout people and the act of repair was also one of devotion.

Out in the square an old man with a little ice cream cart had appeared and he tinkled a bell in the forlorn hope of attracting customers. A pair of children played with a plastic ball, while time continued its patient work of delay.

Returning to the Toyota dealer, I half-expected the lunch hour to have been extended. But no, the staff had returned dead on time, even if there seemed little for them to do. I explained my situation: two punctures and no likelihood of repair until much later. Could I buy a tyre, or maybe even two? I told them the model of my vehicle.

Unfortunately, they said, they could not do as I asked without the permission of the Ministry of Transport. This was the harvest season (I suspect that for the purposes of tyre sales it always was) and so all transport resources such as tyres were being diverted to the harvest sector, as a matter of national priority. However, if I received permission from the Ministry, they would be glad to sell me one.

And where, I asked, did I obtain the permission of the Ministry of Transport?

In Managua, of course. To get there I should have to go by bus; the return journey, to say nothing of the actual negotiations in the Ministry, would take at least two days. When all the talk was of sabotage, chaos, enemies, crisis and so forth, I thought it unlikely I should persuade the Ministry, even supposing I found the right man in the labyrinth to speak to, that the uninterrupted journey of an English bourgeois was more important than bringing in the coffee. I thanked the people in the Toyota agency for their trouble.

The electricity supply having been restored, however, the

vulcanizador repaired my tyres and I was able to leave Estelí, which I did without deep regret. I took the road to León, giving a lift on the way to a group of Nicaraguan students. A pretty girl sat in the cabin with me. She was studying literature at the university and before long had started a litany of complaint.

Her father was originally a staunch supporter of the Sandinistas and had spent the last few years of Somoza's rule in exile in Costa Rica. When the revolution succeeded, he returned at once to Nicaragua, despite entreaties from his family to wait awhile to see which way the wind blew. But he was impatient to help build the new Nicaragua. Gradually he became disillusioned, until his disillusionment reached such a pitch that he was an avid listener to the broadcasts of the Contras. As for his daughter, she believed in neither the Sandinistas nor the Contras, but only in emigration. Anywhere would do as a destination.

She had little money to live on, and though such foodstuffs as were rationed were cheap, they were not enough to last the month, and the black market purchases necessary to supplement them were very expensive. Her economic prospects were dim: the monthly salary of a first year teacher was 160,000 *córdobas*, less than $4 at the Managua black market rate. She could increase her rations by belonging to one or other Sandinista organizations, but this she absolutely refused to do. It was bad enough that at the university she had to sit through interminable lectures on Marxism-Leninism, and even take exams on the subject. All students had to do this regardless of faculty, and there were some, of course, who took to it with aplomb. But she wanted as little to do with politics as possible: she preferred poetry and dancing to dialectics.

We reached León towards evening. The road had been almost empty of traffic, except for large, Russian-made military trucks. In León I said goodbye to the students and tried to find an hotel. They were all full, except for one near the station, which had little rooms with cardboard partitions that seemed to trap and concentrate the already considerable heat of the city. The little bedside fan, besides rattling ferociously, only blew fiery gusts of hot air. Omar Cabezas, the Sandinista fighter and later chief of secret police, devotes an eloquent paragraph or two to the heat of his native city in his memoir of the years of struggle, *Fire From the Mountain*:

Holy Week in León is hot, blistering hot; the pavement is hot, the dust is hot, the park benches are hot, even the water out of the tap

is hot. Everything in that town is hot . . . The hair on your head is
hot, your thoughts are hot . . . Look, it's so hot there are
practically no cars in the street . . . You know it's hot when you
see the dogs trotting along the edge of the sidewalk exactly where
the people walk, because that's where there's a little bit of shade,
and even the shade is hot . . . So that's how hot it is León.

He also describes his city before the revolution, a place of charm
and intrigue, difficult for the poor to live in but no hell, either. From
his description, it had more life then than now.

The streets – once more the grid pattern, once more the single
storey to defeat earthquakes – were ill-lit, as though in permanent
expectation of an air raid. I peered into the houses, many of them
open to the street. All had circles of rocking chairs in the front room,
the family gently rocking in the still evening air. In many homes,
television now replaced conversation or reading as the focus of
attention. The screens cast pale, flickering light into the street, and
watching the soap operas rendered silent by distance, one could not
but think how foolish the human face appears without its accom-
panying words.

León was calm and prosaic that night. One would scarcely have
guessed that a war was raging not far away, that the country was at
the centre of international intrigue. The question preoccupying
Nicaraguans that night was not whether the Sandanista regime
could or should survive, but whether Manuel would propose to
Juanita. For the answer, they would have to wait for the next
episode . . .

I had dinner in the square, next to the vast cathedral. At last it was
something other than pig-skin: six prawns. They and two beers cost
five weeks of a teacher's salary.

Next morning the wing mirrors of my truck were gone, removed,
I must admit, with great skill so as not to damage the panels of my
truck. On the only other night I left my vehicle unguarded in
Nicaragua the insignia and the fuel cap were likewise stolen.

It was the shortages, of course, that explained this thievery. In
Guatemala, if you had money you could buy things; but in
Nicaragua access to scarce goods was controlled by political
influence. Price is a relatively impersonal way of rationing goods,
and in my view greatly to be preferred: it has a much less corrosive
effect on the human personality. I say this as a matter of empirical

observation around the world, after a youth in which I believed precisely the opposite.

León is a city with a surfeit of churches. The first one visits with ardour, the second with enthusiasm, the third with pleasure, the fourth from duty, and the fifth with weariness. In the end, I preferred to watch children play baseball outside one of the churches. How carefree was their laughter! I thought it odd that the two Latin American countries with the greatest love of baseball – Cuba and Nicaragua – were precisely the two to cock a snook at the Colossus of the North. Could it be that the inhabitants felt guilty at having adopted as their own a game so strongly associated with Latin America's auld enemy, and therefore felt the more obliged to rebel? Or was it simply that they had more experience of US occupation?

Above where the children played, on a pock-marked wall of the church was a plaque:

At nine in the morning on 15 February 1979, Comrades Julio César Ayerdis, Francisco Rubi P., José Benito Jirón H., Oswaldo Lanzas and Mauricio Diaz Muller were engaged in an act of peaceful protest in the bell tower of this church and were brutally murdered by the Somocista National Guard.

For these deaths, our deaths, we demand punishment of the guilty.

Understandable sentiments, of course, but I wondered whether they were appropriate to the walls of a Christian church.

I leave it to theologians to decide.

ELEVEN

On the way from León to Managua, I picked up two gringos, a Canadian couple who had come to pick coffee in Nicaragua as a means of expressing their support for the revolution. They belonged to that large foreign fraternity known to sceptics as *Sandalistas* on account of their political opinions and their intellectual footwear. They are from either western Europe or North America, and – as with sufferers from certain illnesses – they fall into two age groups: the young just setting out in life, and the old whose careers are over. Mostly, they are of comfortably middle-class origin.

My couple were brimmingly idealistic, untouched as yet by any paralysing sense of life's complexity. One of them, Cindy, had spent a year at Sussex University's Institute of Development Studies, which did not predispose me in favour of her opinions, for I had seen the results of the Institute's efforts in Tanzania, another country once favoured by young idealists but long since abandoned as being beyond any cure but the strongest International Monetary Fund medicine. Steve, her boyfriend, planned to pursue Latin American studies when he returned to British Columbia, with the aim of assisting Nicaragua's economic development afterwards. Hard up and on their way to Honduras, from which there were cheap flights to North America, they were spending a week in Managua to wind up their affairs in the country (for the time being), and for much of that week we were companions. As people, they were open, attractive and decent, characteristics which for me were more important than any differences of opinion we might have. Is it not the beginning of totalitarianism to judge people solely by their political standpoints?

They had spent a couple of months in Nicaragua and had never before met a foreigner who was openly sceptical of the regime. At first, Steve rode in the cabin of the truck and Cindy behind – it was her choice. I explained to Steve my suspicions of the Sandinistas: that their ideological training had invaded schools and universities, that the police were called the Sandinista Police, the army the Sandinista Army, the television service the Sandinista Television, that the party flag flew everywhere beside the national flag, that the political iconography was both totalitarian in style and ubiquitous, that the rationing and universal shortages gave immense powers of patronage and privilege to the political elite, and so forth. All this led me to suppose that the Sandinistas were not just one party among others, competing on equal terms, though they had not yet installed themselves quite as thoroughly as parties in some countries I could name. When we came to a halt at some obstruction in the road, Steve stuck his head out of the window and said to Cindy:

'Hey, this guy's real interesting. He's got some weird ideas.'

Managua is weird too. It is on the shores of Lake Managua, a lake now so polluted that bathers in it risk dissolution by chemicals. The effects on the city of the 1972 earthquake have not been overcome; indeed, no effort appears to have been made to overcome them. Somoza was too corrupt, the Sandinistas too preoccupied with other matters. And so there are very large tracts of what was once the centre of the city that have reverted to scrub. The wrecked cathedral, once grandiose rather than grand, now deconsecrated and deserted, looks out over wasteland in which graze zebu cattle. The whole enormous edifice, with its crumbled walls of reinforced cement painted to look like marble, seems to mock the vanity of Man's aspirations. Why rebuild when everything is destined for decay? The grass which grows in the cracks in the floor and bends before the wind that gusts through the ruined church made me think of six words: ashes to ashes, dust to dust. The detritus of sanctity lies everywhere, unclaimed; at the foot of what were once the cathedral steps gather a few unemployed men, hopeful of a small income from washing the few cars that pull up. Across the square is the National Palace, still intact and draped with a red banner, before which the government holds its giant rallies to prove to itself and the world that it is still popular, rallies which, I was told, do not draw crowds as large as the congregations at the outdoor masses of the Cardinal Archbishop.

Managua now has no identifiable city centre. One of the only landmarks to have survived the earthquake is the Intercontinental Hotel, a Hollywood-Mayan pyramid. In the middle of a flattened quarter of the city stands a large black statue of a muscular but slightly deformed guerrilla bearing aloft a Kalashnikov from which streams a red and black banner. On the plinth are inscribed some words of General Sandino's:

ONLY THE WORKERS AND PEASANTS WILL
GO TO THE END

This was not a comforting message to such of the Nicaraguan bourgeoisie as had not already fled.

Cindy and Steve wanted to go to one of Managua's markets. They had been in the countryside, where there was nothing to buy; furthermore, they wanted to change money on the black market and knew of a trader there with whom it was safe to do so. They were ashamed of this: when they first arrived in Nicaragua they vowed never to change money on the black market, for they had come to help Nicaragua's economy, not undermine it. But they were now too poor to lose more than half the value of their money by changing it in a bank. In vain did I argue that the speculators, spivs, hoarders and black marketeers were a consequence and not a cause of Nicaragua's plight: that it was the shortages that called the black market into being, not the other way round; that I had seen these phenomena many times before, in different parts of the world, when a government tried to control economic life; that there was nothing more immoral about a black market than an artificial exchange rate; and that therefore they could act with a clear conscience. I could not persuade them. Not only did they wish to believe that Nicaragua's problems had nothing to do with its policies, but they had an insatiable thirst for guilt. It gave to their actions a significance they would otherwise have lacked. But they went ahead all the same – prices were rising every day.

From the market, where vegetables and poor quality general goods were sold (at prices Nicaraguans found expensive), we went to the dollar store, the *Diplotienda*. Here was another pretext for the pleasures of guilt. The *Diplotienda* is patronised by diplomats and employees of international aid agencies, who arrive in vehicles with tinted windows. Nicaraguans with dollars also shop there. Inside, the *Diplotienda* is just like a supermarket, icily air-conditioned, with prepared foods, toiletries, European wines and liqueurs and expensive electronic goods. To anyone accustomed to the empty shelves of Nicaraguan stores, it must have seemed like paradise after purgatory. So it was with Cindy and Steve, transported with guilty delight at the prospect of a fresh apple and some chocolate. Being poor, they had to spend their two or three dollars carefully: they chose their chocolate by bulk, not quality. Other customers took trolleys and indiscriminately shovelled pink cake mix, stuffed olives, Rice Krispies, packets of reconstitutable hollandaise sauce, tinned tuna, maraschino cherries, anchovies, instant potatoes and sanitary napkins into them until they could carry no more. It was I who let the side down by buying nothing at all. I noticed that the women assistants in the *Diplotienda* were elegantly dressed, bilingual and had heavily varnished nails.

Nothing of this world was visible to the hangers-on outside, except the large cartons of groceries which they were employed to carry to the customers' cars. Cindy and Steve ate their chocolate quickly, finishing it before leaving the building because they were sure it would melt in the heat of the city. I mentioned the dollar stores I had seen round the world: in Mozambique (where they accepted South African rand as well as dollars), Tanzania and Burma. I said the appearance of such a store in Managua was not an encouraging prognostic sign. But so absorbed in the lushness of their guilt were Cindy and Steve that they did not take the point.

They decided to stay in one of the few hotels where it was still possible for foreigners to pay in *córdobas* rather than dollars. It was in a bleak part of the city, next to some railway tracks, where the only buildings were a few ruins rising from the coarse grass that had grown up everywhere. I was reminded of pictures of Hiroshima after the dropping of the bomb. Was it really not possible to start on reconstruction fifteen years after the earthquake? Guatemala City and San Salvador had suffered earthquakes too, more recently, and both Guatemala and El Salvador had fought or were fighting wars; yet only Managua retained its Richter-scale desolation.

I stayed in a comfortable, but still cheap, hotel where, however, one had to pay in dollars. In the office, above the telephone, was a notice encouraging Nicaraguans to call foreign countries and reverse the charges, thereby helping to develop the *patria* by earning foreign exchange. (The list of countries one was encouraged to call did not include those of the eastern bloc.) The hotel was in a residential district of the middling sort, where children played baseball in the street and there were cheap restaurants that served meals for only half a month's wages, restaurants that were open intermittently because of power failures. The water supply was very uncertain too – sabotage at the pumping stations, it was said. For most of the time, nothing came out of the taps or shower except dry coughs or gurgled protests, an inconvenience in a climate as close and hot as Managua's. Often one had to get up at two in the morning to have a shower, for it was then that the water flowed; perhaps it was hoped that people would be too tired to use it.

There was another inconvenience on the first night of my week-long stay. Early in the evening there was a power cut that lasted until three in the morning. The guest in the room next door to mine had been listening to the radio when the cut occurred and had forgotten to turn it off. When the power was restored, it played again at high volume, causing the wall between our rooms to vibrate. It woke me and would not let me sleep. Eventually, I banged on my neighbour's door, protesting, pleading, begging, threatening. But the radio was implacable, merciless, and the guest – as I thought – must have been either deaf or dead. There was nothing for it but to spend the rest of the night lying miserably awake.

When morning came I protested to the manager, not volubly or angrily, mindful not to appear an egotistical foreign bourgeois, but with quiet forcefulness. He listened to me with a strange smirk playing on his face which I was at a loss to interpret. It was only later that I learned the room was taken by the hotel's prostitute-in-residence, and that she had been away that night on a professional engagement. I talked to an American journalist who was staying in the hotel and had availed himself of her services. He pointed to an elderly New York lawyer who was having a beer at a table a few yards away. The lawyer was a volunteer worker who had come to codify the laws of Nicaragua as his contribution to the revolution, and he visited the prostitute at least three times a week. There was even talk of love, at least on his side. And when I met her I found her to be highly vivacious and attractive, a Costa Rican who spun her clients a hard-luck story according to their political sympathies, involving asylum and escape from tyrannical regimes, unemployment and economic hardship, a thwarted desire to study fine arts and a family shattered by war.

That same morning I received a phone call from Cindy and Steve to say that they had been mugged the night before while walking near their hotel. Three youths had held them at knifepoint, taken their bag containing their money and passports, emptied their pockets and run off. They asked me to help them search the waste ground near the hotel in case the muggers had thrown away the passports as being of no use to them. I did so, but as soon as I arrived I saw how hopeless a task it was. I drove them instead to the police station from which they needed a report for insurance purposes. The police informed us it was a bad area and getting worse. With some reluctance, they typed a report and fixed a stamp to it, though they kept no copy or any other record for themselves: by far the easiest way of keeping crime figures down.

I went on a kind of solidarity tour of the city. In my hotel were staying two Australians: Bill, a real proletarian, and an elderly lady with bluish hair who had been fighting for good causes for half a century, and would have been lost without them. Bill, a boiler-maker, had never been out of Australia before and had gone directly to Cuba on the first leg of his tour. 'They're making great strides over there,' he said, referring to Cuba and presumably using strides in the non-Australian sense of the word.

'What do you think of Managua, Tone?' asked Bill with the affability characteristic of Australians. We were in the lobby of the Intercontinental Hotel, where for one reason or another all foreigners, whatever their outlook, eventually find themselves.

Searching for something bland and non-committal to say so as not to offend the lady who had fought fifty years for good causes, I said it was a difficult city to get to know, being so spread out.

What I said was not quite bland enough.

'Well,' she said, shaking with instant rage, 'I expect the Sandinistas have more important things to do than worry about the comfort of a few tourists.'

I visited the Museum of the Revolution, which is near one of Managua's markets. Outside is an armoured car, constructed during the war by the revolutionaries, and displayed as an example of their resourcefulness. It is a botched job, and looks like a prop from an early science-fiction movie, but was effective, to judge by the small dents made in its armour plating by bullets. And beside the armoured car is displayed the hind limb of a huge equestrian statue of Somoza, laid on its side, with the jagged edges showing where it was dismembered from the rest of the horse. As propaganda, it could not have been bettered – a stroke of genius on the part of whoever thought of it. The single severed limb is sufficient to conjure up the angry but jubilant crowds which toppled the statue in revenge for forty years of subjection. The veins on the hindquarter, so realistically copied, the sheer size of the thing, the vast bronze hoof and horseshoe, reek of *folie de grandeur*. The way the limb lies abandoned on the ground speaks of a contempt beyond other means of expression. Above all, the hollowness of the statue, that had once seemed as strong and solid as the dictatorship itself, was exposed to the casual gaze of the passer-by, a mute but eloquent comment on the absurdity of power.

Inside the museum is displayed another form of arrogance, but a subtler one. Here the revolutionaries worship themselves and their own success by displaying documents, letters, typewriters for clandestine use, pens, guns and other relics of the early days of their struggle. A remarkable struggle it undoubtedly was, one that required faith, courage, vision and – arrogance. Now, of course, it requires the re-writing of history, so that the Sandinistas can present themselves at the pinnacle of history.

But the star exhibit of the museum is not a revolutionary relic, but a relic of the *ancien régime*: Somoza's tunic covered with the medals he awarded himself, and his jewelled marshal's baton. How preposterous they are, displayed in a simple glass case and stared at idly by people who once would not have been allowed within a diamond's sparkle of them! Yet all is not modesty that eschews ostentation, and I wondered whether in the long run there was not more arrogance in a little book by Jaime Wheelock, wherein are answered all of Nicaragua's age-old problems, than in the sashes and medals of the strutting tyrant.

On a Sunday evening, I went with Cindy and Steve to the famous Liberation Theology church of Father Uriel Mólina in the Riguero district of Managua. Father Mólina helped the Sandinistas from an early stage; indeed, he had a profound influence on the movement. No one could accuse him of not having given political meaning to his 'preferential option for the poor'.

Riguero is poor. When we were still some distance from the church, the people of whom we asked the way were unable to help. But as we drew nearer, people pointed directions even before we asked: they knew where all gringo visitors to their slum were headed on Sunday evenings.

When we arrived at the church, there were two buses marked *Turismo* outside. A Scandinavian camera team was there, setting up its arc lamps. Europeans and North Americans were flooding in. The church was octagonal in form, the inside walls covered in murals of high artistic merit, depicting Sandinism as next to godliness. The ungodly were National Guardsmen dressed in grey uniforms, with hard, evil faces of which a Hieronymus Bosch might have been proud. The God of the murals was clearly not a God of forgiveness for one's class enemies. The crucified Christ was an Indian. The principal artist of the murals was Italian.

On either side of the altar were small bands of singers and guitarists, whose music was quite accomplished and jolly, but somewhat lacking in any feeling of religious mystery.

Father Mólina entered and there was a hush. He was a man of medium height with distinguished grey hair and sleek, almost polished skin. He went up to the altar, bent over it and kissed it. Then he went to pat the two altar boys on the head. In contrast to almost everyone else present, they were ragged. Several people closed for the kill with their video cameras.

The service was unlike any other I had attended. If there was a religious dimension, I missed it. Father Mólina spoke of oppression and its opposite, Total Liberation, but mentioned none of the inherent limitations of life for which religion, rightly or wrongly, has provided consolation over the centuries. He talked of political and economic structures; except that he was in vestments and this was a church, he might have been speaking at a political meeting. When he finished his sermon-speech, he called on a representative of a group of peasants who were studying for two weeks at the *Centro Ecuménico Antonio de Valdevieso* (which Father Mólina founded and directed) to give the congregation his interpretation of the meaning of the Gospels. Father Mólina listened to what he had to say with thespian reverence, as though peasant origin were a guarantee of theological insight. When the peasant had finished, Father Mólina prayed a political prayer and then called on the congregation for their impromptu prayers. There were not many Nicaraguans in the church, perhaps a hundred or so, many of them relatively well-to-do ladies with the lacquered hair, prominent jewellery and make-up, and clouds of scent beloved of the Latin rich. One of the ladies stood and thanked the Lord for his kindness in bringing a peasant to church so that Nicaraguans could hear what he had to say. Another thanked the Lord for bringing so many good people from across the sea to help Nicaragua in its hour of need. When inspiration for prayers dried up, the service ended: everyone embraced one another in a symbolic act of reconciliation, though it seemed that everyone was already reconciled. The Nicaraguan youth of small stature and unprepossessing appearance in front of me seemed particularly anxious to forgive the prettiest young women in the congregation, mainly foreign, whom he hugged very closely indeed, and who would have objected in other circumstances but were now trapped by the atmosphere of universal love. As for Father Mólina, he selected a giant blond Scandinavian cameraman to embrace, and had to stand on tiptoe even to embrace his midriff. I retired to the periphery of the church to watch this part of the service, which Cindy and Steve found moving. They thought it was the finest service they had ever attended.

The next evening we went to a torchlight demonstration, mainly by United States citizens either resident in or visiting Nicaragua, in front of their own embassy. This establishment is a source of amusement and mockery as well as anger, because it has a fortress wall with spikes and barbed wire surrounding it that reeks of paranoia. Those who work within it are said to have a siege mentality, the siege being of their own imagining.

Embassy staff gathered in the sentry boxes at the gate in the wall to watch the demonstration. Some were armed with cameras with which, perhaps, they hoped to intimidate the demonstrators. Instead, the demonstrators laughed and blew kisses in their direction. Paradoxically, the light-hearted response of the demonstrators illustrated their basic faith in the checks to executive power enshrined in the Constitution. Would the citizens of a police state have reacted in this way to cameras wielded by secret policemen?

We stood outside the embassy for about an hour, singing protest songs and making small talk. Then we went on a torchlight march through part of the city on our way to the Military Hospital, where we were to make symbolic reparation to the war wounded for the United States' support of the Contras – the wounded were to receive olive branches and flowers. I marched behind an elderly man with a white beard like Ezra Pound's, who wore sandals and carried a little rucksack that probably contained carrot juice. If ever there was a Platonic form of a professor, it was he. He walked ramrod straight, his muscles stiffened by moral resolve, an expression of deep happiness on his face. A general chant began:

'*Entre cristianismo y revolución, no hay contradicción!*'

(Between Christianity and revolution there is no contradiction!)
We punched the air with our raised fists as we chanted.

Just then we were walking through a slum, a district of shacks where a few lightbulbs jaundiced the darkness. A few of the shack-dwellers gathered at the roadside to watch the procession of gringos.

'*Entre cristianismo y revolución, no hay contradicción!*'

The professor ahead joined in, his rucksack riding high on his back as he gently punched the air. Then suddenly and unexpectedly a hail of small stones thrown from somewhere among the shacks struck him on the side of the head.

Were the stones thrown by someone who thought there *was* a contradiction between Christianity and revolution? Or by someone who simply wanted to get to sleep? Or by a mischievous boy who saw his chance for devilry? Momentarily the professor's world view was shattered and a look of anger passed over his face. Didn't these dummies realize he had come to Nicaragua for their own good? This mood passed almost instantly. His back restraightened, he resumed his confident stride, his face took on once more the look of secular beatitude, and were it not for the fact that he insinuated himself deeper into the crowd and a little further from the side of the road, one might never have known he had just been showered with stones.

We reached the military hospital. In the forecourt, the war wounded had already been lined up in their wheelchairs to receive us. It is a terrible thing to see young men who have lost a leg or an arm, or both. Therefore the presentation of the olive branches and flowers was moving: anyone could weep for these wounded.

TWELVE

After a month away from Guatemala – longer than I had intended – I felt 'homesick' for my newly-adopted land. Often I found myself in the position of advocate for Guatemala, when it stood accused by a variety of detractors and would-be prosecutors. It was not so much that what they said was untrue, but it was not the whole or only truth. Generally, they were determined to prove that Guatemala was Babylon to Nicaragua's Shining City on a Hill, and used any argument to do so, without realising that the countries of Central America were very different – which was why, after all, they were separate countries.

In my hotel in Managua there stayed an American nurse who had come to Nicaragua to find work in the field of public health. She had worked in Africa and was therefore unafraid of harsh conditions; indeed, I suspect she courted them. But the bureaucracy in Nicaragua had been so inefficient that she had spent three months in the hotel awaiting permission to start, and her enthusiasm was beginning to wane. She found Managua boring; I persuaded her to come with me to a vigil of protest hunger strikers outside the American embassy. There were about twenty of them, including a Japanese Buddhist with a shaved head and saffron robes who struck a small drum with impressive, if maddening, regularity every ten seconds. They were undoubtedly sincere, but if insincerity is always a vice, sincerity is not always a virtue, nor is it incompatible with other, questionable traits. One of the fasters was a veteran of the anti-Vietnam war movement, who had been arrested many times in his native Chicago for breaching the peace; he had symbolically dyed red the public fountains so many times that the police now refused to arrest him for it. It was clear that if there had been no good causes, he would have invented them, and he admitted that he found protest a more fulfilling life than being a high school teacher, which was the alternative for him. To rationalise his choice, he claimed that all citizens of the United States, even those conducting their lives as privately as possible, were guilty of crimes against Nicaragua unless they were actively trying, like he, to stop them; indeed, strictly speaking there was no such thing as private life, no man being an island, etc. I objected that his argument was the slippery slope to abject totalitarianism, for it gave social and political significance to every act or omission, however trivial, of a person's life; and that this gave governments an excuse to regulate every detail of existence. But this was a conclusion from which he did not shrink: underneath his casual and anarchic exterior, there was a Philosopher-King trying to get out. And he did not accept that if everyone was guilty, no one was . . .

Also at the vigil was a nun who ran a health clinic in a rural district much affected by the war. She at once offered the nurse a position, who was overjoyed at thus bypassing the bureaucracy. She was to set out next day.

We had dinner together that evening to celebrate her good fortune. A short distance away from us in the restaurant was a table set with twenty places, and while we were eating limousines accompanied by motorcycle outriders with blue flashing lights arrived. Comandante Tomás Borge was entertaining a delegation – Scandinavian from the look of it – to dinner.

The Comandante was dressed in a drab olive uniform with red flashes on the shoulder and heavy boots. He was middle-aged, slightly stooped, not at all a martial figure. He did not sit at once with his party, but made a tour of the restaurant, greeting the diners – mainly foreigners, in view of the prices – with a friendly but proprietorial air. (That, according to one ambassador I met, was probably because he *did* own the restaurant).

He said *buenas noches* to me and I replied with the same words: not exactly a memorable conversation, but still it was something to have shaken the hand of a man who had been a professional revolutionary since his twenties, when the cause seemed hopeless, had been eighteen years an outlaw, was once imprisoned and who, for good or evil, had made history. Suddenly I felt my own life to have been a pale and insignificant thing, though I also wondered whether such loyalty to the ideas of one's youth was not a sign of dangerously arrested development.

Not everyone admires Tomás Borge. An embittered Nicaraguan exile compiled a scurrilous book called *Quien es quien en Nicaragua* (*Who's Who in Nicaragua*). Printed in Costa Rica, it gives brief biographies of everyone of any importance in or to the country, eulogising Contra leaders and ascribing hereditary degeneration to Sandinistas. Of Tomás Borge, the book has this to say:

The son of a lawyer . . . who was a trafficker in historical
documents and archaeological pieces . . . is an aficionado of the
luxuries he never knew before . . . a collector of cars . . . he has
facial massages and invariably hides himself behind his glasses,
disguising his intentions . . . A drug dealer and businessman, he
owns the special diplomatic store and is a black marketeer in
dollars.

According to an ambassador to whom I spoke allegations that
several of the comandantes, including Tomás Borge, had salted
away substantial sums in Swiss bank accounts, were true. I
mentioned this to the American nurse and to my surprise she did not
deny the allegations.

'I'm sure,' she said primly, 'that if they have money in Switzer-
land, it's for the use of the Revolution.'

I had forgotten briefly to what extent belief in the latest utopia was
a religious phenomenon.

On the way back to the hotel, through another blackout, I
mentioned my affection for Guatemala. The nurse was horrified. It
was a country, she said, to which she would never go. I asked why
not, though I already knew. She replied that there was so much
repression and political violence there, and it would be wrong for her
dollars to condone it.

At once we started on one of those political discussions as broad-
ranging as they are without conclusion: in a couple of minutes, we
had both forgotten or changed the point at issue, not once but
several times. I argued that to travel to a country was not necessarily
to lend support to its government. She said that she wouldn't travel
to the Soviet Union either because it was nothing more than a giant
prison camp. I found myself in the unaccustomed position of
defending the Soviet Union. She turned to Guatemala, calling it a
charnel house, as chronicled by Amnesty International and
Americas Watch, to which I replied that if one took the murder rate
for Guatemala as a whole last year, the United States had a higher
rate and some *cities* had a much higher rate. I suggested that
Guatemala should therefore send human rights observers to Miami
to advise the authorities on how to bring the violence there under
control. Not surprisingly, these remarks did nothing to calm the
argument or make it any more rational. She said the difference was
that in Guatemala the murders were political, while in Miami they
were only criminal; I replied that even if so, the difference was small

consolation to the victims (though in my heart I knew the distinction was an important one). She continued that the violence in Guatemala was attributable solely to the bad distribution of land; I said the conflict was more complex than that. Sarcastically, as though it were *a priori* impossible, she asked me how. By this time I was shaking with rage (and enjoying it); I said there was a deep ethnic and cultural conflict in Guatemala. What ethnic and cultural conflict, she asked, still sneering. Between Indians and *ladinos*, I replied. She then revealed she did not know what *ladino* signified, and was surprised to learn it was as much a cultural as a racial term, having supposed until then that *ladino* meant the one or two per cent of pure Europeans who enslaved everyone else in Guatemala. I said that if she were so ignorant of these matters, she had no right to institute a personal boycott and feel morally superior about it.

These remarks were not emollient either, far from it. She said she trusted the reports of Americas Watch more than she trusted anything I could say; that lawyers of international repute sat on the board of Americas Watch who measured their words carefully; that they had called Guatemala the worst human rights violator in the western hemisphere. This was good (or bad) enough for her. I was goaded into remarking that at least some of their observers were not without axes to grind, one of them, at least, supporting the guerrillas (I was thinking of Jean-Marie Simon). I knew of two places where the guerrillas had carried out massacres, that it was widely known the EGP had used barbarous methods, but that this was regarded as of little consequence. She replied it was impossible for guerrillas to behave in the way I alleged, for they wanted and needed the support of the peasants and therefore had no reason to kill. I repeated that I knew of one place where they had murdered twenty people.

At this her fury reached a new pitch. All inhibitions were gone.

'So what?' she shouted. 'What do Americans care if the guerrillas kill a few little Indians?'

THIRTEEN

On the way back to Guatemala, I wanted to stay in the northern Nicaraguan town of Matagalpa (twinned with the heroic London borough of Lewisham), but the town's hotels and guest houses were full of foreign *brigadistas* come to pick coffee. And so, venturing along a road said to be dangerous even by day, I went to the next small town. It was then the dead of night and the mountain road was foggy; I peered into the swirling fog ahead for Contras standing in the road, guns at the ready. But I met no one. A few days before a bus had been ambushed and people killed. It was my fortunate fate always to miss action.

I passed once more through Honduras, this time without trouble, and I parted from Cindy and Steve. I was there only three days, but in that time I gained what I imagined was an insight into the Central American military mind. When I saw a soldier standing at the side of the road, I stopped to offer him a lift. I did not act from kindness. Rather, I guessed that with a military man on board the attitude of soldiers and officials at road blocks would change completely. My prediction was confirmed. Whenever I was stopped by a soldier, his manner altered at once on seeing my travelling companion. Previously hostile and arrogant, he would become the soul of helpfulness, as though nothing were too much trouble for him. As for examining my papers, God forbid that I should be put to the inconveneince of it, the mere presence of the soldier in my vehicle being sufficient guarantee that they were in order.

I had previously found Honduran soldiers without any trace of common humanity. But with one of their number abroad, they chatted, joked, laughed, asked after families and generally behaved like normal people. They must have been trained, brainwashed, to believe that the Honduran army was the elite of the human race, the Guardian of the Nation, and therefore not bound by the normal laws of social intercourse, which enjoin the use of words such as please and thank you.

Did my glimpse of the Honduran army help explain how the Guatemalan army had been able to carry out so many massacres and yet remain full of sane men? For there is no doubt that, accretions of propaganda notwithstanding, the Guatemalan army was responsible for many deeds of unfathomable depravity. Open almost any book about Guatemala on almost any page, and there will be a reference to the unspeakable. Here is an example from Amnesty International's latest report (I have not sought the worst thing in the book):

A few survivors of the massacre . . . gave the following account of how the villagers were killed. At 11 am on Saturday 17 July the army arrived . . . [It] had previously visited the village on 24 June and had told the inhabitants that they would be killed if they were not found peacefully working in their homes and fields . . . On 17 July some 600 soldiers arrived on foot . . .

The people were told to assemble for a discussion with the colonel . . . The villagers first sensed that they were in danger when a man whom survivors said had been 'tied up like a pig' was brought before them by the soldiers. They knew he had not been involved in anything and yet saw he was being 'punished'. They also saw how 'angry' the commander appeared to be . . . The men were then shut up in the courthouse . . . The women were . . . shut up in the church, many of them carrying young children tied to their backs. The catechists told the men in the courthouse to begin praying 'to make their peace with God', as they were about to suffer. A survivor described how: 'We pray, 11 o'clock, 12 o'clock passes. By now, everyone has come into town and been shut up. And then, at 1 o'clock it begins: a blast of gunfire at the women, there in the church. It makes so much noise. All the little children are crying.'

This witness went on to tell how the women who survived the initial gunfire were then taken off in small groups to different houses by soldiers where they were killed, many apparently with machetes. After they had been killed, the houses were set on fire. This witness and others . . . described a particularly atrocious killing they had seen, the murder of a child about three. The child was disembowelled, as were several others, but kept screaming, until a soldier smashed his head with a pole, then swung him by his feet and threw him into a burning house . . .

This witness continued: 'At 3 o'clock, they began with the men. They ordered them out of the courthouse in small groups, and then blasted them with gunfire. It went on and on. They tied up the men's hands and then "bang, bang". The killing took

place in the courtyard outside the courthouse, then they'd throw
the bodies into the church. They killed the three old people with a
blunt machete, the way you would kill a sheep. They cut their
throats.'

Another witness described how the old were killed: 'The old
people said "What have we done, no, we are tired and old . . . We
can't do anything anymore." But they said, "You're not worth
anything anymore, even if you're tired. Get out of there." They
dragged them out, and knifed them. They stabbed and cut them
as if they were animals and they were laughing when they killed
them. They killed them with a machete that had no teeth. They
put one old man on a table, and cut open his chest, the poor man,
and he was still alive, and so they started to cut his throat. They
cut his throat slowly. He was suffering a lot. They were cutting
people under the ribs, and blood came rushing out and they were
laughing . . .

'By now it was about 6.30 pm. It was getting dark outside.
They threw a bomb in the corner of the courthouse. It was
bloody, two were killed. How the blood ran! It ran all over me.
Then they fired at the remaining people in the courthouse. Then
they threw the bodies in a heap. They dragged people by the
feet . . . They threw me on top of the dead bodies.'

I trembled when I read this for the first time. The massacre at the
Finca San Francisco which it describes undoubtedly took place (I
spoke to two people who investigated it) and over three hundred
villagers were killed. The question arises and demands an answer:
what dreadful compulsion could possibly make people act like this?
And behind that question there lurks another, equally troubling
one. Are there circumstances in which I myself would behave in the
same way?

For political analysts, of course, the explanation is simple. The
maldistribution of land in Guatemala provoked the peasants to
rebel. The landed oligarchy, through the army that serves its
interests, responded by a campaign of terror and massacre. The
purpose of the campaign was to teach the peasants that all resistance
was futile.

There is no doubt truth to this, yet still there seems some
explanatory distance between such an abstract scheme and the
concrete horror of the events described. One still needs to know how

a man can disembowel a child, smash his head, swing him by the feet and throw him on a fire, then eat his supper and sleep soundly.

Back now in Antigua, I met a young woman whose brother had attended the *Escuela Politécnica*, the school for officers of the Guatemalan army. He had not completed the course; he resigned (and paid back the cost) before the first few months were over. He said he could stomach the cruelty no longer.

I said I should like to meet him, to hear his story in person. He was now working as a teacher in Guatemala City and his sister was doubtful if he would agree because he had never spoken about his experiences in the *Escuela*, except immediately after leaving. Not only might he be afraid to speak for obvious reasons, but the whole subject was intensely painful to him. Nevertheless, she agreed to ask him, and much to my satisfaction (and her surprise), he said he would come to Antigua the following Saturday. We arranged a place to meet.

Saturday arrived, but I waited in vain. Later I learned that he had come to Antigua as promised, had met his sister, but at the last moment could not face the trauma of the past. He had returned to Guatemala City, apologetic but distressed.

His sister told me the part of his story that she knew. The first three months of the *Escuela* were the worst. It was then that the recruits underwent the brutalisation that either broke them or changed them for ever. Perpetually underfed, they rose at four in the morning to do hard physical exercises for several hours before breakfast. There was study in the afternoons, more exercises, then bed at nine. At ten they would be woken by cadets in the class above and made to do pointless work, like shifting mounds of earth from A to B and back again, completely in the nude. Eventually at two in the morning, they would be allowed to return to their dormitories, only to find that their beds had in the meantime been soaked in cold water and their uniforms dirtied by other members of the class above them. Next morning they would appear haggard and dishevelled at inspection before the colonel, who would therefore put them on punishment exercises, such as running round the athletics field a hundred times on their haunches . . . This treatment continued for months on end. Those who survived not only felt themselves to be an elite with no links to the rest of the human race, but learned to behave with the utmost cruelty to those beneath them, secure in the knowledge that it was essential training. Had they not undergone it themselves and emerged the finest men that ever were?

The sister told me how, when she met childhood friends who had passed out of the *Escuela Politécnica* as lieutenants, they scorned to recognise her, though they had always been very friendly before.

I phoned the *Escuela* with no great hope of being allowed inside, but was invited to tour it that very afternoon. It was near the village of San Juan Sacatepequez, 50 kilometres from the city. When I asked the way there of the villagers, was it my imagination that a look of fear passed over their faces? Would I have noticed anything had I not spoken to a cadet's sister?

I arrived an hour early and spent the time by the gate, where I met two Indian guards. The army had taught them Spanish, and also to read. They were conscripts, not recruits, men, not officers, and felt little gratitude for their education: they wanted to leave the army as soon as possible and return to their villages. They came from the class of young men that the army press-gangs. In towns and cities, the army waits for them outside dance halls and cinemas and drags them into military trucks. In villages, the methods are even less subtle. The upper classes escape this treatment, and seem almost unaware that it exists. From time to time an advertisement addressed to the mothers of Guatemala appears in the *Prensa Libre* and *El Gráfico*, warning them what to expect if the revolution comes to pass:

> Guatemalan Mother
> This is what will happen to your sons
> when the SANDINISTAS arrive!
> You will suffer the same Calvary as the Nicaraguan
> mothers. You will have to hide your sons for fear
> that they will be carried off to the war. Communist
> soldiers will break into your house at midnight. You
> will howl like a lioness trying to hold on to her
> little cub. But it will all be useless. No one will
> hear you. Your cries will be lost in silence. They
> will take away YOUR SON . . . and then THEY WILL
> DELIVER
> A COFFIN

The mother referred to in the advertisement is like the 'everyone' of the gossip columnist's 'everyone was at the party'.

I was shown into the *Escuela* by a recruit with a shaved head, a shako, and red stripes down his trousers. He handed me over to a cadet in a more utilitarian uniform and I was taken to meet the major who was to be my guide.

The institution is built on a treeless upland plateau, over which the wind whistles eerily. Dominating the plateau are two concrete office blocks of ten or eleven storeys. Near them are symmetrical rows of dormitories and classrooms, large fields for sports and square-bashing, a huge concrete gymnasium, tennis and squash courts, an Olympic swimming pool, and an engine room, all drilled into geometrical order by an architect with a military passion for order and parades. Everything has a scrubbed appearance which – by contrast with the usual Guatemalan anarchy – serves all the more to isolate the school from the society out of which it grows.

I was shown to the sixth floor. The entrance hall to the block was a huge, sterile concrete chamber with a full-length portrait of General Rufino Barrios, *el Reformador*, founder of the school. The hall echoed to the sound of boots on the polished floor. On one side was a glass partition, behind which were displayed, like idols, shop's dummies dressed in the various uniforms of the armed services.

I was shown into the major's office. Large windows behind him overlooked the exercise fields. Suddenly, an Indian file of cadets burst out of one of the buildings and began high-stepping as though directed by a martial Busby Berkeley. They were chanting as they ran, probably something like, 'We're the toughest sons-of-bitches in the world, we'll kill you if you don't agree', but their mouths moved like those of goldfish in a bowl: up on the sixth floor, the only noise to penetrate from the outside world was the wind whistling round the tower.

The major was director of education at the *Escuela*. He greeted me affably. I was astonished that I had got this far without anyone asking me to prove I was who I said I was. A series of telephone calls to the major allowed me to inspect the contents of his bookcase. They were mainly works by the enemy: Lenin, Marx, Engels (*The Condition of the Working Class in England*), Mao, and Che Guevara. Fanon's *The Wretched of the Earth* was also there. I began to wonder whether my idea of all army officers having brains made of bone was perhaps a little simplistic.

The major was the son of General Ríos Montt, the former director of the school, and once President of the Republic. The son was stocky, mild-mannered and soft-spoken. Before we started our tour, I asked him a few routine questions about the numbers and social origins of the cadets. They were chosen entirely by merit, he said, and came from all classes except the lowest, who had no education, and the highest, who had no inclination. There were 1,500 applicants for 200 places every six months. Of the 200 chosen, a third completed the course. He, of course, had been one of the successful third, and was now inclined to put on weight, as successful men in authority often do. I asked him about the allegations of cruelty, watching his face closely for the fleeting look of anxiety that often precedes dissimulation.

He was either a practised spokesman or was genuinely undisturbed by any such suggestion. He admitted that life in the *Escuela* was hard, especially in the first few months, for a young man who had never left home before, but – speaking from experience – one soon adapted to the hardships and then ceased to notice them. Why, then, did only a third of cadets become officers? He denied it was because the others were driven away by maltreatment and that only the psychopaths survived. He said they failed in their studies or in their physical training or in their conduct. And I admit that the major seemed to me perfectly normal and well-adjusted; it was not easy to imagine him being gratuitously cruel or even enduring gratuitously cruel behaviour. He spoke of his family with tenderness and would not have minded if his own son became a cadet. He was a religious man, and when I asked him whether he was a Catholic or an evangelical, he replied, 'I am a Christian' – the very words his father uses. The possibility of agnosticism or atheism was not open to him, and indeed all cadets at the *Escuela* are required to practise a religion, lest they fall prey to alien ideologies (evangelical Protestantism having been awarded honorary Guatemalan citizenship). Yet for all his piety and normality, I could not entirely believe the major, however much I wished to do so from the personal viewpoint. Perhaps he had been sheltered from the worst of the school by the eminence of his father – who, however, was famed for his integrity and abhorrence of nepotism and corruption. But the school was the architectural embodiment of cruelty, it was impossible to imagine normal kindness developing there . . .

The major showed me round, not without pride. We walked through fields of cadets doing press-ups, into the classrooms, science laboratories and the library, where the classics of English, French, Russian and Spanish literature were all available, mainly in yellowing, turn-of-the-century editions. Were they for show, or did the cadets really use their spare time reading Chekhov? I pulled out a volume or two to see when they had last been borrowed: not long ago, but not frequently either. Literature as recreation was a poor second to going to Guatemala City at the weekend.

Discipline was severe at the school: weekend leave could be cancelled for having dirty finger nails. This attention to detail was completely at odds with the normally relaxed standards of Guatemalan life, another distinction, no doubt, that encouraged the cadets to think of themselves as standard bearers in Guatemala of the higher civilization that would one day redeem the *patria*. Near the squash courts we met the gymnastics instructor, and he looked exactly like the kind of sadist that every school employs to make the fat boy jump over the horse, impossible though this is until the laws of physics be abrogated. We entered the gymnasium, huge and echoing, with a boxing ring in the corner. We visited the school auditorium, immaculate and cold, and the clinic where the doctor's unctuous joviality seemed slightly sinister. He told me the cadets suffered mainly from musculoskeletal complaints while the men had venereal disease (VD was punishable among the cadets but not among the men). We went to the kitchens, with shiny stainless-steel vats dedicated more to hygiene than flavour. Finally, we went to a recreational hall for the cadets, a great spartan chamber with crates of soft drinks (no alcohol allowed) and fibre glass stackable chairs. A few pool tables had the warmth of absolute zero, but everything was clean. The officers' club was smaller but not different in style. Round the concrete walls were brass plaques presented by equivalent institutions in other countries, mainly Latin America. Outside, startlingly incongruous in the context, was a little formal garden with transplanted colonial fountains. These fountains introduced curves into a harshly angular world, an element almost of femininity into a masculine environment where to be a real man was to be unfeeling. We sat to have a cup of coffee (served by the only female I saw in the school). I asked whether the officers ate the same food as the recruits. Yes, said the major, they did.

I had grown to like him in the two hours he spent with me. He was proud of the *Escuela Politécnica*, and, as he showed me out, we paid our respects to two busts of the Spanish officers who had been the school's first directors. This was the shrine of an institution that worshipped itself. I should have found my visit much less troubling had I found the major utterly despicable. For all his assurances, I thought the school frightening. At the same time, I was reluctant to believe that any real evil could emerge from it because he seemed so ordinary and decent a man. I felt like a youth who plucks the petals of a daisy to discover the truth: she loves me, she loves me not, she loves me . . . but the words that alternated in my mind were decent, horrific, decent, horrific.

I had no experience of other military academies with which to compare it. Perhaps all military education isolates its recipients from the rest of humanity; what was undeniable was that the army, commanded by graduates of this same *Escuela Politécnica*, had committed innumerable atrocities. And had not the major told me, when I asked whether discipline in the school was not a little too severe, that before a man could command he had to learn to obey? Dr Otto Rasch, the head of an *Einsatzgruppe*, understood the psychology of atrocity:

> In his view every man . . . must partake of its collective guilt; the scenes of horror witnessed in common were to form the bond of comradeship holding the unit together; collective blood guilt was to be its cement. Rasch insisted that every man . . . take part in executions; the individual had to 'overcome himself'. There was hardly a man . . . who did not suffer from 'the most horrible dreams' . . . nevertheless, the aim was achieved – the camaraderie of guilt.

Yet still there were questions unanswered about how such terrible things could have happened in Guatemala. The officers trained in the *Escuela Politécnica*, but what about the men? They did not come from the privileged classes, and had no political order to preserve, but they were necessary to do the actual killing. Many of them came from villages very like the ones they destroyed. Why had they not revolted, why had they not turned their guns on their officers?

Perhaps the answer is not a simple one.

FOURTEEN

The major's father, General Efraín Ríos Montt, was now the pastor of an evangelical church whose headquarters were in California. I vaguely remembered newspaper articles about him from the time of the coup in 1982 (which he did not engineer himself) that brought him to power. In those days I had not developed a special interest in Guatemala, but I remembered that the articles sneered at him for his Christian fundamentalism. Later, he was portrayed less as a figure of fun and more as a ruthless dictator, one who systematically perpetrated massacres in the countryside. The word genocide was bandied about. His piety was regarded as a disguise for his lust for power; he was compared with Nazis.

This being so, it was odd to find his name, or rather that of his wife, in the telephone directory. If what they said about him were true, it was rather like finding the name of the wife of a prominent Nazi leader in the Frankfurt telephone directory. But Ríos Montt's was not the only name listed that I should not have expected to find. Guatemala had a strange openness in this regard, violent and dangerous as it was. For example, the names of Generals Benedicto and Romeo Lucas García were also in the telephone directory. They were chief of staff and president respectively in the worst government in Guatemalan history. Listed also were Juan Manuel Arévalo, the former revolutionary president, and Mario Sandoval Alarcón, the leader – by popular repute – of the death squads. I glanced at the yellow pages to check there was not a section, convenient for writers, listing ex-directors, presidents, generals etc.

But in any case, what I had heard in Guatemala about Ríos Montt was rather different from what our newspapers had written about him, and different too from what most authors had written. Whatever he was like, he was clearly a key figure in recent Guatemalan history, and I thought it important that I should meet him. I did not conduct a proper survey or investigate the history of his government in any depth: I am no scholar. But still I was surprised by the extreme divergence of what was said about him and what I read. Even those who disliked him admitted he was not personally corrupt, no small virtue in Guatemalan conditions. And it was generally agreed that the atmosphere in the capital changed overnight when he was installed in power; towns that were deserted every evening because of an unspoken curfew came alive, it being safe once more to walk in the streets. Ríos Montt insisted that public servants arrive at their posts on time, leave no earlier than they should, and treat the public with respect rather than disdain. He would pay unannounced visits to government departments, firing anyone on the spot whom he found insolent, dishonest or incompetent. He made civil servants wear a badge that said, *I don't rob, I don't cheat, I don't lie*, and for a few months it was almost true. Suddenly the police grew polite and teachers were no longer permitted to appear before their classes looking like scarecrows. Every Sunday throughout his eighteen-month presidency he gave a sermon on television, telling Guatemalans not to fornicate, get drunk, or otherwise fall from grace. He asked how the country could be expected to improve when everyone in it behaved so badly. What Guatemala needed, he said, was a change of heart. At first people listened, then they laughed, finally they grew bored.

Not everyone I met approved of Ríos Montt, however. On the way from Antigua to Escuintla, along an unmade road of surpassing beauty, I gave a lift to a schoolteacher on her way home. For something to say, I mentioned that I had interviewed General Ríos Montt.

'A terrible man,' she said shaking her head vehemently.

'Why do you say so?' I asked.

'When he was president,' she said, 'he ordered all the teachers in the department of Escuintla to attend a meeting with him in a cinema in the city. There were five hundred of us.' She was almost choking with rage at the recollection of it. 'Do you know what he did?'

'No,' I said.

'He told one of the teachers to put out his cigarette.'

I didn't know what to say, so I said nothing.

'Is that any way to speak to professionals?'

'No,' I said, feigning shock.

'Then he said that the teachers were not doing their work properly. He called us lazy. Is that any way to speak to professionals?'

If they are lazy, I thought.

'No,' I said. 'It isn't.'

There was a pause in the conversation as I drove over some ruts in the road. The teacher was still raging at the recollection of the humiliation.

'But some people say,' I resumed, 'that when Ríos Montt came to power things got much better. They say there was less killing.'

'Oh yes,' she said. 'Before Ríos Montt we used to see trucks go by with bodies when we stood by the road waiting for a lift. Then, after his coup – no more.'

I looked at her as I drove. It was a dangerous thing to do but I wanted to see whether she was serious. She was, and so I concluded that the episode with the cigarette weighed more with her than the disappearance of trucks laden with bodies. It was a curious scale of values, and one that helps explain the appearance of the trucks in the first place.

The *Iglesia del Verbo* (the Church of the Word) where General Ríos Montt preached was an old skating rink, a huge empty hall with a green tin roof on the Avenida de la Reforma. The receptionist in the little lobby stood in front of a bookcase with volumes of North American suburban piety, translated into Spanish, for sale. The covers of the books had middle-aged couples standing on front lawns gazing happily into each others' eyes, secure in the love of Christ. One might have supposed from the pictures that the first duties of a Christian were to take out life insurance and to lacquer one's hair. The horrible smugness of the pictures gave me the urge to scream. I wanted to shake the woman behind the counter and say, 'Can't you see it's all false, a sham?' But she smiled at me, with that terrible valley-of-the-shadow-of-death smile, and I knew she had a hard protective shell of serenity. By her counter was a box for *diezmos* and *donativos*, tithes and donations.

I was led across the skating rink, reclaimed from sin, to the office of the general. He was shorter than I expected, with black hair and clipped moustache, dressed in a brown tweed jacket, brown tie, brown trousers and brown shoes. With him was a taller man, who offered his services as a translator, but who in reality seemed more like a minder or bodyguard.

I had never met anyone who had been compared to the Nazis before, and very few ex-presidents, so I was not really at ease. I examined the general's face carefully for the mark of Cain, but it was not there. He did, however, have very dark eyes that seemed to bore through you like gimlets; his look was intense and undistractable, whatever occupied his mind occupied it completely, and his

movements were quick, precise and very military. His clothes gave
the impression of an ordinary, tidy *petit bourgeois*: but everything
else about him dispelled that impression.

His words were few but fast, spoken at the rhythm of a machine
gun. Each word was categorical, irreplaceable by any other. His
sentences were as clipped as his moustache: he did not inhabit a
world of nuances. Strangely enough, I had not thought of any
specific questions to ask him but in any case it was his character I
wanted to know, not his opinions. So when he asked what he could
do for me – not an unreasonable question in the circumstances – I
couldn't think of anything to say. My first question, conceived in
panic, was what part he thought his religion had played in his
removal from office. After all, he was an evangelical in a still Catholic
land.

'I have no religion,' said the general.

I must have looked astonished. Was he not the well-known
religious fanatic who could not utter a sentence without bringing
God into it? Had he not been known as *Dios Montt* (God Montt)?

'But. . .' I said, and that was all that was necessary.

The general repeated he had no religion. Journalism, he said, law,
medicine, business, they were religions, systems of belief, but he
was a Christian, that is to say a man who made no distinction
between life and belief. To make such a distinction, he said, was
Pharisaism.

'You know the Pharisees?' asked his bodyguard-minder in
English.

'Slightly,' I replied.

To be Christian, continued the general, was to live the upright,
moral life, to follow Christ in everything. But socialism, capitalism,
communism were all religions. The word religion was clearly not
one that evoked his approval.

His sincerity was unmistakeable, burning and a little alarming. I
wasn't quite sure I followed his line of reasoning, however. I
continued by asking him how he expected the street children of
Guatemala City, for example, to do right when they had no parents,
went to no school and owed allegiance to no one.

He replied that even for them a change of heart was necessary.
How was Guatemala going to change if Guatemalans did not? The
gospels were a call to individuals, not to groups. Without God, he
said, men were slaves to their selfish desires.

Whenever he finished speaking, he had the disconcerting habit of appending *Qué más?* (What else?), as if time were short. It was an effective way of emptying an interviewer's mind. Each new question, therefore, was snatched from the jaws of an awkward silence.

I asked him straight out about the allegations made by Amnesty International and others, of massacres in the countryside during his rule. What did he have to say about them?

He must have been asked the question many times, but it still had the power to stir him up. He stood and paced in a little military circle around the room. I could tell his pulse was racing.

'Go into the countryside and ask,' he said. '*Qué más?*'

Was his excited state the effect of a guilty conscience or of being repeatedly accused of terrible crimes that he did not commit? It is impossible to answer such a question after a short interview. Yet I found it hard to believe that the man before me, whose integrity it is impossible for anyone who meets him to doubt for even a moment, could have ordered or condoned the horrible things that happened.

'Do you deny,' I persisted, 'that innocent people were killed?'

'It was *una guerra sucia* [a dirty war],' he replied. '*Una guerra sucia.*'

The phrase was an unfortunate one, irrevocably associated with the *desaparecidos* of Argentina. But was it without justification? Perhaps the general was tired of explaining to people whose idea of conflict was a discussion round a dinner table what guerrilla warfare was like, that it considerably shortened the temper to be shot at by unseen enemies who never declared themselves, who made a point of being indistinguishable from the surrounding population, and how it was neither surprising nor unprecedented that soldiers sometimes vented their frustration and anger on unfortunate innocents who, of course, might not have been innocent. Even to a man so given to self-righteousness as General Ríos Montt, my question must have seemed self-righteous.

'*Qué más?*'

I asked him how a soldier dedicated to war could be a Christian. Did not the gospels enjoin people to love their enemies?

Yes, but the gospels also told people to render unto Caesar those things which were Caesar's, thus to respect constituted authority.

Did this mean, for instance, that he supported the Sandinistas against the Contras, now that they were constituted authority?

He repeated what he said before: that those thing which were Caesar's should be rendered unto Caesar. I could interpret it as I saw fit. I wanted to ask him about his attitude to changes in authority brought about by revolution. If, for example, the Guerrilla Army of the Poor succeeded in overthrowing the government, would he stand in obedience to it? But he was showing signs of impatience at my foolish questioning, and I took my leave of him.

Out in the street, I tried to collect my thoughts about this man. He was not just a figure of fun, a charlatan or an evil hypocrite, the puppet of dark and murderous forces, as had been suggested. He was far from stupid, though the light of his intelligence was intense rather than broad. Though he believed things to which very few could give assent, and many found ridiculous, he inspired respect and even affection. His integrity was of cast iron. And when I asked him whether he would like to be president again and he answered that it was up to God, not Man, to decide, I think he meant it in all humility (when he received the call to be president, he was sweeping the floor of the Verbo church). Yet I found his absence of self-doubt chilling. In the end, I could not fit him into any of the procrustean categories with which I furnished my mind.

In fact, Guatemala is not a country for those who want the world to be neatly divisible into good and evil. Perhaps such countries do not exist. But to restore my confidence in my ability to recognise evil when I encountered it, I sought an interview with General Benedicto Lucas García. I had tried to contact his brother, General Romeo Lucas García, but he was never at home on his *finca* in Quiché. Whenever I called, he was either in New Orleans or in Guatemala City at an unknown address. Once I tried calling him from the central public telephone office in the city. The woman behind the counter asked for the number I required and the name of the person to whom I wished to speak. When I said, 'General Romeo Lucas García,' she remained commendably impassive, but there was a stir in the queue behind me, which began to melt away, the people having remembered more urgent things to do than make telephone calls. But the man immediately behind me said he knew Romeo because he came from the same village. He stayed.

When I called General Benedicto at his *finca*, on the other hand, it was his wife that answered. She said her husband was presently in the capital and she would pass on my request for an interview. Shortly afterwards I received a call from the general and we arranged to meet next day at the house in which he was staying.

Benedicto was known to be more intelligent and articulate than his brother. Both of them spoke the Indian language of Quiché fluently, and this gave them a certain following amongst the Indians. Benedicto had studied at the French military academy of St Cyr and was a parachutist during the Algerian war. He was a fitness fanatic and was said to love dangerous sports. It was also said that he was the real author of the somewhat more sophisticated approach to guerrilla warfare that had brought the army from the brink of defeat to near-victory, or at least to containment – until, that was, the next escalation.

I found the house where I thought we had arranged to meet. It was in a comfortable but not opulent street. I rang and the door was opened by an attractive housewife. I said I had an appointment with General Benedicto Lucas García.

'He is not here, señor,' she said.

I looked at my piece of paper with his address and telephone number. I said I must have made a mistake and asked to use her telephone. She looked nervous but agreed. It turned out I *had* taken down the number of the house wrongly: it was 1374, not 1364. In Guatemala, house numbers often skip along by leaps and bounds, and 1374 was next door. When the housewife learnt who was staying in her neighbour's house, she paled. She said she was not a political person. I calmed her by saying I was not a friend of the general's either, only a journalist seeking an interview with him. I do not think my unexpected visit did much to improve her morning.

I went next door. My ring was answered by a servant who showed me into a room that was furnished richly, but not to my taste. I have always found mock eighteenth-century French furniture ridiculous, especially in the suburbs. I had just sat down with my arm resting on a cherub when the general made his entrance. Wearing slightly tinted spectacles (the sign of a psychopath, a distinguished professor of psychiatry once told me, and I believed him until I experimented with a pair myself), he radiated fitness and daring. He was dressed casually, except for his shoes, which were highly polished, thick-soled army issue. I wondered whether a supply of such shoes was part of his pension. He wore a gold chain round his neck and a gold ring on his little finger of knuckleduster proportions. His manner was amiable and charming, and it was only with difficulty that I reminded myself that he was one of the officers covered by the amnesty law which the military government passed just before handing power over to the civilians; under this law no soldier could be charged with any crime committed during the counterinsurgency. Unlike a similar law in Argentina, this one had never been abrogated.

It happened that the night before I had heard the rumour of a coup, and I asked the general whether he would welcome it.

He said that he would, though he would personally play no part in it. Guatemala was drifting aimlessly under civilian rule, the Christian Democrats were corrupt, operating a spoils system under which all jobs went to their friends whether they were capable or not of doing them, taxes were increasing yet people in the country did not receive from the government the things they needed, no member of the government ever left the comfort of the city to see what was happening in the countryside, money was being printed to increase inflation and debase the currency (this was a plot by the communists who had infiltrated the Christian Democrats). Only a military government could save the situation.

Benedicto Lucas García went on to say that the security situation was deteriorating once more. This was partly because the government was so nervous of a military coup that it kept moving commanders from one place to another, usually every two months, so that none should have a power base from which to plot. It also meant, of course, that they could not do their job properly. The army was losing ground: the very day before there had been two unpublicised confrontations with the guerrillas in both of which five soldiers had been killed. Furthermore, army intelligence knew of at least seventeen guerrilla cells in Guatemala City, preparing for a campaign of urban terrorism. Under present circumstances, the army could not win. Another problem was the attitude of Mexico: it gave refuge to the guerrillas and refused the right of hot pursuit to the Guatemalan army.

I asked why this should be when, for all its radical rhetoric, Mexico was a conservative country.

Mexico and Guatemala had never been friends, of course, but according to the general, there was a deeper reason than traditional enmity for Mexico's attitude. He said there had been a secret agreement between Mexico and Cuba, to the effect that Cuba would do nothing to aid the guerrilla movement in Mexico if Mexico did nothing to impede the guerrilla movements in Central America. I didn't know whether we were in the realm of madness, fiction or fact.

I asked him about the massacres. Momentarily he grew excited. He said that as chief of staff he had been responsible for all military operations. He was a man of the people, he had grown up in the country; moreover, as a lover of children and animals, how could he have ordered massacres? Was it possible, I asked, that some of his juniors had exceeded their orders? No, it was not possible. But often the guerrillas dressed up as the army, and then the army was blamed for what the guerrillas did. And often the guerrillas had the cooperation of the church. For example, when he had entered the village of Chajul, he had found the saints in the church dressed in guerrilla uniforms.

'Do you know what I did?' he asked, chuckling. 'I made the villagers put army uniforms on the saints.'

When I went to Chajul, all that remained of the uniforms was a camouflage kepi on St Peter.

I knew the general was telling me far less than the truth: I could hardly have expected anything else. I was asking him to confess to being a mass murderer.

He talked of his early career in the army: how in 1954 as a cadet at the *Escuela Politécnica* he had taken part in a revolt and spent three months in gaol as a result. The revolt had been against Castillo Armas, the man who overthrew Arbenz. It was not that the cadets wanted Arbenz back; rather, they were protesting about the attempt by Castillo Armas to make his little invading force an elite corps in the Guatemalan army proper – the army that had failed to defend Arbenz. It had all seemed of great importance at the time, but now the general laughed at the recollection of it.

Before I left him, I had a small mission to perform. A friend of mine, who knew Guatemala far better than I, had heard that one of the worst of the army commanders, by all accounts a sadistic psychopath, had been reappointed to the command of the area where he had committed his worst atrocities. The people there were terrified for their lives, and there were rumours of his atrocities starting up again. My friend asked me to slip the word to General Lucas García who, though retired, still had a great deal of influence. If I let it be known that a foreign writer was aware of the situation, it might just help to have the man removed before he could do further damage . . . Like a character in a Le Carré novel, I passed on the cryptic message which I only half understood myself, with just the right amount of fear: for if the general were the man he was reputed to be, it might be me rather than the commander who was removed. I scanned the general's face for a trace of emotion, but there was none, not even the faintest tremor of an eyelid. Shortly afterwards, the commander *was* removed; I felt vindicated, though his removal had nothing to do with my intervention.

The general saw me to the door, slapping me on the back. I thanked him for his time.

'Not at all,' he said. 'And if there is anything else I can do for you . . .'

As a matter of fact, there was. I wanted to meet his brother, but was having difficulty in contacting him. Perhaps he could help me . . .

Unfortunately, he could not. He and his brother had not spoken for more than two years; they had very different ideas. His brother was a multi-millionaire while he had only his army pension to live on, which was why when he came to Guatemala City he had to stay with friends. Neither did he possess huge plantations like his brother, nor did he go abroad, nor did he own a car . . .

I thanked him again and he slapped me on the back again.

'*A sus órdenes*,' he said. At your orders.

Once more I was confused. I despised myself for liking the general, for not having asked penetrating enough questions, for having allowed myself to be so easily influenced by his superficial charm and affability, for not even having asked why, if the army had done nothing wrong, it had decreed an amnesty for itself. I should never be a prosecuting counsel; I felt my weakness as an investigator and as a man. I had met actors in a drama too large for my comprehending and was out of my depth.

I met only one more general in Guatemala, and he was a relic. He was the last surviving general from Ubico's time, and I thought it would be fascinating to meet him. In the event, I was disappointed, for his memory was going and all that remained was a blind loyalty to Ubico about whom he could remember nothing specific, only that he was a splendid man in every way and very strict without being cruel. If a dog could speak of a stern master, I imagine it would speak thus. The only other thing the general remembered was that it was time for a whisky highball, and he assumed that I, as a Briton, was devoted to Scotch (nothing could be further from the truth).

The general's house smelt, alas, of incontinence, the humiliating fate of the elderly across the world. As I left, the ancient general returned to his television soap opera and it would have taken a more original mind than mine not to have reflected on the transience of life, the vainglory of power.

FIFTEEN

After the restoration of democracy in 1986, the tourists had returned to Guatemala, and nowhere more so than to the shores of Lake Atitlán, the lake that Aldous Huxley called the most beautiful in the world. Certainly it is magnificent: from the southern shore rise the dark green volcanoes of Tolimán, Atitlán and San Pedro, and the lake itself, on a fine day, is the deepest colour of sapphire. But the lake for me was interesting more for the strange activities around it than its splendid landscape.

I reached the village of Panajachel on its northern shore by a route, part of which everyone told me was dangerous. From Antigua, it took about two and a half hours in total. Buses were frequently ambushed along it, bandits posing as guerrillas fighting for a cause stole cars and even stripped passengers of their clothes. The village of Patzun on the way was famous – notorious – for the atrocities committed there by the army. It was inadvisable to take that route.

That is why I went. I took Indian travellers with me, thinking they would be some kind of protection. In Guatemala, the Indians have costumes of unequalled splendour. Every municipality has its own many-coloured costume, though the everyday use of *ladino* clothes has spread among Indian men as being cheaper and more practical. These Indian costumes have both pre-Columbian and colonial elements: in colonial times (and after) they allowed the domicile of any Indian to be known, and therefore acted as a form of control. Aficionados lament that the costumes are now coloured by garish chemical dyes rather than the more restrained vegetable ones of earlier times, but those who lament have probably never prepared natural dyes. The designs of the costumes are said to have symbolic meaning, but with the passage of time many of the meanings have been lost. Still, an Indian market in Guatemala is incomparably the most colourful event of its kind that I have ever seen, the exuberance of the apparel contrasting with the sober and dignified demeanour of the wearer. An Indian market in Guatemala is not just a place to sell but a place to meet, an occasion of ritual . . .

I reached Panajachel safely. It is an ancient Indian settlement, though you wouldn't think it now. Panajachel has been turned into a hippy town, a Central American Kathmandu or Goa, whose main street leading down to the lake is lined by souvenir shops and stalls, cafés, bars, and hippies trying to sell their costume jewellery. Some of the hippies are ageing, too old to keep rejecting society but too old to rejoin it; many look racked by hepatitis and vegetarianism, too poor to eat *and* smoke dope. Jean-Marie Simon expresses outrage in her book that the hippies of Panajachel were once searched *en masse* by the army. Of all the army's many crimes, this seemed to me the least, for drugs are everywhere in Panajachel, and there must be few hippies who never break Guatemalan law by taking them. As the citizen of an *imperium*, however, Jean-Marie Simon considers that her fellow-countrymen have the right to flout with impunity the laws of so inconsiderable a state as Guatemala.

I sat in a café with tables outside in the sun. At the next table sat a middle-aged man from San Francisco, wearing shorts, glasses with elaborate frames like cantilevers, and his hair slicked down over a bald patch. Opposite him was a lady of indeterminate age who, though by no means slim, was squeezed into the shortest of short white skirts, a skin-tight white sweater that showed her enormous bust if not to advantage, then at least very clearly, and a pair of long, fur-lined boots that would have been fashionable in the days of her youth, but which must have been hellishly hot in the warm sunshine. The man from San Francisco had arrived in Guatemala that very morning and had made straight for Panajachel. I could not help overhearing their conversation. Pretending to write a letter, I took notes.

'The people in the world,' he said, 'who get most advantage taken of them are those that give out most straight away. I'm one of those . . . I radiate energy.'

'It's all right if people want to live in hell – that's all right,' the lady responded. Her command of English was part of her capital. 'Let them. But you want to be divine with me? I have mind control. You can be divine with me . . . I teach Spanish. That's the first thing I teach you.'

'I have cycles,' said the man. They were not so much conversing as indulging in two monologues that touched each other tangentially. 'Last night I was so relaxed it would have taken major stimulation to open up new levels of energy.'

Just then a jeep went by full of soldiers, their guns pointing outwards.

'What are those military here for?' he asked.

'They're looking for rebels,' answered the lady.

'They're playing war games. I know they're burning the forest down, beautiful animals . . .'

'You see,' she said, 'they're working with physics, but they don't understand.'

'But why do they burn down villages?'

'They've lost contact with their bodies, their physical selves, and with the astral body. They're lost in the dark side of their minds and they kill you. They become a machine.'

This was a theory of the Guatemalan conflict I had never heard expounded. The man from California changed the subject.

'I haven't looked in a mirror today. How do I look?'

'Good.'

'Natural? Do I look natural?'

'Completely.'

'Rusty?'

'A little.'

'What hotel shall I stay in?'

With that, they left the café and I was able to laugh, though a waiter thought me mad.

In Panajachel I met an American juggler. He worked half the year as a street artist at home in Colorado and half the year as a juggler in the Circus Bar, the best cabaret in Guatemala. The bar was run by a German who never rose before midday and was a fine flamenco guitarist. The second time I went to the bar his left hand was in a bandage, the result of a late night brawl. He employed Argentinian singers, Paraguayan harpists, a German one-man band, and fire-swallowers and jugglers of all nations. He had managed to recreate something of the atmosphere of Weimar Germany in Guatemala: the swirls of bluish smoke, the waiters with their bottles of wine on trays held above their shoulders as they tried to make their way through crowds of tipsy customers, the talented artists on the tiny stage, the feeling that anything went (at least until the re-establishment of dictatorship), reminded me of the cartoons of Georg Grosz.

I did not see the juggler perform – he was preoccupied with learning the tightrope at the time. I met him in his rented house. It had once been a small holiday cottage for a bourgeois family from the city, but there was no possibility of mistaking it for one now: it was sixties alternative lifestyle in pure culture. The chaos was studied. In the garden, on what had once been the lawn, was parked a beaten-up station wagon with hundreds of stickers on it wishing the world peace. It was festooned with psychedelic decorations and was obviously the veteran of many mishaps, major and minor. It was in this vehicle that the juggler proposed to return to the United States, as he had come. He was not apprehensive about the journey, though his vehicle was sure to attract the venemous attention of every uniformed inquisitor from Guatemala to Colorado. Of course, he needed their unpleasantness as much as any addict needs his drug.

He asked me whether I should be interested to meet a painter who had lived many years in Panajachel and had just opened a gallery for his work in his home. George was a German with a remarkable history: during the war he had deserted from the German army and joined the Danish resistance. He had been captured, taken to a concentration camp and more than once sentenced to death, only to be reprieved at the last moment. His life had been saved by the Liberation. Disillusioned by the civilisation that had given rise to the horrors of Auschwitz, he had travelled in the east and turned to oriental mysticism for inspiration. Then he was imprisoned for six months in Sri Lanka for having outstayed his visa. He and his wife had taken refuge from the world on the shores of Lake Atitlán. Alas, the world had come to join them there.

His house, too, had once been bourgeois, but George had transformed it completely. Outside the front door was a little Zen rock garden. Whitewashed poems in English were painted on the rocks, on the theme of their sentience, how the rocks had thoughts of their own, feelings, a soul, etc. and how therefore one should treat them well. Inside, everything was shaded from the light of the sun. The rooms smelt of joss sticks and incense, and Korean music, with ethereal tinkles and occasional deep booms of a gong, played over concealed loudspeakers. Shells were suspended on strings in the portico to tinkle in the wind. On the walls were displayed George's paintings, an interweaving of Buddhist, surrealist and psychedelic themes. Fairy lights flashed on and off at what appeared to be a shrine, and sometimes the Korean music was interrupted by a recording of waves lapping against a shore.

A servant asked us to remove our shoes as we toured the rooms. I wanted very much to meet George, and eventually he emerged to give us that most graceful of oriental greetings, the hands held together pointing upwards which, however, always seems false and even phoney when performed by occidentals. He welcomed us to his 'temple'.

The juggler had told me that George was an enthusiast for long philosophical discussions, and talked for hours once embarked on serious questions. The time was not propitious, though, because his children by his first marriage were visiting: a daughter married to an artist from New Mexico who believed that we all had Art within us if only we could 'access it', and a son who had reverted to Teutonic type, a man temperamentally unsuited to temple life in Panajachel, who craved routine, discipline, structure and fixity of purpose, a real clicker of life's heels.

George was over seventy, with white hair and goatee beard, and wore the brown corduroy trousers of an intellectual. He spoke in barely audible whispers, as though afraid to disturb the peace of the universe. Whatever his eccentricities, one felt he had more than earned the right to them: a man who had experienced so much could scarcely be as others, and anyone who had deserted the Nazi army for the Resistance was worthy of eternal respect. But I thought less charitably of his wife, who was just as eccentric. She was from Santa Barbara, California, and was still in her early thirties. She had borne George three children and like him had turned her back on western civilisation. The juggler told me she did not like to speak English, and sometimes refused to do so, because she said it was a language that falsely divided the world (which was One) into parts; she preferred to speak Tibetan. Unfortunately, not many people in Panajachel spoke Tibetan, and the Indians who came to her to sell tomatoes were somewhat bemused to be greeted in that language. When forced to speak English, she adopted a strange and stilted accent and grammar of her own, designed apparently to make English less analytic and more synthetic. Unfortunately, this also made it incomprehensible, and even the juggler, no enemy of mysticism, found it absurd. Furthermore, she had once told the juggler that she would not teach her children to read and write, for this would only make them oppress the Indians when they grew up. She went barefoot, wore Indian *traje*, carried her latest baby Indian-style on her back and ground her own corn by hand to make her tortillas. All this would have been her own business had she not been more accusatory in her manner than a prosecutor, more virtuous than a saint. It seemed to me that she had the egotism of a Tolstoy without the literary achievements and that her sacrifices were but a form of self-indulgence.

As for her children, one feared for them. They were the human grist to the pedagogical mill of a woman strong in character but deficient in education and common sense. The oldest of the children, a smudge-faced little girl with dirty blonde hair, got out like her mother in Indian *traje*, was old enough to exhibit the consequences of an upbringing in which no moral difference was allowed between mild chastisement and the outbreak of World War Three. Not surprisingly, the child was a monster. Every time she passed me she gave me a pinch on the leg or a kick in the ankles: not a playful one, but one designed to produce as much pain as possible. I thought at first it might be my fault, that somehow I had communicated hostility towards her; but then I saw her behave (when she thought no one was looking) in exactly the same way towards her little brother, the juggler and anyone else who came within pinching distance of her. Discreetly, so as not to offend her pacifist and vegetarian parents, I let her know that if she pinched me again I should give her what is known in mystical India as *one tight slap*. She stopped attacking me at once.

I left George and the reincarnation of Mrs Jellyby and returned to Antigua. Travelling with me was a young Dane whose fine, corn-gold hair was done into a bun at the back of his head, and who wore Schubertian or Kierkegaardian spectacles. He had been George's disciple for several months and he, too, rejected western civilisation, except for things like air tickets back to Denmark and lifts in cars. He was pursuing a project, financed in Germany, to prove the superiority of Mayan to western culture; but this would take some while to arrange, and in the meantime he wanted to go to Ecuador to help defend a group of Indians in the forest against the depredations of oil prospectors. A friend of his had already been killed there doing precisely this, killed by the CIA, he said. I asked how he knew it was the CIA, but I discovered that he had the habit of swiftly changing the subject when anything other than assertion of sentiment was required.

The Dane spoke of George. He was a great artist, he said, because he had suffered so much and was so sincere. I said these attributes might be necessary, but were certainly not sufficient, for the production of great art. There was much suffering and much sincerity in the world, but there was only one Mozart. Again, the subject changed abruptly.

I had met these travelling Scandinavians before. They produced a peculiar sinking feeling somewhere around my diaphragm. They were depressingly the same, all with their worthy opinions, all determined to do good, all blissfully unaware of deeper currents in life (and most of them blinking at the world through little gold-rimmed spectacles with round or oval lenses). They were well-educated and intelligent, speaking English better than the average Briton; yet somehow one never expected to hear anything interesting from them, or a remark that would set one back with a jolt. And as for laughter . . .

Panajachel is all the more bizarre and incongruous because on the opposite shore of the lake a guerrilla war has raged for more than a decade. I went there several times, driving along the unpaved track, on one occasion just after a bus had been ambushed and burned by the guerrillas, and two military commissioners (civilian spies for the army) killed. Another time, an army patrol had just come under mortar fire. I saw no action, but once I was stopped by a group of armed men who had just come down from the mountainside. They asked me who I was. More to the point, who were they? They were in uniform, but instead of boots wore basketball and tennis shoes, and their buttons were sewn on with coloured thread, red, yellow, blue, anything that could be found. If they were soldiers of the Guatemalan army, they were the first I had seen in such a ragged condition, but it was possible they were returning from a long patrol in the bush. On the other hand, they might have been guerrillas (the army accuses them of dressing up like the army, and they accuse the army of dressing up like them). Anyway, I didn't think it polite to ask. And they gave me no trouble, waving me on.

The guerrillas of the *Organización del Pueblo en Armas* (the Organisation of the People in Arms, ORPA) have a better reputation than those of the *Ejército Guerrillero de los Pobres* (the Guerrilla Army of the Poor, EGP), though they have united in the *Unión Revolucionaria Nacional Guatemalteca* (the Guatemalan National Revolutionary Union, URNG), which includes also the *Fuerzas Armadas Rebeldes* (the Rebel Armed Forces, FAR). Unlike the EGP, which tries to hold 'liberated' territory and organises civilian populations, the ORPA is purely military, using guerrilla attacks to inflict whatever damage it can in the hope that the state will eventually give up in despair, or the people will rise up to overthrow it. The ORPA is said to enjoy support particularly among the migrant workers of the southern region where there are large plantations, for it uses protection rackets to ensure the plantation owners pay at least the minimum legal wage (3.20 *quetzales*, or $1.30, per day) to their workers, which, if left to their own devices, they rarely would. A

British journalist, Ambrose Evans-Pritchard, spent a week with a guerrilla band of the ORPA and found them among the finest people he had ever met, though this did not cloud his larger judgment that their victory would usher in no golden age, that they had very little idea of what to do if they found themselves in power. But of late, even the ORPA had turned to more drastic methods of recruitment and supply, according to my very reliable source (in writing of the south side of the lake, it is better not to be specific). For example, the ORPA had recently offered a man in one of the villages 200 *quetzales* per recruit he raised, an offer he would be ill-advised to ignore. The money came from 'revolutionary taxes' on landowners, kidnappings and bank robberies. I found it difficult to believe that men, however idealistic, could long remain uncorrupted by these methods. My source traced for me the boundaries of the ORPA and EGP operations, and I thought of Chicago during Prohibition . . .

The town of Santiago Atitlán is visited by almost every journalist who comes to Guatemala, for it is relatively easy of access and has an unrivalled reputation for violent nastiness. Since the tourist boom, the morning boat across the lake from Panajachel, which arrives at ten o'clock, deposits twenty or so tourists and takes them away again an hour or two later. Just before they arrive, the owners of the little stores along the cobbled street that leads from the shore to the main plaza hang out their *típica* – bags with multicoloured, machine-embroidered quetzal birds – and a café owner turns up his ghetto-blaster until the ground shakes. Later in the day, when the town has returned to normal, the café owner – deaf and drunk – reveals a penchant for brass band funeral music.

What is normal in Santiago Atitlán? On my first night there, the main square was the scene of an evangelical revival meeting. On one side of the square was a banner proclaiming that the army and people were working together to defeat communism; on the other, a banner proclaiming that Christ was the only hope. This was strung across a stage erected for a preacher and his entourage. Further up the hill was the large whitewashed Catholic church, all but empty, with a commemorative plaque on the wall to Father Stanley Rother, the parish priest from Oklahoma who was murdered there in 1981. A little way from the square, in an ostentatiously unornamented chapel, were hundreds of Indians in *traje*, down on their knees, beseeching and muttering in tongues. As the light failed, the faithful – or perhaps the curious and bored – gathered in the square to hear the preacher. Before long the preacher was accusing his congregation of every sin imaginable. Behind him sat a panel of saved Indians, who had graduated from *traje* to lumpy, ill-fitting *ladino* suits, unpressed collars and ties as wide as Nancy Reagan's fixed smile. Sin, however, could be forgiven if . . . Here the preacher broke into the Indian language. Then the singing started, horrible hymns magnified even louder than the café owner's ghetto-blaster. The preacher's voice shook to the vibrato of cheap emotion, distorted by the overloaded sound system. Among those listening to him, the few elect had chairs, the waverers stood behind, while the outright sceptics and mockers, and the plain bewildered, held their distance. There were a thousand people that night in the square. I thought most of them must be there for the novelty.

For the novelty! I was forgetting that Santiago, which is no vast metropolis, has had on average a murder every month for years, and therefore does not stand in need of sensation. The week before the revival meeting, the bodies of two women had been found, raped and naked, near the road just outside the town. The received wisdom was that the army was responsible; someone who knew the town well said it was the guerrillas, because the two women were dealers in *típica* for tourists and had failed to pay their suppliers and were generally regarded as exploiters. And an hour before the revival meeting, I happened to meet a doctor who was chatting to one of the town's firemen. The doctor told me that 80 per cent of Santiago's children were infested with the giant roundworm, *Ascaris lumbricoides*; the fireman told me a cousin of his had just been murdered. I asked him questions, but he would tell me neither the motive nor the perpetrator, though I suspected he knew both. All he would add was that the people of Santiago lived in fear.

Further along the south side of the lake is the town of San Pedro de la Laguna, where there has been peace for several years. Superficially, the town does not look much different from Santiago: a little more prosperous, perhaps, for the people own a little more land, but otherwise much the same. The parish priest of San Pedro, Father Vessey, is from Brooklyn. He is a controversial figure, as men with firm opinions often are. Rumours about him abound. It is said that he was forced to leave Paraguay, where he served many years, because his parishioners threatened to kill him; and that he was similarly evicted from the parish of Santiago Atitlán, where an enraged mob attacked the church one night and he was saved only by the intervention of a twenty stone nun who kept the mob at bay while he hid in the belfry. The next day he was smuggled out of the town hidden in some laundry. More recently, he had been involved in controversy over some religious statuary in the little town of San Pablo, adjacent to San Pedro and within the confines of his parish. The statues belonged to the *cofradías* of San Pablo, the lay religious associations whose worship Father Vessey considered unorthodox and even idolatrous, embodying as it did the syncretism of Catholicism and pre-Columbian religious belief almost universal in the Indian parts of Guatemala. A man of unbending faith and principle, as well as the representative of the one true church in his parish, Father Vessey confiscated the statues of the *cofradías* and insisted, moreover, on controlling their very finances. The people of San Pablo rose up against this partial re-enactment of the Conquest, and went to Father Vessey's bishop to demand his recall. Their demand was not met, and feeling ran high for a time. There was talk of Father Vessey's imminent murder. A party of people from San Pablo went to Guatemala City and occupied the cathedral there. Eventually, the Archbishop worked out a compromise solution, whereby Father Vessey kept his parish but agreed never to enter San Pablo.

Victor Perera, the author of *Rites*, told me that when he visited Father Vessey he formed the impression of a man with a martyr complex, of someone determined to follow Father Rother violently to the grave. His cause was not political but religious, and he wanted desperately to be canonised. Victor thought him mad, in the most literal and psychiatric sense: a man who perceived things that were not there, who believed that everything was directed at or against him, who thought he had an ordained place in God's plan for this corner of the universe, and who knew he was surrounded by a miasma of evil that only someone with his special faculties could discern.

Arriving at the priest's house in San Pedro early one afternoon, I was told that the Father, having that morning returned from a long journey, was asleep. The house was next to a school and as I sat waiting a nun shepherded a large group of laughing children into the schoolroom. The nun was not dressed as other nuns I had seen in Central America, either in mufti or a kind of truncated grey habit that was neither formal nor casual but only ugly and undignified; she was in full medieval regalia, with a long dark blue habit and a starched wimple as white and beautiful as any in an early Flemish painting. It was glorious to see, its very impracticality in the circumstances a demonstration of faith, its association with an ancient tradition an assurance there are truths beyond fashionable ideas (whether they exist or not is another question). And her attitude to the children was self-evidently one of love, so that she controlled them without an external form of discipline.

Father Vessey rose from his sleep. He was dressed in a T-shirt and blue tracksuit trousers. This surprised me; there are some priests who are ideologically committed to wearing ecclesiastical costume as little as possible, but I doubted whether Father Vessey was one of them. He had the bluest eyes I have ever seen, bluer than the sky, so blue that any portrait would be discounted as an exaggeration. Like the eyes of General Ríos Montt, they did not merely look at, they bored into, whatever they were turned upon. Another man, I thought, with categorical ideas.

Why, I asked without bothering with small talk, was Santiago so violent when the towns to either side of it, San Pedro de la Laguna and San Lucas Tolimán, were at peace? It was just the kind of question that Father Vessey liked.

'Because San Lucas and San Pedro have turned their backs on evil,' he replied, the stare of his eyes so intense, so ablaze with the importance of what he said, that it was easy to understand why some thought him mad.

Certainly the difference in respect to violence between the towns required *some* explanation. The articles that appear in the world's press about Santiago scarcely mention it, preferring to arouse the warm glow of readers' outrage by sensational accounts of grisly horrors. Whether Father Vessey's answer was the correct one, appealing as it did to the irreducible freedom of human conduct, I cannot judge, but it was not one that would appeal to sociologists, economists or psychologists, who prefer to think of differences in income, employment rates and the like. They believe that to understand all is to forgive all. But what is it to understand all, there being in the final analysis no final analysis? Explanation is like an onion with an infinite number of skins; one stops peeling when continuation becomes too painful.

Therefore I did not find Father Vessey's explanation quite as fatuous as others might think it. He saw choice where others saw only predestination. He was strongly against drink, obsessively and inappropriately so according to his critics, for ceremonial drunkenness had long been part of the culture of the lakeside Indians, and the church had traditionally been lenient and accommodating about it. But Father Vessey said drink ruined the lives of drinkers and those of their families, turning them into something less than fully human. But still it was a matter of choice: without a change of heart by the drinker himself, nothing could be done. He had preached that very morning against the evils of drink (so fervent was he on the subject that I began to suspect a personal interest, like an erring parent or a chequered past). His campaign was increasingly successful, he said; the children of former drunks were better nourished, the wives remained unbeaten. The Kingdom of God is within you.

Extrapolating from drink to murder, he said it was clear that the difference between San Pedro and Santiago was moral and religious, not economic or social. A short while ago, the towns were as violent as each other. Where, Father Vessey asked, had the violence come from? The traditional answer was that the army killed anyone who demanded rights, allegedly supported the guerrillas, was a leader of the community, questioned the *status quo*, was malcontent, or stood out in any other way. The people of the south side of the lake were usually portrayed as being the passive victims of this violence, contributing nothing to their own immolation. But this, said Father Vessey, was not true, or it was such a simplification that it amounted to untruth. And here I must add that Father Vessey's testimony was confirmed by those who knew the lake better than he.

Violence was not a new method of settling disputes in the area. Once the civil war was under way and there were trigger-happy soldiers everywhere, the citizens of the towns took advantage of their presence to denounce their enemies. You had only to tell the army that your neighbour supplied food for the guerrillas effectively to sign his death warrant. He disappeared at once. In the climate of fear and repression that developed, when no questions were asked, it was possible to remove creditors, competitors and enemies, and carry on vendettas, entirely by denunciation. Well, the towns of San Lucas and San Pedro had decided they would play this deadly game no more, that no one would denounce anybody ever again, and the killings stopped. Only Santiago stuck to the old ways.

But even there things had changed, so I was told: there was more 'justice' in the killings than before. The army had become almost discriminating. It searched out the brightest citizens to appoint as *orejas*, ears, whose task it was to pass on local intelligence. It was an appointment one could not refuse, from which one could not resign, and in pursuit of whose duties it was advisable, from the longevity point of view, to be diligent, for negligence was rewarded with death. Failure to denounce those who should have been denounced was fatal but – an important innovation – so now was false denunciation. The army no longer killed without grounds of suspicion (this was an improvement!) and many of the *orejas* supposedly killed by the guerrillas were in fact killed by the army, dissatisfied in one way or another with their service. Thus the only hope of peace in Santiago lay in a halt to denunciations, which in turn depended on no one supporting the guerrillas. It was not a stupid strategy by the army, and accounted for the greater desperation and virulence of the guerrillas.

Of course, these complexities undermined the clarity of Father Vessey's vision. If both the army and the guerrillas issued mortal threats, then the decision to eschew denunciation was not quite like the decision to eschew strong drink. But if Father Vessey was unable to provide a completely satisfying account of the south side of the lake – and by extension, the rest of Guatemala – neither was anybody else I ever met. He was not the half-mad figure of fun I had been led to expect.

SIXTEEN

By far the most sinister place in Santiago Atitlán was an extraordinary half-completed pleasure garden and hotel complex on the shores of the lake. That no expense had been spared or detail overlooked was clear, and made it all the more grotesque. The gardens were laid out with infinite care: there was a huge, dry, irregularly-shaped swimming pool; various ponds with bridges over them; a castellated café built on an artificial rocky outcrop in the middle of a man-made lake painted turquoise but without any water; a hotel building whose design committee must have included at the very least Suleiman the Magnificent, D. W. Griffiths and General Pinochet; and surrounding walls appropriate to a prison camp, over whose gates I expected to see the words 'Pleasure Will Make You Free'. Everything was constructed of dark grey rock, so that even the airiest of designs would have been heavy and forbidding. Silence resounded through the gardens. Though all work was in abeyance, pending resumption in more propitious times, both the gardens and the buildings were scrupulously maintained, and though open to the public – that is to say, the entrance was not closed – they were deserted. Around the flower beds, I noticed that a single thread of barbed wire had been strung, no doubt to teach rabbits and small children a proper respect for flowers.

Who could have built such a monstrosity with so much pride and devotion? My guess was that it was a retired military torturer who, having corruptly amassed a fortune, looked around for an investment, decided on an hotel and pleasure garden and then tried to remember what it was like to be a child. Actually, I learnt from a 1983 brochure that the *Turicentro Tiosh-Abaj* was the brainchild of a Señor Jose Jimenez Romero, 'who with futuristic vision proposed this beautiful project'. Appended was a photograph of him in dark glasses, looking exactly like a retired torturer.

The parish priest of Santiago was another American from Oklahoma, who preferred cowboy clothes to vestments. He was altogether more relaxed about sin than Father Vessey; he was professionally opposed to it, of course, but recognized that without it he would soon be out of a job. He knew that he could impose no Catholic orthodoxy on the people, and saw nothing wrong with their religious syncretism. After all, what now counted as orthodoxy was nothing but the syncretism of past ages. As for the challenge presented by the Protestant, evangelical and pentecostal sects, he was not tortured by thoughts of heresy as Father Vessey was; he did not want to save the Indians from eternal damnation, whose prospect was as real to Father Vessey, but not to him, as tomorrow's breakfast. When I asked him what percentage of his parish was now non-Catholic, he said twenty, perhaps thirty, but this included people who spoke in tongues one day and prayed in front of the Virgin Mary the next. The Indians did what they had always done, took elements that suited them and used them as they saw fit. The sects were a bubble that would burst. In any case, he was not prepared to coerce the Indians into a doubtful orthodoxy by forbidding them this or that practice, or frightening them with morbid ideas of hell-fire and damnation.

He did not seem like a man with strong faith. I wasn't quite sure what he believed (I had no such problem with Father Vessey). I even thought he took traditional Catholic beliefs as a bit of a joke, or at least seriously open to doubt: a position one expects in a layman, in certain novelists even, but not in a missionary priest thousands of miles from home. When it was time for a service ('the people are waiting for me,' he said), he donned no vestments in preparation, merely removed his cowboy hat. He spoke of services as though they were superstitious and barbaric vestiges, which he performed not with delight in the transcendent mystery but as a regrettable part of the job. Yet he was clearly a man beloved of his flock who put his faith into life rather than into doctrine.

A priest in Sololá – a town high up in the hills on the other side of the lake and the seat of Santiago's diocese – was less sanguine (from the Catholic point of view) about the religious changes occurring in Guatemala. He thought the further spread of North American sects inevitable. This was for several reasons, most importantly because there were no more than 500 priests in the whole of Guatemala, that is, one for every 17,000 people, of whom not more than 200 were Guatemalans. The rest were foreigners – mostly North Americans, Belgians and Spanish. His own parish had over 30,000 parishioners spread in 24 villages, the majority of which he could visit only once a month or even less, and the inhabitants of which therefore remained strangers to him. The sects, by contrast, had thousands of pastors:

the local baker or candlestick maker was a preacher on Sundays, one who moreover knew and shared the joys and sorrows of his congregation. The women of Guatemala appreciated the sects' strong stand against drink, while the Catholic church (except for Father Vessey) remained tolerant of the drunkenness that for them meant only beatings and poverty. The Catholic church had tried to respond to the challenge by training lay catechists, but they had been selected by the army for death or disappearance. The catechists were tainted with the social doctrine of the church, the army mistaking liberation theology for Marxism pure and simple.

Was this totally unfounded, I asked? After all, I possessed a book, published in Mexico but bought in Guatemala (a sign of the more liberal times) that contained interviews with foreign priests working in Guatemala who had joined up with the guerrillas and equated Catholic orthodoxy with revolution. What conclusion was an army officer, unused to drawing subtle distinctions and raised on crude geopolitics, expected to draw?

The priest explained that the sects had escaped army repression because their doctrine was one of personal salvation, not social improvement. Joining a sect, therefore, provided the peasants with a measure of protection. While catechists were slaughtered, pastors remained safe. And when a village was rebuilt after its destruction by the army, the sects were able, thanks to their wealthy North American connections, to offer material aid such as tin roofs, while the Catholic church in Guatemala had to rely on its own meagre resources.

And in times of uncertainty, he said, people needed not less but more doctrine, not tolerance and vacillation but a laying down of the law. This the sects were able to do. When people were moved by suffering to ask why such terrible things had happened to them, they wanted to know it was because of something they had done or omitted to do, that it was just retribution, for otherwise the world lost all meaning, and reward and punishment were random events over which they had no control. Better a harsh God than unfeeling chance.

The priest at Sololá, unlike Father Vessey, was unconcerned by the almost pagan nature of the *cofradías*, the lay religious fraternities. His God was a God of understanding and love, not a tetchy paterfamilias who laid down rules and consigned people to eternal flames for bad table manners.

The most famous of the *cofradías* in Santiago is that of San Simón, more widely known as Maximón. His relation to any figure of the Christian religion is tenuous, to say the least, and no-one knows exactly when his cult started. Probably it grew in the time of Rufino Barrios, when orthodoxy was at a very low ebb after the expulsion of foreign priests, who remained in exile for seventy years. Most of the time the figure of Maximón is kept in the roof of a house which also contains a figure of the dead Christ in a glass coffin. The underside of the roof is decorated with a jungle of plastic fruit and foliage; the room is filled with the scent of copal incense, and there are bottles of *aguardiente*, cane spirit, everywhere (Maximón is a drinker). His guardian offered to show me the idol for ten *quetzales*, but we agreed on five. He climbed into the roof and levered Maximón down. My first inclination, which of course I suppressed, was to laugh: he was a dumpy little fellow, without arms (cut off, according to one legend, to prevent him from sexually assaulting the women of Santiago), with stumpy legs ending in platform shoes, a smooth but crudely carved wooden face with a slightly hangdog expression, a large but ill-rolled cigar stuck in his pouting mouth, and dressed in a patchwork of colourful cloths like silk handkerchiefs, wearing also the San Pedro trousers of white and black stripes lovingly embroidered at their hems with colourful birds and flowers that indicate the Indians' intense love of the natural world.

A single glimpse was sufficient to tell me that I should never be able to enter imaginatively into the world of people who believed in the powers of this statue, not if I lived among them for the rest of my life and read all the anthropological texts that ever were. Some gulfs are beyond the capacity of goodwill to bridge; that, in part, is Guatemala's tragedy.

Yet, surprisingly enough, there are *ladinos* who are devotees of Maximón. Nor are they only the poor and ignorant. There is another statue of Maximón in the town of San Andrés Ixtapa, not very far from Antigua. He has his own chapel there, and on Sundays one may see BMWs and Mercedes from Guatemala City parked outside while the owners give thanks, the Maximón of San Andrés being celebrated for his help in economic affairs.

The road to his chapel is lined with stalls that sell candles, incense, reproductions of the 'saint', and sizzling meat on skewers, the sacred and profane being intermingled as everywhere else in Guatemala. The chapel has a little forecourt, and here incense is burnt. A notice on the wall explains the use of different coloured candles:

Red – Love, faith and goodwill

Green – Business and prosperity
Dark blue – Work and luck
Pink – Health and hope
Black – Against enemies and envy
Brown – Against vices and bad thoughts
Light blue – Money, happiness, journeys and studies
Yellow – Protection for adults
White – Protection for children

In the chapel, a building without ornament, are eight stone-topped altars, on which the worshippers light their candles, sprinkle *aguardiente*, offer up food and cigars, and behind which they pray. Above them, on a dais, is Maximón himself, preserved in a large glass case. There are steps up to him, and the worshippers each spend a few minutes buttonholing him with their petitions. The relations between him and his worshippers seem surprisingly equal, for there is in their manner of prayer just a hint of threat, that if their petitions are rejected, he will receive no more cigars or *aguardiente*.

The Maximón of San Andrés is a little different from his namesake in Santiago. The first statue in San Andrés was burnt to ashes in a fire. Judging from the photographs he was the very image of a nineteenth-century German coffee *finca* owner, of whom the peasants would have said he was severe but just. His son, the second statue, is similar, but, being a second-generation Guatemalan, is less Teutonic, having softened a little, and being less obsessively methodical, more tropical. Still, with his dark suit and tie, pork-pie hat, jet black moustaches and right hand clutching a shotgun (while still smoking a cigar), he is severe enough. Sometimes he is dressed in military uniform, a symbol of power. To his right are plaques testifying to and thanking him for the miracles he has performed; to his left a warning to those who come to pray to him:

Dear Brothers:
I, Simon, beg you not to come to me with a handful of candles to request evil for your brothers, because the harm that you ask for them will be done unto you; therefore do not waste my time coming dressed as a sheep if deep inside you are a wolf. I, Simon, give thanks to you.

This spirit of forgiveness was something new in the cult of Maximón. An old notice gave the purpose of black candles unashamedly as *revenge*, and there were many black candles lit whenever I visited the chapel.

I returned several times to Santiago, and once heard the strange rumour that there were twenty-four Argentinians in town, instructing the army garrison there in techniques of torture. Times were lean at home for torturers, and they were part of an export drive. But I never met them or anybody who knew them. I was with a young American reporter at the time, to whom I had suggested many dangerous enterprises. His appetite for risk was somewhat reduced, however, when back in Guatemala City he pulled over to the side of the road to consult his map and three men jumped into his car, held a pistol to his head, told him where to drive, and then relieved him of his car (which the police later recovered).

We went for a walk on the lower slopes of the Tolimán volcano, an area of almost unnatural quiet, as though the birds had fled the war; we thought that every step might be our last, for our imaginations planted mines everywhere. The path we followed petered out near a cave, in whose shade we sat. It was time, as it says in Russian literature, to talk philosophy. There is nothing quite like danger (real or imagined) for making you think about the purpose of your life. We decided that we would pay a visit to the army garrison, to hear what the soldiers had to say.

We expected them to be a little wary of two strangers who turned up in the middle of a war and started asking questions. On the contrary, they were relaxed, almost casual. The camp was defended by a fence of chicken wire, outside which Indian women gathered to sell fruit to the off-duty soldiers. We told the sentry we wanted to speak to the commanding officer – on reflection, a somewhat arrogant request, though it seemed perfectly natural to us at the time. Anyway, the sentry meekly did as he was asked, and before long a captain and lieutenant came out of one of the makeshift buildings that comprised the camp. They took us to a round thatched pavilion made of pickets and asked us what we wanted.

The two men were very different. They would have made a classic interrogation team: one reasonable and accommodating, the other brutal and direct. The captain was a slight man with a pock-marked face whose glasses gave him an intellectual bearing. He spoke quietly and with a melancholy that made one wish to probe his thoughts and memories, to discern the cause of this melancholy. The lieutenant, on the other hand, was full of energy and enthusiasm, untouched by any sense of irony, still less tragedy. Perhaps he never would be. He struck me as a man whose ambition was so great that he would find sophistical justifications for anything

he did or ordered done. He would always sleep easy. He spoke with
absolute conviction, his eyes blazing, his words like shotgun pellets.
When excited, which was most of the time, or when he had made
what he considered a telling point, he would pace round the pavilion
like a caged lion. His favourite form of argument, not surprisingly,
was *tu quoque*, you also, turning the accusation on the accuser
(without ever noticing that it was also an admission of guilt). When,
for instance, we asked about the fate of the Guatemalan Indians, he
turned on us and vehemently asked about the fate of the Indians in
North America, a question he would not permit me to evade by
saying I was not North American, for we were *anglosajones* – Anglo-
Saxons – together. The Indians of Guatemala, he said, had never
been systematically exterminated, unlike those of North America. It
was strange to hear him speak of Indians as though they were an
alien race, for though of Hispanic culture, he was of almost pure
Indian descent.

Throughout his diatribes, which were clearly expressed and by no
means those of a fool, his commanding officer remained silent, as
though he had deeper knowledge of life which, however, was not so
easily communicated.

Our discussion continued for two hours. It was a model of illogic.
When one side stated something, the other would counter with a
statement that was neither a refutation nor wholly irrelevant. Thus:

Many innocent people, mainly Indians, have been killed in the
war.

But in English colonies the Indians were exterminated.

That was a long time ago.

The few survivors are still badly treated.

Before long, everything had been dragged in: the Falklands, or
Malvinas, War, child pornography in the United States, the
aborigines of Australia, drug addiction and crime rates, all with the
purpose of demonstrating that Guatemala was not worse than our
own countries. And from his nationalist standpoint, I could see it
was a valuable tactic, one with which I secretly sympathised. For
like him, I was tired of people who used Guatemala as a kind of
psychotherapy to assuage their self-important need for righteous-
ness and guilt. How tiresome were those ladies who thrilled to the
wickedness of Guatemala, but would not dare venture out after dark
in their own country!

But still there remained the fatal flaw in the *tu quoque* argument.
The captain and the lieutenant invited us to lunch. I was for

accepting, but the young reporter said no. Later, he told me that his journalistic ethics prevented him from accepting anything from people about whom he might write, lest the gift relationship affected what he wrote. I found his code, while magnificent in its way, a trifle rigorous. I felt I was a writer, not a prosecutor, and if I wanted to understand people, or hear their unguarded thoughts, I could not afford to be so sea-green incorruptible.

The soldiers told us that the war was, to all intents and purposes, won; that while the guerrillas could still inflict casualties on the army if it went into the bush in search of them, they lacked the strength for an all-out attack. This did not quite tally with the fact that the Military Hospital in Guatemala City was at that very moment full to overflowing with wounded soldiers; yet what they said was in essence (though only for the moment) true. The captain thought there were only 150 ORPA guerrillas in the field; no doubt in his estimate he was torn between a desire to minimise their numbers to show how slight was their support, and to maximise them to show how difficult a task the army faced. The guerrillas were split into bands of five or six; without helicopters the army was not sufficiently mobile to engage them other than by chance, and was therefore operating at a disadvantage. I met a Scandinavian photographer who spent two months with the ORPA and had photographs of many successful ambushes. He, of course, was one of those guerrillophiles who so abound in western Europe; he rejoiced at the deaths of Guatemalan soldiers. Whether they died to any purpose was beside the point. Born rich into a world of poverty, but unable to abandon his privileges, he projected the drama of his guilt and self-hatred on to distant lands.

The last day I spent in Santiago was the Wednesday before Easter, at the end of March. By tradition, Maximón spends this day in the municipal offices before his removal to a little chapel near the church, where he remains until Good Friday. On Wednesday afternoon he is carried from the offices to the chapel to the accompaniment of drums. Colourful as this ceremony is, the crowds are growing ever smaller. The *cofradías* are losing their hold in Santiago: election to office in one of them involves expenditure of much money, perhaps a man's entire life savings, and cannot be refused. Avoidance of such office, therefore, is yet another motive for conversion to evangelical and pentecostal sects.

This time I was in the company of a German journalist, and he too wore the round, gold-rimmed spectacles of the vicarious revolutionist. Together we paid a visit to the headmaster of Santiago's school. He was a *ladino*, but had lived a quarter of a century in the town. Times were hard for teachers in Santiago. Of the twenty staff of his school, four had recently fled to the capital. Their names were among the 180 that appeared on a death list allegedly found by the army in the knapsack of a dead guerrilla, and which the army then showed to all the people on the list, hinting darkly that their safety could not now be assured. In the nearby village of Cerro de Oro (Hill of Gold), another six teachers had fled because two of their number had encountered a well-dressed man along the road who informed them that they and their colleagues might be killed if they stayed. They had never seen the well-dressed man before, but in these times and in these parts one took such gnomic utterances seriously. The teachers in another nearby village, Chacaya, took the hint and also fled.

In 1987, the headmaster said, twenty or twenty-five people had been murdered in Santiago. So far this year (it was only March) an equal number had died. Five were murdered on one single night in February, in different parts of the town. These deaths were never investigated. The people of Santiago were peaceful by nature, he said; they wanted work, roads and schools, not war, the army, civil patrols and the guerrillas.

This cycle of murder and revenge sounded hopeless, yet the headmaster was not entirely without hope. In certain respects, things had improved. The army was less a law unto itself, he said, and sometimes the civil authorities even listened to what the people had to say. When he first came to Santiago there were only two hundred pupils at school; now there were 1,200, but the population had only doubled. Illiteracy was on the wane, and now there were two doctors resident in the town, whereas twenty-five years ago doctors paid only the rarest of fleeting visits.

That night, a strange group of foreigners gathered for dinner in an ill-lit *comedor*, or cheap restaurant. First there was an American in Indian *traje* and dark glasses. His face and arms were adorned with plasters that covered the wounds he had received when he was attacked in Antigua by a man with a knife. His voice was loud as he talked of himself and of his parents' disappointment in him. His brother and all his contemporaries were yuppies, with expensive homes, wives, foreign cars, children and other possessions. He had opted out of this meaningless existence at an early age, returning to the world of commerce – selling T-shirts at pop festivals – only when he needed money to live. But though he knew meaninglessness when he saw it, he had yet to discover meaning.

Second was a bearded Danish teacher and radical, who was so certain of his judgment in favour of the guerrillas that he told me any peasant in Guatemala who spoke against them did so out of fear of the army. He would write articles when he returned, and it was not difficult to guess their content or tone. He was also gathering teaching materials for his class at home. It was important, he said, that children should learn reality.

Third was a retired English physiologist, soft-spoken but full of virulent hatred. Mrs Thatcher was the particular object of his odium: government cuts, he said, had threatened the institution to which he had devoted his life. Seeing the writing on the wall, he had taken early retirement. But it was really western civilisation as a whole that he hated and he had come to Santiago to escape it. Of course his renunciation did not go quite as far as his pension or the rent from his house in London, but I had long since ceased to expect perfect consistency from human beings. At heart, he was a romantic, seeing in the Indians all that was missing from his own life: a sense of continuity, a oneness with Nature and the like. But still I wondered whether, if he had achieved a chair, if he had held the title of 'professor', he would have raged quite so bitterly against the evangelicals who, he said, were destroying the Indians, turning them materialistic, ruining their manners, teaching them to be dirty and creating in them an appetite for junk food. When anyone disagreed with him, or said something with which he disagreed, he at once ascribed to them the worst of motives or plain stupidity, which made for a lively if acrimonious discussion.

The last at dinner was a Vietnam veteran, an odd, silent man. He had been a volunteer, not a conscript, the member of an elite corps of undercover killers, a man who had been trained to survive in the jungle, to cut throats silently, to say nothing. He had been involved in some particularly horrible battle, after which he lost his memory and was invalided home. For many years afterwards his concentration was poor, he could not sleep, he avoided company. He went to live on his own in the woods, a kind of hybrid of Thoreau and Rambo. Eventually, he recovered a little, at least sufficiently to return to college (Vietnam had interrupted his education). Now he had a year to go and he would take the awarding of his degree as a sign of his complete rehabilitation. But still he was strange. For long periods his expression would be vacant, his eyes would stare glassily.

Then suddenly he gave the impression of hyper-alertness, as though there were enemies in the darkness. Perhaps he had come to Santiago to test his sanity.

It was a good test and in my opinion he passed it. George, the English physiologist, launched over soup into one of his diatribes against western civilization. What, he asked, could we teach the Indians about agriculture? Nothing, absolutely nothing. We would only teach them to pollute with our fertilizers, insecticides, fungicides, herbicides and other death-dealing chemicals; we would poison the earth that they had been successfully cultivating for thousands of years. And in the process, we would smash their beautiful, gentle society.

Very quietly, almost inaudibly, the Vietam veteran mentioned a fish-farming project he had seen. The Indians round the lake fished very little, in part because fish stocks were low. He could see nothing wrong with teaching Indians to farm fish, especially as the use of chemicals was not required. And it would improve their diet, he said.

George did not address the question of fish farms directly. Instead, he spoke against ploughs. They ruined the land, he said, dug too deep, exhausted the soil, destroyed patterns of land tenure, induced greed, promoted new and unnecessary crops,and cost a lot of money; in short they were a menace. The Indians had been using hand hoes for centuries. What need then of ploughs? Who would benefit but the odious plough salesmen?

There were several answers one might have made, among them that to extol the hand hoe was clearly the prerogative of a man who had never had to use one. Or one might have answered that hand hoes were once as alien as ploughs, having been brought by the Spaniards to replace the digging stick. But the Vietnam veteran stuck to his point.

'Fish farms don't use ploughs.'

George, however, had the bit between his teeth and next he attacked the corrupting influence of foreigners in Santiago. (He had awarded himself citizenship after his brief stay.) You could already see the effects: surliness, shoddy workmanship, loss of traditional values, radios everywhere, soft drinks, in fact the whole catalogue of evils that plague the correspondence columns of the *Daily Telegraph*.

All of a sudden, quite without warning, the Dane was shaking with rage. He brought his fist crashing down and would have hit the table a tremendous blow had he not recalled at the last moment that he was a Scandinavian and therefore a man of peace. It appeared he was tired of hearing all this hypocritical nonsense about the inviolability of Indian culture. Was not most of it based on ignorance and superstition? Did it not give the Indian a false view of the world that had allowed him to be exploited for centuries? What they needed was Marxism, not Maximón.

Luckily for the Indians, all of us around the table knew what was good for them. The only slight problem was that everyone knew something incompatible with what everyone else knew. I recalled a passage from *La patria del criollo*:

> The enthusiasm that certain aspects of Indian culture once evoked – its antiquity, its 'authenticity', its simplicity in some ways, its 'esoteric depths' in others – must suffer a severe blow when it is demonstrated that all those aspects are the outcome of a concrete process of several centuries of colonial oppression, the very oppression they still reflect. This blow, however, is an indispensable step towards a scientific and revolutionary conception of the Indian . . . This conception sees backwardness and anachronism where others ignorantly see venerable antiquity and authenticity . . . sees infantilism and poverty of resources where others like to see simplicity; sees superstition and magical thought, the outcome of ignorance, where others falsely see exoticism and spirituality.

But whether intellectuals finally come to see the Indians as repositories of ancient wisdom or of childish nonsense, of one thing they may rest assured: the intellectuals will never *ask* them what they want, and be satisfied with the answer.

SEVENTEEN

It is not easy to find the truth of anything in Guatemala.

The *Tigre* of Ixcán, Don Luis Arenas, was a famous – or infamous – landowner in the mountainous and forested Ixcán region of Guatemala. In 1975, when in his seventies, he became the first victim in the EGP's revolutionary campaign. His death at their hands was their declaration of war, as it were. When his death became known, the army descended on the Ixcán and 'disappeared' thirty-seven peasants from a nearby village in reprisal.

The *Tigre* was killed at Finca la Perla while he was paying out wages to his workers. One of his assassins, Mario Payeras, wrote a short book of memoirs called *Los días de la selva* (*Days of the Jungle*), in which he described the death of the *finca* owner in detail. The purpose of his death was to ignite a rebellion.

June 1 was payday, which made it easier for us to approach the offices where the workers were to collect their wages. They clustered in front of the manager's office waiting for their money. Standing in front of the manager and looking like a bird of prey, the lord of the land was counting his coins . . . When we ordered him to raise his hands, his eyes rested for a second on his associates and he instinctively reached for his gun. A quick burst of gunfire killed him just as he was pressing the trigger of his revolver.

Not believing what they had just seen, the crowd nervously listened to the explanation, in their own language, that we offered then and there. As the indictment progressed, recalling Arenas's injustices and depredations, voices began to be heard among the crowd, interrupting the speaker and adding justifications of their own for the man's execution. Finally shouts of joy burst from throats accustomed for centuries only to silence and lament . . .

We did not take a *centavo* of the money . . .

Two days of fiesta at Ilom, a neighbouring village, was the best proof of the people's joy over the event.

I met Don Enrique Arenas, the son of the *Tigre* and present owner of La Perla, and he asked me whether I would go to the *finca* for a week or two, there having been no doctor there for a long time. Nothing could have suited me better, for I sensed that the events at Finca la Perla and the personality of Don Luis were somehow at the heart of the Guatemalan matter.

It was only possible to reach La Perla by light aircraft, for there was still guerrilla activity all round. I prepared for the journey and my stay by reading the rest of *Days of the Jungle*, and also by reading in Mike Shawcross's archive the story of Nick Blake, an American journalist who disappeared with a friend in the hills of the Ixil Triangle, not so very far away. He was trying to contact the EGP to write a story about them.

Blake was a freelance journalist who came from a prominent family of Philadelphia bankers. Their summer home was next to that of President Bush, who was also a friend. Nick was the black sheep of the family, wanting to be a writer rather than a banker, and he came to Central America to make his name. He had been with the guerrillas in El Salvador and had published articles in several newspapers, but he needed a big story to establish himself, and many journalists had written about the Salvadorean guerrillas. He felt it was make or break. No one had ever succeeded in going with the EGP, and so he set out with his friend to contact them in the hills above Nebaj. He was never seen or heard of again.

In Mike Shawcross's files are some melancholy letters from a mutual friend of theirs. Before Nick's departure, the escapade sounded almost like a student stunt, though there is already just a hint of apprehension:

Nick tells me he's running around the jungles looking for g's . . . If he makes it out OK I hope you can talk him into sticking around for at least a beer or two . . .

Three weeks later, the writer has not heard the news. The tone is the same:

I trust Nick arrived OK from his trip and that it was a success. Please give him my best and tell him I look forward to consuming an excessive number of drinks with him. . .

But five weeks later, there is only whistling in the dark:

I have felt so utterly useless in this whole thing with Nick and have often questioned what kind of friend I am to have done nothing except pray and know he's coming out safely.

At first the Blake family thought it must have been the Guatemalan army that killed Nick. His younger brother Sam told a newspaper: 'They [the army] may get away with it with these peasants, but they're not going to get away with it with me.' Even allowing for the emotional upset of losing a brother, one can hear the hard edge of privilege in these words. The Blake family worked through the then Vice President Bush to have all American aid to Guatemala suspended until the guilty were punished.

The Guatemalan army, however, mounted a large-scale sweep through the hills in search of Nick, and in the process lost seven of its men. This helped to persuade the Blake family that it was the guerrillas who killed him. Sam Blake then told a newspaper: 'Either [the guerrillas] admit their role or take the consequences.' The consequences were that the Blake family would try to influence George Bush to step up United States aid to the Guatemalan army.

The most poignant aspect of the whole affair was that Nick Blake was writing a novel at the time of his death. It concerns a young journalist called David Seeker.

David Seeker had come to Central America for a variety of reasons . . . Like so many other young journalists, he was there to make a reputation. Escape the glacial process of dues-paying journalism back in the States.

But it wasn't only ambition. He had been nurtured on revolutions, starting with television images in the sixties and later in his reading. It exhilarated him to see people rising in mass catharsis . . . Seeker felt his life had begun in Central America.

Is it coincidence that revolution should be described as though it were a collective psychoanalysis? Or that revolutionary romanticism should have started, like sales of a new toothpaste, with 'television images'?

Life sometimes imitates art. On the last page of the novel Seeker and a companion have gone into the jungle to meet the guerrillas. They meet them: 'short, ragged men, with bandanas tied over their faces, Jesse James-style.' Seeing that they are about to shoot, Seeker throws up his hands and shouts *'Periodista!'* ('Journalist!') To no avail: 'Bullets from an automatic tore into him and his companion. They were still shouting when the shots knocked them over into the mud.'

Was Nick Blake's last utterance '*Periodista!*' with his hands in the air? I began to wonder whether my visit to La Perla was not a little foolhardy.

However, I was so engaged by *Days of the Jungle* that I simply had to go. The book that affected me so deeply is short, scarcely a hundred pages, written by an educated man with a genuine feeling for nature. It tells the story of what in the Spanish version is called an *implantación*, an implantation, a word that, curiously enough, is missing from the version in English, perhaps because it gives too much away. The book describes how a handful of would-be guerrillas entered Guatemala from Mexico with 'commandeered' supplies, and found the local population either indifferent or hostile to their calls for revolution. 'On learning of our presence, the inhabitants either locked themselves into their houses or fled into the hills . . . Some of us were forced to chase the runaways and warn them to return.' There is no mention of the method of persuasion used, but then, like most memoirs, *Days of the Jungle* is a curious mixture of self-disclosure and evasion.

The peasants did not rush to the aid of the little band of intellectuals and urban *petit bourgeois* who were fighting on their behalf. 'We could see, in the granaries of the very people who told us they had no corn, mounds of what we needed so badly to survive.' And this was not surprising, for Mario Payeras admits that the guerrillas' idea of fomenting revolution in the area predated any real knowledge of it. 'Our days in the village taught us much about the conditions of our people . . . We had [not] delved deeply into . . . their aspirations.' This surely is a breathtaking admission, and it expresses with radiant clarity the way a disposition towards revolution is often anterior to its alleged justification. But never mind their ignorance; the little band knew enough to teach the peasants. 'This was the best way of explaining what the poor of Guatemala must do.'

The guerrillas' idea was to spread military action all over the country. Somehow, this was to be done without evoking too strong a response from the Guatemalan army. The attacks of the guerrillas should be:

. . . limited so that the enemy's reaction would not exceed either what the people were prepared to understand or what we were capable of withstanding and defending at the local level. The wind we set in motion should not be so strong as to strip the blossoms from the tree.

This last image is surely of Maoist inspiration: people as blank sheets of paper on which the most beautiful characters can be written, or blossoms to be shaken or not shaken from a tree. The idea that a tiny group of men could somehow have titrated the response of the Guatemalan army is puerile even by the standards of undergraduate revolutionaries: criminally puerile, one feels inclined to add, for the brutality of the army was already known and its response to the murder of Luis Arenas was warning enough.

As for the society that was to be created after victory, Mario Payeras was less than precise. But his book provides clues. He calls dialectics 'the most useful of all sciences', more useful than mere physics, for example, or biochemistry, because it allows one to establish any conclusion one wishes. He rhapsodises about an experiment in 'rudimentary communism . . . a new kind of social consciousness' which the guerrillas encourage, an experiment which has the habit of turning nasty beyond the wildest dreams of sadists, as the history of the twentieth century amply attests. But, as several peasants told me, the guerrillas did not at the same time hesitate to promise them land, goods and wealth to be held as private property, in order to secure a tactical alliance with them until after the revolution, when of course a different tune would be hummed.

To judge from the book, the new Guatemala is also to be a prig's paradise. Every event, every feeling, every thought, is invested with earnest meaning, in the manner of adolescents. The philosophising is banal: 'We were materialists, and we therefore knew that death is the result of chance and cannot be foreseen, although one can scientifically consider it as one of the possibilities of war.' There is wrestling with the problem of good and evil, in the manner of Protestant tracts: when one of the desperately hungry guerrillas licks the empty sack of sugar instead of putting it in the collective coffee to boil, he is made publicly to confess, and every guerrilla inwardly swears never again to be prey to the cancer of *petit bourgeois* individualism. Yet this vice keeps rearing its head:

The guerrillero who had the foresight to preserve a cigarette butt through storms and overturned boats, and who set out to enjoy it in his hammock after a gruelling day, was inevitably reprimanded by a *compañero* with less foresight for 'acting like a thief, giving free reign to his individualism'.

In the world of guerrillas, as in that of religious enthusiasts, deprivation and suffering are the *sine qua non* of virtue. The worth of a cause is proportional to the lengths to which its adherents are prepared to go to further it. But there are backsliders and renegades, described in the very terms a missionary might employ. A young *compañero* called Efraín deserted during the first year because 'unknown factors' in his early life had undermined his revolutionary convictions. And when another *compañero* expressed his scepticism about the guerrillas' chances of sucess, they decided to execute him. At first they preached at him, like good evangelicals, appealing to his better nature, but at length his fate was sealed. History itself demanded nothing less than the death penalty:

We shot him one April morning when many birds were singing. This was one of the world's lovely sounds that he would no longer hear . . . We returned to our posts. A profound silence reigned. The unit had reached maturity. Perhaps from that moment each of us was a better person.

A better person for having killed a former friend! This is what another philosopher of death had to say on the subject:

Most of you will know what it means to see a hundred corpses – five hundred – a thousand – lying there. But seeing this thing through and nevertheless . . . remaining decent, that is what has made us hard. This is a never-recorded . . . page of glory in our history.

The words are those of Heinrich Himmler.

I wanted to go to La Perla to verify or refute those parts of *Days of the Jungle* that referred to it. If anything would provide me with the golden key to Guatemala, I thought, this investigation would. The light aircraft was waiting at the airport: the other passengers were Mike Shawcross and Don Enrique, the present owner. The pilot was a young man who did not tell me until much later that he crashed the first time he landed at La Perla, broke both his legs and spent several months in hospital. A short time after I departed from the *finca*, he crashed again, or at least came to the end of the landing strip there without taking off. I remember feeling relief at his air of quiet confidence and technical competence. Another thing he did not tell me until much later was that he had once landed at La Perla to find the guerrillas waiting for him. They burned the aircraft and made off with the workers' wages he had brought from Guatemala City. For neither of these actions did they earn the gratitude of the people of La Perla, whose wages were already low enough without being made non-existent, and for whom the aircraft was literally a lifeline. This happened in the early eighties.

Our first attempt to reach the *finca* was abortive. Although a radio link to La Perla had told us the weather was fine when we started out, by the time we reached the highlands there was complete cloud cover, and our little craft could fly only very slightly higher than the mountains themselves. Without navigational aids, we had little alternative but to return to the city.

The next day we tried again, without Don Enrique, in another small aircraft. I had thought the first one rickety enough, but the second was absurdly decrepit, a thing of rags and patches. There were no seats inside, except the pilot's. We sat on plastic tanks of aviation fuel: it was like flying in a Molotov cocktail. So overladen with cargo was it (no one bothered about weight) that I sat with my face against the cockpit window, my neck craning horribly. The automatic starter did not work, and the pilot, a different one who struck us as somewhat insouciant about life and death, got out to crank the propeller by hand. We took off and wobbled in the crosswind. 'Oh Lord,' I prayed, 'I didn't mean it when I said You didn't exist.' There's nothing like flying on a gas tank for taking Pascal's bet.

We climbed slowly. I remembered all those news bulletins about aircraft that crashed five minutes after take-off. Unnoticed by the pilot (the only one of us, of course, with a seat belt) his door opened somewhere over Guatemala City. Mike leaned forward to close it, but the mechanism was faulty, so he held it shut for the rest of the journey.

Again we did not reach our destination. We saw the clouds rolling down the mountainsides like theatrical smoke and returned once more, though not until the pilot had made a couple of kamikaze dives through supposed gaps in the cloud.

The third day we didn't even set out, but sat at the airport's aero club awaiting a radio message from La Perla about fine weather. It never came, but it was interesting enough watching the dark-windowed station wagons come and go, delivering and collecting *finca* owners on their way to and from their *fincas*. Pilots sat in the clubhouse swapping tall stories. It was here that I heard that Don Enrique owned his own aircraft which he used to fly to his *finca* in the south, where there was no danger of its destruction by guerrillas; he hired aircraft to go to La Perla.

On the fourth day the sky was brilliantly clear and once more we climbed aboard our single-seater Molotov cocktail. Soon we were flying over (or rather through) a magnificent landscape of forested mountains, deep ravines and white water. The mountain peaks were high above us; it was exhilarating to fly in the valleys. How tiny was our aircraft, how small our lives! I thought of the brief but beautiful ball of orange flame we should make against the mountain if the pilot made an error. Would anyone see it? I was surprised that even in the most inaccessible valleys, where there was not so much as a track, rectangles of forest had been cut down. Was this for the timber (but how could it be transported from so inaccessible a place?), or was it to clear the land for a *milpa*, a corn field?

If the latter, for whom was the corn destined? Guerrillas? Refugees from the war? I could not tell.

We swung left into another valley and ahead of us was La Perla, the Pearl. It was indeed beautiful. The village clung to the dark green hillsides, a small white church dazzling by contrast. The landing strip ran up a small hill and between flights served as a playground for the children of the *finca*. On our left as we landed was the coffee processing plant of whitewashed wood, built on pillars of cement. In front of it was a large and perfectly flat concrete yard where the coffee beans, having been separated from the red husk of the berry and soaked in tanks beneath the plant, were laid out to dry, raked by workers into patterns resembling those of the pebble gardens of Kyoto. Above the processing plant was the house in which Don Luis used to live, but now it was the headquarters of La Perla's garrison of 160 men, with a flagpole flying the sky-blue, white and sky-blue flag of Guatemala, and, a little way beyond, a helicopter landing pad on the top of a hillock. On the other side of the valley, atop another hill, was a small graveyard, and it was here that Luis Arenas was buried in a simple tomb among those of his workers, the inscription giving only his name and dates of existence.

Waiting for us at the landing strip was La Perla's only vehicle, an open and battered jeep that looked and sounded as though it might

at any moment disintegrate into a heap of parts. How had it reached
La Perla? There were only mule tracks there. The only road went to
a distant part of the *finca* called Santa Delfina, a road which the
workers had built by hand in defiance of threats by the guerrillas.
The jeep had been flown to La Perla by helicopter, and was therefore
a precious vehicle. It drove us the few hundred yards down the
muddy track to the processing plant, in the quarters of which we
were to live.

The rooms were large and airy and wooden shutters opened on to
a view of green hills. Below us we could hear the grinding and
slurping of coffee bean extraction. We were served lunch by a
motherly servant of the family, Doña Caterina: soup, meat and
tortillas, accompanied by a pickle of burnt-tasting chillies, to which
I soon grew addicted. While talking to Doña Caterina, she let slip
that her husband had been murdered by the guerrillas, for reasons
that she did not understand. Not long after we arrived she was called
to Guatemala City, where Don Enrique's mother was ill and needed
Doña Caterina as a nurse. The woman who replaced her was short, a
ladina who spoke no Indian language yet dressed half in the Indian
way. She told me that her husband also had been killed by the
guerrillas, and her son. The guerrillas burst into their hut one night
and shot them. She had no idea why; we were poor people, she said.
Were they military commissioners, I asked? No, she replied. After
the killings, she had fled to Nebaj, a day or two through the
mountains, and there, *gracias a Díos*, she had heard an evangelist
preach and she had 'accepted Christ', as she put it.

But why, I asked, had she changed from her ancestral Catholicism?

'*Por mucha tristeza*,' she replied. Because of much sadness.

When later I recounted this to assorted journalists and solidarity
workers, they said it was impossible; the women had mistaken the
soldiers for guerrillas, or they were afraid to say it was the army. But
when I told them the women were well able to distinguish, and were
moreover unafraid to acknowledge the army's killings in the area, in
the course of which whole villages had been destroyed and scores of
people murdered, they remained incredulous. No, they insisted, the
women were afraid to speak . . .

Later, the pilot told me the guerrillas would have known of my
presence in La Perla. How he knew, I did not inquire; presumably
there were guerrilla *orejas* (ears) in the village.

After lunch, I went to the clinic. It had been built by the *Hechos de*

Fé (Deeds of Faith) mission. Apparently, a posse of Californian believers had descended on La Perla and, much to the astonishment of the local people, had worked all day and night until it was complete. They left behind a missionary and his wife, Doña Victoria, who was a nurse. Later, she became ill with an ear infection and, after an operation, was advised not to return to high altitude. The *Hechos de Fé* clinic was left in the hands of Luis, a young *ladino* who had done a little first aid training in the army. Luis first came to La Perla during his period of conscription, and had returned to marry an Indian girl there.

Poor Luis! He was a devout evangelical and had exchanged a riotous life for sobriety, but he was quite out of his depth at the clinic. The medicines came from the United States; my heart sank when I saw yet again that terrible hotchpotch of physicians' samples, time-expired stock and patent medicines that good people in Europe and North America so assiduously collect to send to clinics in poor countries, warming to the glow of lives saved thereby. I had seen exactly the same selection of drugs all over Africa. If only one could get it across to good people that what was needed was a large quantity of a few cheap drugs, not samples of the latest anti-hypertensive sufficient only for three days' treatment. I found banana-flavoured slimming tablets that swelled in the stomach to give the sensation of fullness and thus reduce hunger (a North American cocoa leaf), cartons of vaginal deodorants, bottles of the latest vitamin supplement thought to grant eternal youth if taken at breakfast. There were some useful drugs too, but in much smaller quantities. And Luis, who was barely literate in Spanish, who wrote with his tongue protruding and whose spelling was uncertain (he put h's where there were none, left them off when they should have been there, and mistook b for v and v for b), had to read the names and instructions in English, of which he spoke not a word. The result was that he had to guess the purpose of the lotions, capsules and ointments by their external characteristics. The people of La Perla, therefore, were rubbing lurid green fluoride toothwash into their hair to rid themselves of lice. For all I knew, it worked. Here, perhaps, was a subject for pathbreaking research. I found it difficult to imagine the little creatures surviving long in the green fluid. (Back in Guatemala City, I mentioned the misuse of the toothwash to an American human rights activist, and, far from laughing, he saw it as just one more example of imperialism at work.) Luis was dispensing anti-indigestion tablets for coughs and anti-inflammatory eye drops for wax in the ears. Man, however, is a tough organism and can withstand – within wide limits, much to the relief of doctors – misprescription.

Mike Shawcross had only two or three days to spare, and so we set out to see something of the nearby villages. We had a guide and two mules and a pony, though it was not clear whether these latter made our journey any the easier. Unused to riding, at the end of several hours in the saddle my thighs ached and my buttocks felt like those of a masochist after a good night out. But it was worth the travail a hundred times over, for the steep and muddy mule tracks over which the beasts fastidiously picked their way, at their own pace and no other, passed through scenes of astonishing loveliness, always to the accompaniment of the sound of running water. The dark green coffee bushes on the more accessible slopes were hung with crimson berries. From the sides of ravines grew huge and noble trees, ceibas with hundred foot trunks that suddenly opened up into broad canopies of foliage. All around were wild dahlias, tall as a man standing on another man's shoulders, bearing mauve flowers; and white trumpet lilies, perfect in form, that seemed to call for the loving work of a Victorian flower painter to capture them on the page of an exquisite volume. Vistas opened up of green mountains against blue sky. I drew my mule up sharply just so that I could drink with my eyes.

We descended into a deep valley. On the way we came upon a deserted mill with old, possibly Edwardian, English machinery. How had this massive ironwork been brought here? One shuddered to think of the human labour involved. But now the mill had only the vague melancholy of any abandoned building in a wild place. A grove of orange trees had been planted all around and we stopped to eat some: they were by far the most delicious I had ever eaten. Then we continued our descent, the temperature of the air rising with every step downwards, until we reached the valley floor, with its greenhouse heat, where La Perla's second crop, cardamom, grew. In the dark groves of cardamom shrubs, where the mud sucked underfoot like the tentacles of an octopus, huge butterflies with dull brown underwings but with brilliant iridescent overwings, flitted by silently and tantalizingly, disappearing ahead of us into the jungle darkness.

Cardamom: a spice whose flavour and aroma I knew and appreciated in Indian cooking and Arabian coffee, but of whose natural history I knew nothing, whether it grew in pods, on trees, underground or waving in the air. I had never suspected that it grew at the base of bamboo-like bushes, or that it would give so refreshing a scent to all the air around it.

But the cultivation of cardamom as a cash crop illustrates all too well the problems that countries like Guatemala face in their attempts to diversify their economies. In the early seventies, shrewd Guatemalans realized that the Arab countries, with their untold funds, had a vast appetite for the spice, of which there was then a shortage. For several years, at times of high prices, Guatemala enjoyed a near monopoly in the cardamom trade. Many fortunes were made. But other countries got in on the act; before long there was a glut and the price plummeted to below the cost of production. Producers kept going because there was nothing else they could do.

And we continued, too, until we reached a mountain meadow of great size and lushness, where horses and cattle grazed. At the far end of the meadow ran a river, of limpid water crushed into foam by rocks. On the banks of the river hosts of brilliant butterflies played in the sun, as if for joy of living. If ever there were an earthly paradise, I thought, this was it.

Across the river was slung a suspension bridge of wire and wooden slats. Many of the slats were broken or missing, the wire was worn and looked as though it might snap at any moment. When one stepped on to the bridge, it began to oscillate with considerable violence, like a dog shaking off water. To reach our destination, the village of La Estrella (the Star), we had to cross the river, but the animals clearly could not use the bridge and we sent them across what we mistakenly thought was a ford. But the water was deep and the current strong, and within a couple of minutes the terrified animals were struggling for their lives. One of them would neither go forward nor return, and when at last he tried to go up river, it was into deeper water still. His eyes stared wildly, as in a painting by Géricault, and we thought we had lost him, but, with what seemed his very last strength, he managed to drag himself ashore. I watched the drama from the bridge, to the centre of which I had gone to conquer my fear, and so absorbing was the drama that I did not notice until it was over that the bridge swung with almost every breath I took.

So we did not reach La Estrella, but it happened that we met a few men from there on their way to La Perla. We sat by the riverside and talked to them. Oh yes, they had known disaster: the army had attacked their village, burned their houses, killed scores of people.

They had gone to live in the mountains until it was safe to return.
They were no longer afraid of the army, but before . . . We heard
similar stories in other villages. One of them had once consisted of
more than 600 households but now there were only 97. It was true
that people were still coming down from the mountains, but it would
never return to its former size.

Whenever I heard these stories, what struck me was the great
dignity with which they were told. The people were neither self-
pitying, nor asking for pity. Neither were they thirsting for revenge,
at least to all outward appearances. Yet they were not apathetic
either: there was something about them more positive than that, as
though they were in possession of a philosophy that put them above
the world of dreadful appearances. Perhaps it was the old Mayan
idea that all that happens goes in cycles. At any rate, *something* must
have given them the strength, the desire, to go on living, the ability
still to laugh after having witnessed the scenes that their laconic
descriptions of events implied. Still they wanted children. And they
even took part in village football matches with enthusiasm. I
remembered my rage at life when a telephone number I had rung
was busy, and was ashamed.

Mike left La Perla a few days after we arrived, and his plane out
was the last we saw for two weeks. Every day thereafter the clouds
poured down the mountainsides, and sometimes they threw sheets
of rain at the *finca*. Supplies in the village grew scarce. The little
stores with the simple necessities of Guatemalan rural life in the
muddy main street either failed to open or opened but had little to
sell. With the guerrillas still active in the vicinity, the whole area was
dependent on the aircraft to bring meat, vegetables, oil and even
corn and beans. This, of course, meant that everything was very
expensive, and wages were low (the servants earned only two
quetzales a day, with corn at forty-five centavos a kilo). Moreover,
the *finca*'s produce – coffee and cardamom – also had to be
transported by air, the coffee to Nebaj, fifteen minutes away, the
cardamom to Coban because it was too valuable to be sent by road
from Nebaj. There were bandits along that road looking for
cardamom. Of course, this did little for the *finca*'s profitability. Yet
the worst days were over, the early eighties, when the settlement of
La Perla was surrounded by guerrillas on the mountain tops, and it
was too dangerous for anyone to venture out into the coffee
plantations. (Even now, the pickers often took escorts armed with
old mausers.) For two years running there had been no harvest; La

Perla was plunged into debt. At one time it looked as though it might have to be abandoned altogether, but then the tide turned in the war. A battle was waged to lift the siege, a battle the guerrillas lost and in which twelve of them died, including a woman from the nearest village. The guerrillas never recovered their stranglehold, but past indebtedness still ate up the *finca's* income. And for the people of La Perla, the need still to use the aircraft to travel to Nebaj was little short of a disaster. It cost thirteen *quetzales* to fly there and the same back, the equivalent of eight or ten days' labour, when before the war it took them two or three days to walk there and back. I heard very little gratitude expressed at La Perla for the attempts of the guerrillas to liberate it.

People came to the clinic. We tried to tidy it up, rearranging the drugs in rational order. While doing so, I came across an evangelical magazine called *Charisma*, which Doña Victoria had left behind. It contained an article about Jimmy Swaggart, the television evangelist, before his ignominious downfall. 'There is no telling,' concluded the author, 'what God can do with this ministry.' I also found a book with multiple choice questions for children about the Bible: Abraham did not sacrifice his son Isaac because a, b, c or d; tick the correct answer.

Every corner of the world has its pattern of disease. At La Perla, gastroenteritis, dysentery, intestinal worms and *mal de ojos* (conjunctivitis) were so common as to be practically normal. Every house in La Perla had its proper latrine, but when the rain fell the world dissolved into mud, making it impossible to keep clean, and there was little running water except for the streams. Of course there were other diseases too: asthma, epilepsy, pneumonia. There were plenty of minor complaints originating in the hard conditions of existence: headaches, general fatigue, fleeting pains that made work impossible that day. In England such complaints irritated me, but not at La Perla. The life there was one of such unremitting toil that no one could begrudge the people their aches and pains. One day as I was walking to the clinic a young Indian boy, no more than five years old, passed me with his back bent at a right angle by a sack of coffee he was carrying to be processed. As he passed me he raised his hand in respectful greeting; but such was the weight of his load, so delicately was it balanced on his back, and so slippery was the mud, that the slight gesture upset his equilibrium and he fell over in the mud. He tried to get up but like an exhausted pack animal could not. I had to lift him.

Childhood in La Perla, as in other parts of the Guatemalan highlands, is not the prolonged period of learning and lack of responsibility that it is in the industrialised world. From the very earliest age possible children fetch and carry. It is not uncommon to see tiny girls in *traje* carrying either babies or bundles of firewood on their backs, performing their duties with the gravity of adults at an age when the heaviest burden on such a child in Europe or North America would be to put away the toys at the end of the day. And not only do they carry heavy burdens, but they carry them up slopes of sixty degrees, not for a few yards but for miles.

There are certain statistics about Guatemala that have become true by repetition, and scenes such as the one above lend them plausibility. The most commonly quoted of these statistics is that seventy per cent of the land is owned by two per cent of the people; but this is a fact that requires a certain legerdemain to prove, since a third of the national territory is owned by the state, and much of the land in the highlands is excluded as uncultivable, though it is actually under cultivation. Nor is it often mentioned that the land whose ownership is undoubtedly most concentrated, in the south of the country, was largely uninhabited until after the Second World War, because it was so fever-ridden.

Another statistic that had acquired the status of almost un-questionable truth is that eighty-five per cent of Guatemalan children are malnourished. If it was true anywhere, it was true at La Perla. Many of the children were obviously malnourished, and all were infected with the repulsive giant roundworm, *ascaris lumbricoides*, that has often seemed to me a decisive argument against the goodness of God. Yet when I saw the children playing tag or football on the landing strip, I found the figure hard to believe. And if it was not true here, where could it be true?

Mothers came with their children and simply said '*lombrices*', worms. I asked the mothers if they knew where the worms came from and they looked at me with astonishment, as if I were mad. Did worms *come* from somewhere, then? Were they not generated spontaneously, something that all children developed as they grew?

'Do they come, for example,' I asked, 'from the sky?'

At this, they laughed. No, of course not. Perhaps there was a point to my question after all.

I gave an explanation, as brief and clear as I was able. But as I described how children could avoid reinfection once they (and their family) had been treated, I would hear the rain fall, remember the mud, and wonder whether I was achieving anything. Later, I was replaced by an enthusiastic young Guatemalan doctor, just starting on his career and idealistically anxious to bring health care to the rural poor. He arranged a programme with a health fund in Guatemala City to provide all the inhabitants of La Perla with vermifuges to be taken simultaneously in the hope that once banished, the worms would never return.

The *Hechos de Fé* mission had scores of sacks of milk powder, a Gift of the People of the United States, and hundreds of cartons of tinned soup. I decided to distribute them to the people of La Perla, though I was worried that they should have been kept for some dire emergency such as a famine. On the other hand, if they were not distributed soon they might not benefit anyone, for signs of deterioration were already present. I was also concerned that they should be distributed equally. How to inform the whole village? Luis told me not to worry: if I told a handful of people of the impending distribution, the rest of the village would soon get to hear of it. And so it transpired. Everyone came to claim their milk and minestrone. Some were so poor they possessed no bag in which to carry it away. By the end of the day, Luis and I had distributed two tons of milk powder, and my hair had turned grey with it. Like sand in the Sahara, it got everywhere. But though I felt I had achieved something – brief popularity, if nothing else – I had misgivings. Were not such charitable donations destructive of self-respect? Were they not a drug that produced a craving for more? The thought that the guerrillas would know of my actions and approve comforted me. How could they disapprove of a man who gave milk to the people?

I had another misgiving: that the milk would be reconstituted with dirty water and cause worse dysentery than was already endemic in La Perla.

I grew to know the soldiers, or at least the officers, who lived in the house above me. One of them was an *enfermero*, a nurse, who treated the poor of the village. His supply of drugs was more limited than mine, and his knowledge of the use of them but slight. Once he came to the clinic to ask me to call on the house of a young *ladina* who was having a fit. She was a member of a poor family that lived no differently, except for dress and language, from the Indians. When I arrived, several soldiers stood by her bedside, bewildered and frightened. She was suffering from a variety of spasms that clearly had no physical origin. She was so weak that she was able to do only those things that she wanted to do, not the domestic chores. I took the *teniente* aside.

'Has this girl any problems?' I asked.

It was a fatuous question. One had only to look around the house, or rather the hut. But the *teniente* knew what I meant.

'She is in love with one of the soldiers,' he said, 'but he doesn't come to visit her very often.'

My prescription was more love, less neglect. But just in case the love was not forthcoming, I left a couple of tranquillisers.

The evenings were long, the lights were dim and I had soon run out of reading material. The house had a bookcase with an eclectic collection: Hegel in Spanish; a biography of Lucrezia Borgia; a 1939 textbook of cattle husbandry in English, in which it was stated that the history of civilisation was really the history of the cow; a book called *Los derechos humanos* (Human Rights), by Carlos García Bauer, ex-Foreign Minister of Guatemala, Judge of the International Court of Justice, and Guatemalan representative at the United Nations, inscribed 'For Don Jose Luis Arenas with the esteem of the author, February 1961'; a whodunnit in English by Agatha Christie with the first fourteen pages missing; and several numbers of the technical journal of the Guatemalan Association of Coffee Growers, with scientific reports on how to increase yields. The subscription seemed to have lapsed at about the time the insurgency started. No doubt there were other matters than increasing yields on everyone's mind. On a chest of drawers I found an advertisement for a self-defence training course run by an Israeli instructor in Guatemala City. It taught the skills of entering your house at night when you suspected intruders, how to shoot from moving cars, how to defend yourself at traffic lights, etc.

I spent several evenings chatting to soldiers and officers on the verandah of the processing plant. The verandah had a trap door next to a weighing machine. After the coffee had been weighed and registered in the name of the picker, it was poured through the trap door into the sour-smelling vats below for separation by soaking. Whenever I looked at the trap door I could not help but think of Sweeney Todd and the *desaparecidos*.

The officers were keen to be listened to and vehement in their denial of atrocities, all of which they ascribed to guerrillas in army uniforms. They were proud that they had all but won the war at a time when the United States denied them help, proud too that their uniforms and even their boots were now made in Guatemala, as a response to President Carter's embargo. They were a poor army, they said, without advanced technology, but disciplined and tough. They hoped they would never have to clash with the British army over the question of Belize (as usual, the British had been perfidious, and their opponents less than rational).

The officers were fully aware of the accusations levelled against them. They thought that Amnesty International and Americas Watch were part of a world communist conspiracy against Guatemala, which played the part of first domino in the series *Guatemala, Mexico, United States*. As for the accusation that army officers wished only to enrich themselves, they thought it absurd: who would patrol the mountains of Ixcán for five days at a time, sometimes without food, always cold and wet, with the likelihood of being ambushed, just as a means of enriching himself? It was patriotism and the desire for freedom that drove them on. To prove it, they showed me their wounds: most of them had bullet scars somewhere about them.

They spoke with absolute conviction, but it wasn't proof of what they said. Colonels and generals quickly make fortunes in Guatemala, and the young officers still had time for promotion. When I looked into their faces, I thought it would be decidedly unpleasant to get on the wrong side of them. What I should call an atrocity, they would call a military precaution. But I noticed that their relations with the people of La Perla were relaxed, that the people showed no fear of them (Jean-Marie Simon has a picture in her book of soldiers 'occupying' La Perla). The age of atrocities was past, at least for the time being.

One of the officers consulted me about his knee. He had twisted it in the jungle some months before and it had never been right since. I thought he had a cartilage injury and needed an operation. The prospect of an operation, however, frightened him more than the EGP, even though I warned him that his knee might let him down in a moment of danger. He was frightened by the prospect of an anaesthetic.

I visited their barracks, in what used to be Don Luis's house. The *teniente* had mentioned that he possessed documents captured when his men recently overran an EGP camp, and I was anxious to see them. He brought them for me to read, a thick bundle of closely hand-written pages of exercise books. They were the political catechisms of EGP soldiers: they had been corrected in red ink by an instructor. Much of the orthography was incorrect, and that of the instructor was not much better. When I pointed this out to the *teniente*, he said, with no trace of disdain or condescension, that the writers were *gente humilde*, humble folk. The *teniente* was a soldier of seven or eight years' standing, he had passed through the *Escuela Politécnica*, he had fought with the army in the worst years of the counterinsurgency when, on its own admission, over 400 villages had been destroyed; he must have been at least a witness to horrors, if not the author of some of his own; yet he had spoken with understanding, almost with tenderness. This was something I could not understand.

The catechisms were simple slogans and political statements untouched by qualification. I was convinced of their authenticity: the paper was blotchy and soiled just as one might have expected. No one would have thought it worthwhile to produce hundreds of pages of such stuff for the benefit of the few casual visitors to La Perla. The slogans were dreary in the extreme. They were couched in the language of twentieth century revolutions. Reading them, one had visions of North Korea or Albania.

1. Firm in combat, secure in victory.
2. Because the colour of blood is never forgotten the massacred will be revenged.
3. Revolution or death – we shall be triumphant.
4. With discipline and decisiveness, we shall make the revolution.
5. United, organised and combative, our people will never be defeated.
6. Against reactionary manoeuvres our revolutionary unity!

There followed simple definitions of concepts such as exploitation, discrimination and oppression, definitions that seemed to bear the mark of bitter experience:

Exploitation is robbery of our labour by the rich, on plantations and in factories, where all workers and peasants [*obreros y campesinos*, spelt *hobreros y campecinos*] work.
The way in which they rob us is by not paying us our full wages.

Discrimination is not respecting the language, culture, dress, customs of the indigenous people . . . when the indigenous people present themselves before the authorities, in health centres, public transport [and furthermore, added the instructor in red ink, to discriminate is to make less of a person].

Oppression is when the rich put their ideas into our thoughts through the radio and school. The rich do not want the ideas of the poor to develop: an example of this is to dress like them in both the countryside and the city . . .

A little while later I was sitting in the processing plant when I noticed a bedraggled group of Indians go by, about thirty in all. They were people who had just come down from the mountains, to which they had fled some six years earlier. Their villages had been burnt, but they did not say by whom: an army lieutenant was hovering in the background as we spoke in their temporary shelter where they were to sleep and where the army fed them. They were in sorry condition. The tatters of their colourful costumes were darkened with dirt, their legs were thin, the children had the prominent bellies of hunger, their hair was matted, and many of their scalps had large bald patches where fungus grew. They all had lice.

Only two of the men appeared to speak Spanish, and they described the life they had led in the *montaña*. It occurred to me that what they said might have been the result of army coaching, but they had been in the control of the army for only a day and a half if their story was to be believed (and I am uncertain that it was). Some things they said had the ring of truth; others of propaganda.

The guerrillas had promised them land, cars, everything the rich possessed, when first they came under their protection. They were told that final victory was at hand, but after six years it was no longer possible to believe it. True, the guerrillas gave them land to cultivate, but they requisitioned all the produce, returning practically nothing so that the peasants had largely to subsist on grass and leaves. Salt cost one *quetzal* an ounce in the *montaña*, brought in by suppliers to the *Comités Popular de Resistencia*, the EGP organisation responsible for provisioning. (At La Perla, to which salt was brought by aircraft and was therefore considered expensive, it cost thirty-five centavos a pound – one fiftieth the price.) It was dangerous to talk in EGP territory: the *Fuerza Irregular Local* ensured the peasants did not leave and shot anyone who so much as expressed a wish to do so. At the same time it was impressed upon them that if they ever succeeded in returning to government-held territory they would be killed at once by the army. Since they had no contact with the outside world, and their memories of it were not exactly happy ones, they believed what they were told. Yet they decided to risk death rather than continue living under the control of the guerrillas, who muzzled their dogs lest they barked, broke the beaks of their cockerels lest they crowed, and demanded that they take their babies into the bush to stifle their cries. Fires were not allowed after dark lest the army saw them. It was a life of a thousand fears.

One day they took advantage of the EGP's emergency plan to scatter on the approach of an army patrol. They scattered as planned, but when the alarm was over, they regrouped instead of returning and walked together for four days, reaching the village of Chel, where the army found them. They told me that when they first fled to the mountains and arrived in EGP territory there were schools, but conditions had deteriorated and now there were none. One of my informants had worked as a security guard of the *Dirección Regional*, a middle layer of the EGP leadership. The leaders led hermetic lives, were unknown to their inferiors but controlled by their superiors, whom they in turn did not know. They lived well, at least by the standards of the *montaña*, with privileges and small luxuries. If half of what my informants told me were true, it did not augur well for the utopia the EGP was building. On the contrary, it was another Cambodia in the making.

What I heard from these two men was in part confirmed by a woman I met in the town of Nebaj, who lived in a poor and makeshift district called Las Violetas. She was under no compulsion to speak kindly of the authorities or subscribe to their views: she had seen with her own eyes soldiers drown three peasants by tying stones to their legs and tossing them alive into the river. She and her family had fled from the violence of the army into EGP territory, but had discovered that the EGP was no better. Though she spoke in Ixil (her son who went with her into the mountains translated), one word of Spanish recurred as she described the EGP: *mentiroso*, lying. Instead of the promised prosperity, she and her family had lived off grass and leaves. In the *montaña* they had lived in terror. She said the EGP killed new-born babies, especially girls, because they hindered the war effort. After two years she and her husband fled and had since encountered no difficulties with the army, who had left them in peace. She told me this in her shack, a construction of stick and thatch, in which she was cooking a dish of *boxból*, leaves stuffed with maize flour and served with chilli relish, over an open fire the smoke from which blackened everything. Our conversation was watched by a small child and a baby, both with the perpetual runny noses of poverty. The mother was affectionate towards them, and they smiled at her. She told her story without rancour, and now her family seemed ordinary and happy, an eloquent testimony to the resilience of the Ixil people.

I also spent evenings at La Perla with a man who was witness to the murder of Don Luis Arenas. He was the *finca*'s book-keeper and at the time was sitting at the table from which Don Luis was distributing the wages. His account of what happened differed somewhat from the account given in *Days of the Jungle*. For example, the workers did not stay around after the shooting to listen to political speeches, they fled. And the guerrillas *did* take the money which Mario Payeras says they left alone. Furthermore, the man who told me this walked with a very pronounced limp, and had to use a stick. What he did not tell me was that his limp was the result of the shots fired into his back and leg when he tried to protect Don Luis. This incident finds no mention in *Days of the Jungle*.

I left La Perla after three weeks dissatisfied with my performance as a doctor. The health of the village had not been notably improved by my ministrations and my one success, as I thought it, turned out soon afterwards to be a tragedy. The mother of a man in his late thirties came to me not long after my arrival to ask for my help. Her son was very weak, she said, too ill to come himself to the clinic. Though not old by the standards of Europe or North America, the mother was bent and arthritic after a lifetime of carrying heavy loads, bearing children and sleeping in the damp. She led me to her son who was lying on his bed in his hut which was on the far side of two steep and muddy gulleys. He was so weak he could barely raise himself. For more than a month he had suffered from diarrhoea twelve times a day and in that time had eaten almost nothing. He was feverish and anaemic, his pulse was rapid and weak, his abdomen stretched by fluid. I thought it best to look after him in the clinic: he was illiterate, his mother was illiterate, his entire family was illiterate, so I could not leave written instructions about what medicines to take and how to take them. Besides, there was no one to look after him at home: even his mother was out all day, picking coffee. By a supreme effort of will, therefore, he stood and walked to the clinic, taking a very few steps at a time before stopping to recover his breath. I reached the clinic in five minutes; it took him more than an hour.

Slowly, he seemed to improve. His diarrhoea ceased, his appetite returned. One morning I found him sitting on a bench outside the clinic, warming himself in the early sun. He had never complained, and I rejoiced to see him well. His mother brought him meals and I told her (as I had told the mothers of malnourished children) that he must eat a varied diet with plenty of protein: beans, fish, meat, eggs. I might as well have told her to bring caviar. She had no money, and the price of beans in the shops had risen to ninety-five centavos a kilo, for the aircraft had still not brought supplies and there was a scarcity. It was a bad time to need protein, for the clouds closed in every day. I went with his mother to the shops, saying that I would buy him beans, but we found only one shop with any left, and they had been bored by worms. However, they were better than nothing.

One morning I was surprised to find another patient on a bed in the clinic. He looked a perfectly healthy young man, but there was an intravenous drip in his arm (put there by Luis, the *enfermero*), through which flowed liquid the colour of lager. It was saline solution mixed with vitamin B. At first, I was irritated at this obviously bogus medicine. After all, there was enough real sickness about for us not to waste time or equipment on neurosis. But I thought better of expressing my irritation, for in a world in which deadly sickness can strike at any time and very little in the way of help is available, a little hypochondria is understandable. The young man turned out to be the pastor of one of the protestant chapels in La Perla. As he lay on his bed receiving his infusion of vitamins, he read the gospels. He was a convert from Catholicism, having been converted by a preacher in Nebaj, where he had gone as a refugee from the war. He had been a pastor for five years, though he was still only twenty-six. He was largely self-educated, a man of obvious rectitude and intelligence, who had struggled against great odds, and I suddenly realised how callous it would have been to disabuse him of his faith in either religion or his vitamins. I let well alone.

The health of the man with what I thought was dysentery continued to improve. When I left La Perla, I thought I had saved his life. He was eating well, he was not feverish, he smiled and thanked me. He could now walk more easily and was not nearly so breathless. Two months later, I heard his symptoms had returned suddenly, and this time had not responded to treatment. He died. I heard also the villagers believed he had been fated all along to die by magic, and that medicine could not possibly have worked in such a case. It was foolish even to have tried to save him.

EIGHTEEN

After I returned from La Perla to the city I went to see Don Enrique. I wanted to talk to him at length about his father, about whom I felt I needed more information, but I had not told Don Enrique before I went to La Perla that I was a writer as well as a doctor, or that I was writing a book about Guatemala. I confessed, and far from thinking I had paid him an underhand trick, he talked to me for two hours. I asked him about the story of the fiesta in Ilom recounted in *Days of the Jungle*, and he said that he had read the book (though it was not easy to find in Guatemala). Not only was the story false, he said, but it was the exact opposite of the truth. The burial of Don Luis had had to be postponed because of all the people who came to pay their respects, from as far away as Chajul, two days on foot from La Perla. Would they have made that effort if Luis Arenas had been the monster depicted by Mario Payeras? I asked why he was called the *Tigre* of Ixcán. Don Enrique said it was not because he was fierce or cruel but because in the early days, at the end of the forties, he had gone to the Ixcán with a posse of workers and hacked down the forest with his own hands. (One story I heard was that he lured workers to the landing strip and announced that their wages would be a fraction of what he had promised. Those who did not like the new arrangement were free to leave, but on foot. My informant told me that many had died on their way through the jungle.) The *Tigre* had had many encounters with real *tigres*, the latter always coming off second best. Hence his nickname was not one of abuse but admiration for his determination and bravery.

Don Enrique said the people of La Perla detested the guerrillas, who had done nothing but make their lives more difficult. Once, he had gone to the *finca* to tell the people that they had two choices: they could abandon the *finca*, or sit it out. They chose to sit it out – without much pay, for at that time there was no harvest. They had joined together to build the road to Santa Delfina, braving the wrath of the guerrillas, and now they were joining together to build a road to Nebaj, an enterprise the guerrillas would almost certainly try to sabotage because it meant that La Perla and the whole district would then flourish as never before (and would give easier access to the army). Far from the people resenting the army, he said, he had to restrain them from going out into the *montaña* themselves to hunt the hated guerrillas.

Don Enrique was a thin, nervous man who chain-smoked. On the wall of his well-appointed office was a signed photograph of President Reagan and a framed letter from him. He spoke with intensity between inhalations of smoke, another man whose sincerity it was impossible to doubt. He showed me a photograph album of the workers of La Perla as they built the road to Santa Delfina, pointing to the stream in which had appeared the bodies of three people killed by the guerrillas.

He described the great changes he had recently instituted at La Perla. Deciding that the *finca* was not tenable unless the people who lived there had a direct interest in its success, he had sold them forty per cent of the shares. These they bought slowly, *quetzal* by *quetzal*. Don Enrique used the money raised for community projects, though legally speaking the money was his. He said the people of La Perla had understood the implications of share ownership at once: the harvest had doubled and trebled (admittedly from a low level) since the initiation of the scheme. Once the road to Nebaj was built and the bank debt repaid, there was the prospect of real prosperity. Some of Don Enrique's friends said that had he not been the son of his father, they would have called him a communist. Being called a communist in Guatemala is bad for one's health.

It wasn't difficult to imagine what real Marxists would have made of Don Enrique's scheme. They would have called it an elaborate swindle to deceive the workers. After all, Don Enrique retained a controlling interest; one man owned more shares than four hundred workers put together. Furthermore, since La Perla was not currently making a profit, it was probable that it was valueless on the open market. Therefore, Don Enrique had everything to gain by his share distribution. He had engaged on capital expenditure cunningly disguised as good works, simultaneously persuading the workers that their interests were now the same as his. If La Perla was ever profitable again, he would have lost nothing. The new 'false consciousness' of the workers more than compensated for the loss of shares.

For a Marxist, there is something comforting about this interpretation. Otherwise he might have to confront the fact that a scion of the oligarchy has actually done something for (or at least to) the benefit of the workers. And in any country other than Guatemala, with its phobia of communism, Don Enrique's scheme might have proved a model for social and agricultural advance. He had already distributed a dividend against future profits. And Don Enrique said something that convinced me he was an honest man.

'Of course, if the guerrillas had not killed my father, I should never have thought of selling the shares.'

With these words, it seemed to me, Don Enrique drew attention to the one achievement of the guerrilla insurrection: namely, that it had forced at least some Guatemalan landowners to consider their workers not as inanimate robots, but as people with lives and interests of their own. It was a lesson dearly and incompletely bought.

Don Enrique told me something which I found truly astonishing in its irony. Back in the sixties, his father had often given refuge in his house in Guatemala City to Turcios Lima, the disaffected army officer who was the founder and leader of the first guerrilla movement in Guatemala. It was not that Luis Arenas felt any sympathy for Turcios Lima's political opinions, but he recognised in him a man of principle and honour. And so, as the police and army searched for the would-be scourge of the landowners, he went into hiding – with a landowner.

Guatemala being so small a country, I asked everyone I met who might have known the *Tigre* for his or her opinion of him. In Nebaj is a *pensión* called *Las Tres Hermanas*, the Three Sisters. It is named for its owners, three ageing sisters who have lived all their lives in the town. When I talked to them – spinsters all – in this garrison town, I was irresistibly reminded of Chekhov. Did they sigh, I wondered, for Guatemala City as Chekhov's three sisters sighed for Moscow? I do not think so. It was my romantic preconception that they were trapped by a melancholy Chekhovian fate; actually, I discovered as I got to know them better that they were full of fun and loved recounting stories to those who would listen. I talked to them in their smoky kitchen where they produced nourishing meals for such trifling sums that I wondered whether they did it for money or love. They chuckled as they remembered the time the guerrillas had taken over the town (in those early days of the war the mastodon military trucks did not rumble like thunder through the cobbled streets, nor were there sandbagged look-out posts on the corners). A group of about fifty guerrillas – Indians led by a bearded *ladino* – burst into the courtyard of the *pensión*, waving guns and demanding that everyone, including tourists, gathered in the main square (with its typical whitewashed church but untypical garden gnome atop the municipal fountain) to listen to a political declaration. According to the three sisters, the patriarch of the landowning Brol family, then eighty years old, was shot by the guerrillas for refusing to go. As for the sisters, they had been more afraid to go than to stay, and fortunately no one noticed their absence. They weren't interested in politics. But they remembered the various battles that had raged in Nebaj, the guerrillas at one end of the town, the army at the other, with bullets whistling low over the *pensión*, while they got on with the real work of cooking. They laughed at the foolishness of men who imagined they were doing something important. I asked them whether they had known Luis Arenas.

They knew him well, of course. Often he used to walk to Nebaj from La Perla with the mule train that brought out the coffee and cardamom, and then he would stay at *Las Tres Hermanas* overnight. He was a good man, they said; he used always to eat with his men at the same table and sleep in the same room, with no extra comfort for himself. This made him popular with his men. The sisters knew of no stories of his cruelty.

In Guatemala City, four weeks later, I met a German journalist who had asked the three sisters the same questions as I. He said they had answered cautiously, stating that Don Luis had always been all right with them, but what he was like with others they could not say. From this the German journalist concluded that the *Tigre* had indeed been rapacious, but the sisters were afraid to say so directly. This was the conclusion he had wanted; just as the conclusion I had wanted was that Luis Arenas was neither saint nor monster, but a man with the usual contradictory traits of humanity. No doubt it was wrong to start with a conclusion and argue backwards to the evidence – another all too human trait. But if minds are rarely completely open, sometimes they are not hermetically sealed.

I met two more people who had known Don Luis, and neither flattered his reputation. The first was Jorge Skinner-Klee, a lawyer and politician, the deputy leader of a moderate conservative party. He was a man known throughout Guatemala for his intellect, an intellect of which he was said to be rather too conscious. I was warned that I should find him arrogant and inaccessible, and indeed at first he was wary of me. Writers on Guatemala generally come to do hatchet jobs on such as he, a member of the upper classes, educated in the United States, of European descent, a staunch

Catholic and nationalist while at the same time cosmopolitan, well-read, a bibliophile, and therefore guilty of crimes before history and journalism.

I met him in his chambers in Guatemala City. His inner sanctum was a haven of peace that protected him from the polluted city beyond his door, with its cacophony of impatient drivers, itinerant salesmen, idlers, beggars, drunks, bus queues, shoppers and bellowing diesel engines. Words spoken out loud in the sanctum were muffled by the heavy decor, the deep leather chairs and heavy drapes absorbing and burying confidences. Outside in the waiting room I had noticed old British prints of Belize, sovereignty over which was an old Guatemalan claim (maps in the country showed it as part of Guatemala). Insofar as Don Jorge was irrational about anything, I was told by someone who knew him, he was irrational about Belize.

A man with a high-domed brow accentuated by baldness, one could not have mistaken Don Jorge for anything other than a man of intellect. But intellectuals of his time and class in Guatemala were not contemplative individuals, with noses in books and minds abstracted in a platonic world: they were men of action who not only reflected on history, but lived it and made it. Before long, Don Jorge embarked on a stream of reminiscences whose spring was inexhaustible. Again I felt the insignificance of my own experience of life.

First, though, I asked him why Guatemalan historians wrote from so uniform a standpoint. This elicited just the kind of response I had been told to expect.

'There are no Guatemalan historians,' he said.

I mentioned Severo Martínez Pelaez, whose *La Patria del Criollo* I was rather proud of having read, considering its great length.

'That's not history,' said Don Jorge, 'that's a political pamphlet.'

It was true that the book was written more with the present in mind than the past, that it sought to establish political conclusions already firm in the author's mind. But still Don Jorge's was a harsh judgment. The book was a clear exposition, and certainly not without interest.

'Martínez Pelaez is a schoolteacher without training as an historian,' sniffed Don Jorge. It was only in Guatemala that he could pass for one. Don Jorge admitted, though, that in his later work, on peasant rebellions in the colonial era, Martínez Pelaez showed signs of improvement, and might make an historian yet. As for

Guatemalan literature of other genres, Don Jorge said there wasn't any. I began to understand how he might not be the darling of his country's intellectuals.

Don Jorge was a man of parts. Among other things, he was a director of one of the biggest banks in the country. He told me how bank loans were arranged in Guatemala. First the intending borrower put forward his business proposal, which was then carefully examined by the bank's team of economists and other experts, to assess its viability. They prepared a report which they sent to the board of directors, who discussed the loan at the next board meeting.

'In all my years as a director,' said Don Jorge, 'I have never known them read a single report.'

Instead, the board sat around discussing the relatives of the applicant.

'Isn't he the cousin of so-and-so?' one of the directors would ask.

'Yes,' another would answer.

'In that case, we're not giving the bastard a penny.'

At first, Don Jorge had been outraged at this way of conducting a bank's affairs. But later, after years of very healthy profits, he began to wonder whether it was so very bad after all. Perhaps in a country like Guatemala it was for the best: the corrupt old directors really did know better than the eager young technocrats.

I asked him whether he had known Luis Arenas, the *Tigre* of Ixcán.

'Yes,' he said contemptuously. Don Jorge was good at expressing contempt. He knew how to curl his lip faintly.

I told him what I had heard from Don Enrique, but he dismissed this as evidence, saying that Don Enrique had never really known his father who, by the way, had started out in life as a butcher in the town of Comalapa. I thought I detected in this remark the snobbery and antipathy of a man whose family has been monied for two or three generations towards the man who has made his money himself. Yes, Don Luis was a butcher who took himself off one day to the Ixcán to found himself an empire.

'He was always flying people up there to show them what he'd done,' said Don Jorge. 'One day he flew the President, Castillo Armas, up there to show him how much good he was doing. I went with them. Well, I thought it wasn't a good thing he was doing. He was stealing the land from the people at La Perla. In my opinion, La Perla shouldn't exist. It should be given back to the people from whom it was taken.'

So the version of Don Luis in *Days of the Jungle* was right after all? 'It was inevitable his life would end like that. It had to.'

I concealed my surprise. I had to remind myself I was not talking to some wild adolescent revolutionary, but to a conservative lawyer who lived in a country where conservatives were not of the wishy-washy Thatcherite kind.

It was not on that visit to La Perla that Don Jorge had first met the *Tigre*, however. He met him first in prison, back in 1949. Again I concealed my surprise. This besuited, cerebral lawyer in prison? But it seemed that everybody who was anybody had been there at some time or other. In 1949, of course, he was a young hothead – a conservative hothead – just out of uiversity. Arévalo was president of the first revolutionary government and things were going badly from the conservative point of view. Their candidate in the forthcoming elections, Colonel Arana, was assassinated. Conservatives said – and still say – that the radical candidate, Jacobo Arbenz, was the one responsible; they say that Arbenz watched through field glasses as Arana was ambushed and shot on the bridge called La Gloria.

In 1949 there was a serious uprising against Arévalo (one of many during his presidency). Don Jorge took part in it. He objected to a piece of legislation that he deemed unconstitutional. The rebels thought the end of the world was nigh. For two weeks Don Jorge was an outlaw, hiding and escaping from rooftop to rooftop. He seemed to enjoy the recollection of it: no doubt the question, 'What is the purpose of life?', answered itself.

Eventually, he was captured. In the cell next to his was another rebel, Luis Arenas. They could not communicate, but Don Jorge heard his neighbour undergoing torture. He heard scuffles and screams, and then Luis Arenas's head would be held under water. He would cough and splutter when his head was pulled out of the barrel in which it had been ducked. Sometimes the duckings lasted longer, and then there would be silence, followed by an instruction from a police interrogator:

'It's all right, he's breathing, he's alive, you can put him back under.'

Don Jorge didn't approve of Luis Arenas even then, but he didn't approve of torture either. And being imprisoned next to a man who is being tortured is a kind of torture in itself: naturally, you imagine you are next. But Don Jorge wasn't tortured.

His fortune revived with the revolt of Castillo Armas against

Arbenz. This counter-revolution is generally described as having been carried out by CIA-paid mercenaries, but several participants to whom I spoke denied there were mercenaries involved. They were Guatemalan patriots who thought they were doing the right thing for their country, and none was paid to do it. They were not all of the landowning class, either: there were poor peasants among them. The only non-Guatemalan elements in the revolution were the pilots of the P-51 fighter-bombers (known colloquially as *sulfatos* because of the aperient effect they exercised in the presidential palace) who were North Americans. Still a young man, Don Jorge found himself Foreign Minister in Castillo Armas's government. I asked him whether he could shed any light on the subsequent assassination of Castillo Armas.

My question had been at random, but it seemed to electrify Don Jorge.

'So you've heard, then?'

I guessed I had touched a nerve, and decided to reply evasively.

'Something,' I said.

'Where?' he asked.

'Oh, from people . . .'

'Yes, the rumour's started to go round again. It was that bastard Trujillo who started it.'

The Trujillo in question was the dictator of the Dominican Republic, himself assassinated four years later.

'Have you read his book?' asked Don Jorge.

'No,' I replied.

'Well, he wrote a book in which he accused *me* of killing Castillo Armas. Of course, he distributed it everywhere. That's how the rumour started.'

'Why did Trujillo write it?' I asked.

'When I was Foreign Minister I was part of a conspiracy to bring about his downfall. I thought his influence was unhealthy for the region. Of course, the conspiracy failed. Trujillo was not a forgiving man. After Castillo Armas was killed, he wrote a book to accuse me of the murder. Being the kind of man he was, vicious and crude, that wasn't enough for him. He had to accuse my mother of running a whorehouse as well.'

Once again the literary technique of magical realism seemed more realist than magical.

Trujillo's book was now a rarity, a collector's item. But Don Jorge had heard that a facsimile copy was beginning to circulate in the city, an unreassuring phenomenon. I asked him who was behind it. He said he didn't know, but he had enemies enough; the extreme right wing, perhaps, as a prelude to something worse. He had faced attacks before and was ready for them – not in any physical sense, since his only protection was an ancient and unarmed retainer who acted as watchman in his office – but psychologically. He was once nearly shot by a man in the street. As we stepped from his office into the now dark city, I imagined assassins lurking everywhere. In other climes, Don Jorge would have been a pillar of respectability, who derived his excitement from the completion of the crossword in record time.

Still I felt I had not penetrated to the truth of Luis Arenas, or found the key to the man who would prove the key to the country. I was pleased to meet a German-Guatemalan of the coffee *finca*-owning class who had also known Luis Arenas. My informant had returned to Germany to fight in the war and had spent two years afterwards as what he called 'a distinguished guest of the Soviet Union.' In view of his past, I expected to find a man of crude and stereotyped opinions. But it was my expectation that was crude and stereotyped. When he returned to Guatemala after the war, he threw himself with gusto into the revolution. He wanted there to be social justice such as there had never been before in Guatemala. A surveyor by profession, he worked for the land reform programme that resulted from the famous Law Number 900 of 1952. His work was to survey farms with a view to establishing which lands were liable to confiscation (with compensation) under the law. These lands were to be redistributed to peasants. He remembered arriving in a small town one night and slinging his hammock between the posts of the verandah of a poor man's house. Shortly after going to sleep in the hammock, he heard the clatter of a group of armed men coming towards him. 'Now,' he thought, 'I'm for it.' He took his gun out of its holster and prepared to go down fighting. But the group of armed men were peasants and they had come to protect him rather than attack him, as he was working for the land reform. They told him the local landowners were plotting to kill him but they, the peasants, would guard him with their lives. And so he went to sleep, protected by machetes and ancient rifles.

It was while he was doing this work that he met a young Argentine doctor called Ernesto Guevara who had come to Guatemala because he thought it was a beacon of revolutionary hope to the whole of Latin America. He was pretty fiery and opinionated even then,

given to extremes and long conversations into the night which meant
that he couldn't rise early the next morning. Routine was not for
him. He had recently been casually humiliated by the United States.
After qualifying as a doctor in Argentina, he went there in the hope
of finding postgraduate work; but when he reached the airport, the
immigration officers turned him away, probably with a display of
contumely to which he was more than sensitive.

'Imagine me, a doctor, being treated like that!' the future Che
protested to my informant.

Was this another Cleopatra's nose of history? If the US immigration had welcomed the young Dr Guevara into their country,
would he have ended his days as a dermatologist of radical views in a
dusty provincial Argentine town?

My German-Guatemalan informant had grown disillusioned with
the land reform, and came to the conclusion it was leading to
economic disaster. Whatever the books might now say about it, the
process was messy and often violent. There is an aspect of the
Arbenz government that is rarely mentioned: the increasing atmosphere of terror. I spoke to a man (by no means an oligarch) who
remembered in his childhood watching a truckload of political
opponents go by on their way to the cemetery in Antigua where they
were summarily executed. Several others spoke of massacres of
landowners, not all of them hugely wealthy; massacres that involved
not just a few hated individuals, but scores and even hundreds of
men, disposed of in unmarked mass graves. It was a time to keep
silent, too, for critical remarks could end in death. Many land
seizures took place outside the scope of the law, and these the
government either would not, or could not, control. There was
incipient anarchy that drove many men, not just landowners, to
rebellion. It also explained why hardly a finger was lifted by anyone
to save the Arbenz government.

My informant, however, was not a troglodyte conservative who
saw the hand of Moscow behind every centavo of tax. He was a man
who knew the Indians well, the injustices they suffered, and who
appreciated the dignity with which they suffered them. He was
eyewitness to a massacre at the height of the insurgency. He was
doing some survey work in the department of C— when in the
distance he saw a group of fifteen Indian women walking along with
firewood on their heads. There was a patrol of soldiers on the brow of
a nearby hill. They called to the women to halt. Instead of doing so,
they began to run away, obviously terrified. The soldiers opened fire

and within seconds all fifteen were dead. After this, he had to make himself scarce, for if the soldiers knew he had witnessed their great victory, they would have killed him as well.

But he was not a supporter of the guerrillas. He felt they were led – or misled – by intellectuals who cared more for the purity of doctrine than for actual human life. They had provoked a war in which the Indians were bound to be the victims, and which they did not understand.

'Dr Daniels, Dr Daniels, Dr Daniels,' he said, covering his face and suddenly overcome by emotion. 'They were not ready for it, they were not ready for it.'

Up till then he had spoken in English. Thereafter, he spoke in Spanish.

I asked his opinion of Luis Arenas.

The lowest possible, he said. He had been in the Ixcán when the *Tigre* was carving out a fiefdom for himself. He had thrown people off the land, using goon squads and armed ruffians. He was a man without feeling.

I had now heard a great deal about Luis Arenas, and this last evidence seemed decisive. Yet still I could not quite make up my mind about him. I had heard he was rapacious, unfeeling and cruel; but I had also heard he was a good *patrón*, a man to whom his workers could turn when they had a problem, a man who distributed gifts at Christmas to all the children of the *finca*, a man who shared his food with his men and would never ask them to do something he would not do himself, who had given refuge to a guerrilla leader because of his sense of honour. Had people mourned the death of Luis Arenas from fear, respect or love?

Perhaps the truth was that Luis Arenas was as other men, only more so. His character was not consistent; both his vices and his virtues were big ones, mythopoeic in size. As for his rapacity and land-grabbing, I thought I understood it better for having met his son. Don Enrique described a land dispute on which he was currently engaged with a squatter on the edge of La Perla. It was not the land, he said, which was of little value or extent; it was the principle. If the squatter who claimed to own the land could prove it in court, all well and good, he could keep it; if not, he must clear off, however poor he might be. For Don Enrique was determined to pass on La Perla intact, not only for the sake of his family but for that of the people of the *finca*. It was obvious that for him land was not just an economic asset, but something of spiritual importance, however distorted. No doubt his father felt about it the same way; and once he believed he had legal title to the land, no other consideration weighed in his mind. His ruthlessness was the consequence of radically different conceptions of land ownership by Guatemala's two cultures.

Nevertheless, I felt I had not satisfactorily resolved the contradictions of the man. And if I could not understand a single individual, how could I understand a whole country?

NINETEEN

In the south of Guatemala are the hot Pacific lowlands, great tracts of which are the source of wealth of Guatemala's richest families. They were settled extensively only in the last fifty years, when it became possible to combat their endemic fevers. Here cattle are raised for beef to export, sugar and cotton are grown, and more recently sorghum and soya which need less labour. On the lower slopes of the mountains, coffee is cultivated. I drove four hours from Antigua to the small town of Tiquisate to meet Father Andrés Girón, a priest who rose from obscurity to national – even international – fame in 1986 by leading a march of landless peasants to the capital where, in front of the national palace, they demanded land.

I went without an appointment and when I arrived in the afternoon Father Girón was taking a class of seminarians. Then he officiated at mass. Meanwhile I sat in the parish house, which was furnished simply but without any attempt at discomfort: no one could say that Father Girón had founded his movement of peasants so that he could live luxuriously. Tiquisate was hot and dusty but fortunately a breeze blew through the open louvred windows. The living room had a small bookcase with works of theology and philosophy in English, Spanish and French; they looked neglected, and I guessed that Father Girón considered purely intellectual pursuits a self-indulgence in Guatemalan circumstances. On the wall was his degree from a Catholic college in Louisiana and a framed testimonial from the people of his last parish in the Indian department of Huehuetanango:

FATHER ANDRÉS
Keep this little gift as a recognition of your great work among this your group, who will always remember you as one of the great instruments of Christ.

You may be absent, but your spirit and teachings will remain engraved on the hearts of all those you have loved.

On the floor, I saw a telegram, which I confess that I read. It was a message of support for, and solidarity with, Father Girón's organisation. It was signed 'Licenciado Marco Vinicio Cerezo Arévalo, President of the Republic.'

I passed the time reading a book about the American Catholic mystic, Thomas Merton. By the time Father Girón arrived, it was dark. He was dressed in a white cotton soutane, soiled by a long day in a hot and dusty climate. He was not wearing the other part of his 'uniform' which has become famous throughout Guatemala: a floppy-brimmed straw hat. He looked exhausted. As the priest of a parish with an eighth of a million parishioners, and as a public figure besides, neither his person nor his time were his own; he was perpetually at someone else's disposal. I had been warned he was not a man without ego; but as I explained who I was and why I had come, I felt that the egotism was mine. A book of travels is not so serious a thing as a peasant's land or soul.

He excused himself to take a quick wash, but only after he had let fall a few words.

'The people,' he said, 'want me for president.'

When he returned from his wash, I asked whether he would stand for election.

He thought for a moment.

'I have more power now,' he said, 'as leader of my movement.'

It was said that Father Girón was a close friend of the President's wife.

'But perhaps I'll stand,' he said after some reflection, as though making a concession.

I asked whether he would win, and he said he had no doubt of it. But would he then remain a priest? After all, the Pope was not happy about the involvement of priests in the government of Nicaragua. What if his bishop forbad him to stand? Father Girón had just visited his bishop, who was of a very different cast of mind. In fact, he obstructed Father Girón at every turn. If he forbad him to stand, Father Girón would disobey.

'The bishops,' he said, 'are the evil of the church. There are some good bishops, but not many. Of a thousand bishops, only one is good.'

Father Girón was busy, and we arranged to meet the following week in the other town of his parish, Nueva Concepción, about half an hour from Tiquisate.

I arrived the evening before our appointment and went to eat in a roadside restaurant. There I met a Salvadorean immigrant to

Guatemala and his girlfriend who, though young, was already running to surplus flesh, a fact she tried unsuccessfully to conceal by squeezing herself into the tightest of clothes. The Salvadorean began to boast how easy it was to make money in Guatemala if you worked hard and didn't throw your money away. The trouble with Guatemalans, he said, was that they were lazy, and none too bright into the bargain. When they had money, they spent it all. Salvadoreans, by comparison, were hard workers and shrewd businessmen. For example, his family had arrived in Guatemala with nothing; now they owned a truck, two bars and a brothel. Naturally, this had not made them popular in the town. His small sister, a girl of five, had recently been run over and killed by a truck which could easily have avoided her. This happened a few weeks ago on the street where we were sitting. He and his family were sure she was killed deliberately by another truck owner of the town, trying to rid himself of foreign competition.

Had they gone to the police, I asked.

He laughed. The police would be on the killer's side; as for the mayor, he would side with the police. It would be risking expulsion to complain. For the moment, the family would have to accept their little girl's death. But Nueva Concepción was not a town where people forgot or forgave – to do so was regarded as cowardice, not Christianity – and deaths by stabbing were far from unknown. The family would await its moment. He had drunk a few beers, and I was unsure how far to believe him. But I decided to avoid contentious discussions while I was in Nueva Concepción.

Next morning, I met Father Girón a second time. He had a house in the town, which was as simple as the one in Tiquisate and as lacking in privacy. A woman had come to him with a problem about some land, and while there she thought she might as well ask his advice about the education of her son . . . Father Girón was legal, spiritual and career adviser rolled into one. It takes either saintliness or a large ego (or perhaps both) to play all these roles for all-comers at any time of the day or night.

No sooner had he finished dealing – with admirable forbearance – with this lady's problems than he received a message that his presence was urgently required in Guatemala City. My plan had been to spend the day with him as he toured the agricultural cooperative he had founded for landless peasants. His cooperative was intended as a model of land reform for the whole of the country.

But I had to abandon this plan. If I wished to speak to him at all, it would have to be as he drove to the capital. This would give me three hours to talk to him.

We set out in his beloved old Citroën after he had changed from his sleeveless shirt and track-suit trousers into his white soutane. I sat next to him, while in the back was a police bodyguard, pointing his automatic up and out of the rear window. Father Girón had been threatened with death many times (landowners thought he was a communist), and he had once caught a glimpse of a gunman aiming at him. I asked him whether he felt less or more secure with a policeman to guard him. After all, the reputation of the Guatemalan police was not exactly that of guardians of free speech . . . This policeman, he said, was all right. He was a member of Father Girón's movement.

My truck followed behind, driven by one of Father Girón's assistants and also protected by a policeman with an automatic. Coming from England, I found it difficult to conceive of these precautions as other than melodramatic. Yet most people thought that Father Girón's life expectancy was not very long. And not many months after I left Guatemala, Father Girón was ambushed and his bodyguard killed.

We spoke in English, which the policeman did not understand. Father Girón went straight to the heart of the matter.

'One per cent own eighty per cent. Either there is reform, or there will be bloody revolution.'

Before coming to Nueva Concepción, I had looked up the figures on agricultural holdings. It required no elaborate mathematics to work out that, if the rural population continued to grow at its present rate, and if there were an absolutely equal land distribution, it would be no more than twenty or thirty years before the average holding was eight acres – theoretically, more than enough to feed a family, it is true, but quite likely in practice to lead to terrible erosion, crop failures, etc. In the meantime, the commercial sector would have been destroyed and the country would have nothing to export.

I put this to Father Girón, and of course he knew it already. He said he did not want to divide up the land into parcels: that would be a disaster. If he were president, he would distribute expropriated land to people in need, on condition they farmed it collectively or cooperatively. He would not expropriate all *fincas*, but said it was unnecessary for a man to own seventeen or eighteen of them or, as in one case, fifty-seven – a point of view with which I found it hard to disagree. Father Girón knew also that collective farming had not exactly met with universal success around the globe. But in Guatemala, he wanted farms to diversify and to process more of their produce. He said he was a democratic solialist.

I asked him which country he would like to emulate. He laughed, and said it was a good question: there were no models at the moment.

He had had some experience of 'actually existing socialism,' as cant phrase has it. He had visited Poland and Czechoslovakia and found them sad; all life, all joy had been extinguished by the crushing greyness, he said. As for the model closer to home, Nicaragua, he admitted that he did not find it encouraging. When Sergio Ramírez, the novelist and vice-president, told him how prices were controlled and decided from above, he was shocked. Father Girón agreed that the system of rationing there was a prelude to corruption, not only financial but of the human personality as well. He had been offered an honorary degree in Nicaragua, but had turned it down because to have accepted it would have been to harm his movement.

Father Girón was not the wild revolutionary some had led me to expect. He was a romantic populist, and in some respects deeply conservative. His lengthy stay in the United States had taught him that material prosperity was less important than beauty and friendship, and that the North Americans had lost their way. They led lonely, separated, atomistic lives, and possessed no spiritual values. Life in North America was easy but empty. He contrasted it with life in his Indian parish in the highlands, where people derived enjoyment and meaning even in the midst of hardship, where the unpolluted springs and rivers made up for the lack of everything else. The Indians in their earthly paradise were closer to God . . .

These ideas were not new, of course, and I thought of the famous lines written in 1905 by Ruben Darío, the Nicaraguan poet, in honour of Theodore Roosevelt and his country:

> You are a superb and proud example of your race;
> you are cultured and clever; you are opposed to Tolstoy.
> And taming horses, or murdering tigers,
> you are an Alexander-Nebuchadnezzar.
> (You are a professor of energy,
> as today's madmen put it.)

You believe that life is fire,
that progress is eruption;
that where your bullet goes
there is the future.

No.

The United States are powerful and great.
When they shake, a profound tremble
runs down the vast spine of the Andes.
If you cry out, you are heard like the roar of a lion . . .
. . . You are rich.
You unite the cult of Hercules with the cult of Mammon;
and lighting the road to easy conquest,
Liberty raises her torch in New York . . .

And, having everything, you lack just one thing: God!

Talking of God, I asked him what he thought of Ríos Montt, the preacher-general-president. I expected a stern indictment.

'He was an honest man,' he said. 'He was trying to do his best for the country.'

Father Girón said there had been massacres in the countryside under Ríos Montt, but not as many as before. He was overthrown because his religious harangues were becoming more embarrassing, but also because he was preparing a genuine land reform. Then Father Girón said something that shocked every Guatemalan to whom I related it.

'If Ríos Montt stood for president and asked me to be his vice-president, I would accept.'

Then he asked me – with a great deal of interest – whether General Ríos Montt had mentioned him when he spoke to me, and if so, what the general had thought of him. When I told him that his name had not been mentioned during our discussion, he was obviously disappointed. He asked me another question.

'What do you think would happen if I was president?'

I said he would be dead within two years, and he laughed. Father Girón was no saint and I liked him. After all, total self-abnegation is not an attractive quality close-up.

While the subject of self-abnegation was in my mind, I asked him about the guerrillas.

'They are beautiful people,' he said.

'Even the EGP?' I asked, mentioning one or two things I had heard about them.

Well, perhaps not. They killed innocent people, though not nearly as many as the army. In general, Father Girón was on good, if slightly competitive, terms with the guerrillas. 'If you win, we lose,' a female *comandante* had told him. 'If you lose, we win.'

The guerrillas were patient. Time was on their side. Father Girón said Guatemala was not prepared yet for democracy. It needed strong government. Vinicio Cerezo, the president, was a nice man but not a strong one, and he was a very good liar. Time out of number he had promised help to Father Girón's movement, but he had never kept his promises. Recently, though, he had done Father Girón a good turn. A North American well-wisher, a senator, had presented Father Girón with a new car, which the priest's brother drove down to Guatemala. There the car aroused the envy of a colonel, who coveted it. Why should a parish priest, and a communist one at that, drive around in a swank American car? So the colonel arranged for the import duty to be fixed at 49,000 *quetzales*, a sum he knew it was impossible for Father Girón to pay. The plan was then for the car to be sold to the colonel at a knockdown price, a plan which Father Girón exposed on television. Shortly after, the President telephoned him to say he was arranging for the car to be allowed into Guatemala free of duty, but though this was some weeks ago, he still had received neither papers nor car, which languished in the customs warehouse.

The moral of this story, from Father Girón's point of view, was the weakness of the president. His word was very far from law. I thought it illustrated how far Guatemala was from being a country of laws and not of men.

I left Father Girón and his bodyguard in a suburb of the city. The leader of the movement for land reform was preparing to do battle with the Ministry of Education, trying to provoke it into sending a teacher to the school on the cooperative farm in Nueva Concepción, which so far it had refused to do. The battle had lasted months, but was entering its decisive phase.

After my talk with Father Girón, I paid a visit to a landowner in the south, not a feudal baron, but the owner of a comparatively modest coffee *finca* called El Manzano near the town of Coatepeque. The southern plantations of Guatemala are the lynch-pin of an economic system, giving seasonal employment to highland Indians who have to supplement their meagre subsistence from their tiny mountain cornfields with wages, however small. Don Federico's *finca* was a few miles off the main road, down an almost impassably rough track through groves of coffee trees. Along the way, I picked up an architectural student who was returning from college to see his family, who were labourers on one of the neighbouring estates. He told me that the landowners varied greatly; some paid the minimum legal wage or even more, but others much less. The guerrillas of the ORPA operated in this part of the country, attacking the *fincas* of the landowners who paid the lowest wages. However, it was usually not the landowners who suffered directly, for they lived in the city, but their managers.

I dropped him at his home, a very simple wooden shack in a terrace of such shacks. I thought it a remarkable sign of change and – dare I say it? – of progress that a young man from so poor a background should be engaged in higher education. Of course, the permanent workers on a *finca*, who lived there all year round, were not the poorest of the poor; that distinction remained to the Indians who migrated annually from the highlands. These migrant workers were often herded into the most squalid of barracks, denied all privacy and hygiene, and were prey to malaria and dysentery with little hope of treatment. The education of their children was interrupted by the annual migration. Not only exploited economically, they were subject to racial and cultural disdain. The permanent workers, then, were well-off by comparison. Yet still I doubt whether, twenty years ago, I should have encountered students among their children.

I arrived at the *casa grande* – big house – of the *finca*. It was not in any way architecturally distinguished but it was, more importantly, the kind of house that inspires affection. Built on a single floor, painted white, it was anarchically irregular in shape, and most of its walls were covered by creepers with orange and red flowers. There was a large, cool verandah with cane chairs and innumerable flowerpots; surrounding the house were a small lawn and some flower-beds, ablaze with extravagant tropical blooms. All around was the dark green of coffee bushes, shaded from direct sunlight by macadamia trees. If a man could achieve peace, I thought, it was here.

The owner and his wife, though not expecting me, bade me welcome and showed me into the sitting-room. In a strange way, everything seemed familiar. Suddenly I realized why: Turgenev and Chekhov again. Here, far from 'civilisation', was a grand piano; the chairs were strewn with the scores of Schubert and Beethoven. The bookshelves were filled with French and Russian literature, there were newspapers from the capital (a few weeks old) and the United States. On a small table were agricultural journals for farmers who wished to learn to farm scientifically. Señora Perez had attended the French *lycée* and dressed well, though not fashionably. Her husband had just come in from the fields: his face was brown and weatherbeaten, and his eyes shone with a lively intelligence. He would have disclaimed any pretence to culture, yet he read the best literature and listened to classical music. His wife also read romantic novels. They led a gentry life at the time of its decay.

I had often thought of parallels between nineteenth-century Russia and the Latin America of the twentieth century. They both had an agrarian upper class of very different culture (and even language) from that of the numerically predominant peasantry, an upper class that created islands of western European or North American civilisation in an ocean of peasant backwardness. Both Russia and Latin America had neighbours (western Europe in the case of Russia, the United States in the case of Latin America) to whom they felt both inferior and superior: inferior materially and technologically, but superior culturally and spiritually. There were parallels too in intellectual development. At first the gentry were the bearers of ideas and they alone attended universities. But as access to higher education spread, and educated young men with no economic prospects became more common, intellectual life grew ever more violent, with no sense remaining of the inherent limitations and difficulties of human existence. Just as the intellectuals of Russia had extolled the collectivist traditions of the Russian peasants to justify their revolutionary plans, so the intellectuals of Latin America now extol the collectivist traditions of the Aztec, Mayan and Incan empires to justify *their* revolutionary schemes . . .

Life at Finca el Manzano had an elegaic quality. Don Federico loved his land and the quiet rhythm of his days, but none of his children wanted to continue the tradition: they all had city careers to pursue. And so, when he died, Finca el Manzano would die too, and with it his life's work.

Of course, Don Federico couldn't really blame his children for their decision. In the old days, before the insurrection, the local landowners used to get together for parties and bridge evenings, but now all social life was extinguished, and there was nothing to amuse a young person at el Manzano. All the other local landowners had either been killed or had fled to the city. Only Don Federico among them had never been threatened by the guerrillas, and now he was the last one still to live on his *finca*. His nearest neighbour had been his wife's sister and her husband, but they were murdered two years before.

Was there, I asked, any reason why they should have been killed?

Who knows? came the answer, leaving open the possibility that they had done something to incur the wrath of the guerrillas.

Don Federico showed me round his estate. He took me to his little reservoir and its water mill that provided the *finca* with its power, and the nursery where he raised young coffee bushes, though not with the care he would have wished, for he had neither the land nor the labour to do so. He gathered a bag of macadamia nuts for me. In the distance, across a valley, he pointed to a large white house of some magnificence. It belonged, he said, to one of the richest families in Guatemala, Jewish immigrants from Germany. The family was seldom there, but when they were the house became like a fortress, guarded at every point. The family was good to its employees, providing schools, clinics and even scholarships to university. The *finca* was but a small part of the family's business empire, whereas Finca el Manzano was everything Don Federico owned. He said this without bitterness or envy; it was just a fact, like the fine weather.

I took a last drink with them on the verandah. They were people who had been born too late, after their time. Don Federico was the member of a class that had had its day, that belonged – as the Marxists so charmingly put it – in the dustbin of history. I hoped they would be allowed to live out their days at el Manzano, which they loved. For our century punishes no crime with such severity as that of having been born in the wrong place at the wrong time.

TWENTY

I decided to visit the jungles of Petén, one third of Guatemala's territory, and on my way there, just outside the town of Coban, I saved a man's life. I was driving at night along the metalled road that led into the town when a drunk, lying in the road, appeared in the beam of my headlights. With great difficulty, I avoided him. It was pitch dark and I stopped to haul him out of the road. I walked up to him and told him he had chosen a dangerous place to sleep. He tried to get up but was incapable. I dragged him to the grass verge of the road. '*Amigo, amigo*,' he muttered incoherently as I struggled with his dead weight. How right he was! Seconds later, a forty-ton truck hurtled by at sixty miles an hour. The driver would hardly have seen him, let alone stopped for him.

From Coban I drove with Carmen, a Swiss tourist whom I met, into the Petén jungle. We took the road to Sayaxché; the map we had with us gave us no warning of the road's hazards. Indeed, beyond a certain point, the map proved entirely fictional, plotting the course of roads that did not exist and omitting junctions that undoubtedly existed.

At first, as the road descended to the forested plain below, it was built of sharp flinty pebbles and rocks, to which my unfortunate truck was barely equal. Although we averaged only ten miles an hour, our descent was a massacre of the butterflies, which immolated themselves on my radiator grille like Iranian children going to war. Having reached the plain after several hours, we stopped in a village in a large clearing. It was, as Hemingway might have put it in one of his more descriptive passages, hot; people walked as though tethered by invisible bands of despair and the dogs used up their little energy in panting. We went to a café where even the Coca-Cola was served hot, and asked for coffee, black, no sugar. The first cup made honey seem bitter. It was as though they had not believed we meant what we said. We asked again: coffee, black, no sugar. This time it came just as people who take coffee, black, three sugars, like it. I guessed that they had thrown away the first cup but – to save energy – they had not cleared away the sugary sludge at the bottom before they poured in more coffee. As a Swiss, Carmen was temperamentally unsuited to understanding the problem, and we therefore persisted: coffee, black, no sugar. Third time lucky: there was no sugar in the coffee. The only problem was that there was no coffee in the coffee, either. In my experience, the poorer a country or a community, the harder it is to obtain unsweetened drinks.

We asked the proprietor of the café, who belonged in the hammock from which he watched our little drama as much as any hermit crab belongs in its shell, whether we could reach Sayaxché by nightfall, and he said we could – just.

Looking at our map, which at that stage we still trusted, there was but one road going north and if we followed it we would reach our destination. Our confidence in the accuracy of our map declined after the first two or three unmarked T-junctions, all of which demanded decisions. To go north, should we turn east or west? As the sun went down, we could disguise it from ourselves no longer: we were hopelessly lost. Though the landscape was deserted, Man had had a great impact upon it, destroying forest on both sides of the track, leaving only occasional dead trunks upright, to carve out cattle ranches that needed no trees. We reached a miserable collection of wooden huts on both sides of the road that called itself a village. The entire population was outside, taking the local equivalent of the evening promenade. We stopped to ask the way of them. For the first time in Guatemala, I encountered frank hostility. There was a strange and very striking atmosphere of evil about the place, and I felt that if we stayed there the night we might not survive to see the morning. The people were sullen and half-starved; I thought we might accidentally have wandered into a penal colony, or a settlement where people had been brought by force. As informants, they were quite useless. The first man reluctantly gave us directions, which I took the precaution of checking with someone else. His directions were exactly opposite. The more we asked, the more I became convinced that it was not just ignorance at work, but malevolence, directed at outsiders for whom the Petén was but a place of recreation.

Eventually we chose a direction at random and drove off. We encountered another hostile village further on. But we also found a bicyclist who was friendly and who seemed to know what he was talking about. We had confidence in his directions.

It was now completely dark. The road was treacherous. A hundred yards of comparatively firm, dry surface would suddenly give way to a muddy swamp, churned into deep ridges. The first couple of times we got stuck, Carmen took over the wheel and I pushed, the second time with the help of a passing peasant who was hopeful of a lift. We laid twigs and grass in the path of the wheels to give them some purchase. It took an hour to shift the vehicle, and we emerged stiff with mud but triumphant. At each subsequent sea of mud the peasant would jump out of the back and guide me through it, estimating where it was shallowest. A few miles further on was a large truck that was definitively stuck, tilting at a crazy angle, surrounded by men who, ant-like, were trying without hope to shift it. As we squeezed past, I opened the window to offer our help, only for our small truck to slide, glissando-like, into the mud of a deep ditch. Two hours of effort proved to us that it was futile, we were stuck until a more powerful vehicle could extricate us. The men from the big truck told us that this was guerrilla country. The guerrillas were those of the *Fuerzas Armadas Rebeldes*, so there was nothing to fear from them except boredom. They gave you a political lecture for an hour or two – it hadn't changed in fifteen years – and then they let you go. You weren't allowed to interrupt or ask questions, and it was terribly tedious, especially when you had heard it several times before. It was reassuring to know, however, that the guerrillas harmed no one, and I went to sleep in the back of my truck, thinking how odd it was that it should be so cold at night in the jungle.

Fortunately, at midnight another truck arrived and all the people travelling in it, eight in all, came to our rescue. Everyone laughed – mud is fun, once you lose your inhibitions about getting dirty. We drove off after our release in a convoy of two vehicles. Within a mile, feeling foolish, Carmen and I were stuck again and had to be towed once more from the mire. How, I wondered, could I repay their tolerant, amused kindness? I soon found out. Their truck stuck fast in the mud and our roles were reversed. Alas, my little truck could not pull theirs: as it strained at the rope, its engine screaming, we seemed to go backwards rather than forwards. The truck's owner decided to leave one of his men at the truck while the rest of us, nine in number, drove on to Sayaxché in my truck. I didn't think we would make it, especially as there was now a thick mist swirling at road level, but make it we did, at two in the morning.

The owner of the truck knew of an hotel. The rooms were little bigger than the beds they contained, boxes without windows, separated from one another by the thinnest of partitions. Still, by then we were pleased enough of anywhere to sleep; unfortunately, the local cockerels were particularly assiduous in anticipating the dawn by several hours and seemed to reproach us for being slugabeds. When morning truly came, I was still very tired.

There were Mayan ruins near to Sayaxché, but the owner of the truck wanted to go on to the next town to find help for his marooned vehicle (there was none to be had at Sayaxché). So we missed the ruins, but I consoled myself, as we crossed the great brown greasy river at Sayaxché on a flat-bottomed, eminently sinkable ferry, that there were more and better ruins at Tikal where we were headed. To a non-expert like myself, I continued, one set of Mayan ruins was very like another.

We reached Flores, the capital of the Petén, without further difficulty. It is a town built on an island in a lake called Petén Itza, connected to the mainland by a dusty causeway. Painted pastel shades, it is a hot, ordinary town despite its exotic location. It was not named for botanical abundance (*flores* meaning flowers in Spanish) but after a nineteenth-century military governor. Many young gringos gather there, bringing with them a whiff of Kathmandu in the sixties. One of the cafés they frequent had two live ocelot kittens, and I wasn't sure whether I should suppress my natural inclination to be charmed by them and give vent to simulated outrage that embattled Nature should be so trivialised. Better, I suppose, ocelots in cafés than in coats.

There are two hotels near the ruins at Tikal, and we stayed in the lesser of them. It was owned by an Englishwoman from the south coast who married an employee of the Guatemalan state airline, Aviateca. Business, she said, was picking up, but in the not distant past it had been terrible. For two years they had not a single guest. Then the guerrillas came and burned down the hotel. She, her husband and her four children were left with the clothes they stood up in. I asked why the guerrillas had done it, for even if rich by local standards, they were clearly no plutocrats.

'Because my husband was the manager of the state airline here,' she said. 'It was nothing personal against us.'

They had rebuilt the hotel, necessity being the mother of fortitude. Even if the guerrillas came to burn it down again, the Englishwoman preferred to stay. Rather arson in Guatemala than order in Sussex. I understood completely.

The ruins of Tikal are the grandest, if not the most beautiful, in all Central America. Argument still rages as to which of the four horsemen caused the city's sudden abandonment; the mystery grips you and you wish you were an archaeologist capable of giving the definitive answer. It is a transcendental experience to watch the sun go down from the top of a tenth-century Mayan pyramid that rises above the jungle. But in my case, the curiosity produced by ruins is always short-lived. My mind begins to turn to lunch and dinner, or other unworthy subjects; I let my mind be side-tracked by lesser questions about the past. For example, at Tikal I wondered how Aldous Huxley, in *Beyond the Mexique Bay*, was able to give so fastidious a description of the ruins when every blurb biography of him describes him as nearly blind. Did he *feel* the pyramids? In which case, his rather purple prose was a considerable achievement.

But I hadn't come to Central America for ruins, at least not of the archaeological sort. The recent discovery that Mayan pyramid complexes were of more secular inspiration than anyone had previously imagined excited me less than the recollection by a peasant or an oligarch of Guatemala's recent past.

It was in the Ixil Triangle, where an Indian people called the Ixil, 50,000 strong, lived, that recent history had been most cruel. The ruins there were not enigmatic. So many villages were destroyed, so many people killed, so many fields abandoned, that the word 'genocide' has been used to describe what happened there. In the circumstances it might seem pedantic to object to its use; but it seems to me that the crime of genocide – the deliberate elimination of an entire people as an entity – is so serious that a word ought to be kept strictly apart for it. The Ixil people suffered terribly, but they were not exterminated.

Mike Shawcross ran a relief programme in the Ixil Triangle, and I went with him into the area several times during my months in Guatemala. Sometimes there were just a handful of us, at other times what seemed like a large delegation. In all, I visited about ten villages. The first was Páramos Chiquitos, a tiny settlement a few kilometres into the mountains off the road. A few villagers met us where the track from the village reached the road. We had brought them hundredweight sacks of *atol*, a nutritious porridge-like drink. These tiny men, scarcely two thirds my size, cheerfully lifted these sacks (to me almost immoveable) on to their backs, tied them round their waists and secured a headband round the sacks and their foreheads. Then they began to scamper up the sixty degree slopes while I – unloaded – gasped and puffed my way behind them, inwardly swearing never to walk in mountains again. Only the fear of looking ridiculous prevented me from bursting into tears.

We passed through near-vertical fields of maize and beans; I thought of the harvest and was ashamed of my feebleness. It was cold and there was a fine drizzle which made the track slippery and treacherous, but the Indians, tough and surefooted, kept going relentlessly forwards and upwards.

'From here,' they said to encourage us, 'it's on the flat.'

It was the flat for them, perhaps, who did not appear to notice slopes of sixty degrees even while carrying a hundredweight on their backs, but for me . . . only the appearance of Páramos Chiquitos on the brow of a hill an hour and a half after we started out forestalled an ignominious expression of despair.

The village was small. The villagers told us we were the first foreigners ever to visit it. During the troubles, Páramos Chiquitos had been destoyed – without difficulty, since the people owned little and their huts were highly combustible. The people would not say who had destroyed the village, but they said both sides in the conflict had killed. The villagers fled and had wandered for five years in the wilderness, some of them returning home only three months before our visit. Their huts were simple and provided little protection against the cold. Their clothes, too, were insufficient, in many cases mere rags. The only help they had received from the authorities was roofing: 800 sheets of zinc, brought four at a time from the roadside down below, requiring 200 journeys. So far, they had had no time to use it. They were pleased with the sacks of *atol*, and Mike asked them what other help they needed. Their requests were typical of those he received from villages trying to rebuild themselves after the war: first they wanted a teacher so that their children might learn, second they wanted seeds so that they might plant, third they wanted a water supply that they might drink safely and wash easily.

Mike believed it was wrong to do things *for* the Indians. In their dealings with the authorities he encouraged them to be persistent. A single letter of request to the Ministry of Education was never sufficient, but it was all the Indians ever wrote. They took bureaucratic silence as refusal. Except in rare instances, Mike provided them with seed but not with food. And in construction work, such as the installation of a portable water supply, he provided the materials and technical advice but the villagers had to supply the labour. To give while demanding nothing in return undermined their self-respect.

Before we left Páramos Chiquitos, the villagers insisted that we ate a meal. Though they had practically nothing, they gave of their best: two kinds of tortillas, freshly made and delicious, beans, some hard biscuits and sweet coffee (they apologised for not having milk to give us, and only a little sugar). This meal meant more than any sumptuous banquet. After all they had suffered, the Indians retained their kindness, their charm, their modesty, their faith in the goodness of others. Four and a half centuries ago, Fray Bartolome de las Casas wrote:

> God created these races [the native inhabitants of America] to be the simplest of men, without wickedness or guile, the most obedient and faithful to their natural lords or to the Christians whom they serve; the most humble, most patient, most peaceful and quiet . . . that there are in all the world.
>
> Unto these gentle lambs . . . came the Spaniards . . . as wolves, tigers and lions made cruel by many days of hunger.

But this is not how the army saw the Ixil or any other Indians, all of whom were suspect in its eyes because the guerrillas fought in the name of the Indians. The better to keep the Ixil under control, the army constructed several *polos de desarollo* (poles of development) in the Ixil Triangle. These are model villages, built on the sites of old villages destroyed by the army. They bear little resemblance to the original settlements, which were scattered anarchically among the lands owned by the inhabitants. The model villages, by contrast, are centralized and built on a strict grid pattern. The houses are no longer of adobe or thatch, but of wood and tin, and utterly uniform. Each house has an identical, tiny garden; water stands have been provided at regular intervals, and the villages have been electrified. When I remarked on the fearful symmetry of model villages, an army officer described them as *bien bonito* – very nice. He did not speak with irony: military minds like regularity, their aesthetics are those of the short-back-and-sides haircut. For them, disorder is ugliness.

These model villages have often been described as concentration camps. One of them, Tzalbal, has an army barracks overlooking it from a nearby hill, and in the early days the inhabitants of model villages were not allowed to leave without army permission. These villages are charmless and they enable much closer official super-vision of the peasantry then ever before; yet still I should hesitate to call them concentration camps, for in our century of horrors it remains important to grade the horrors justly.

Evil, like beauty, is in the eye of the beholder – at least to some extent. On one of our trips into the Ixil Triangle, we took with us a bearded North American who described himself as a political sculptor and solidarity worker. He was a serious man; he seemed to be of the opinion that to smile in Guatemala was to be deficient in sympathy with the people. As we walked towards one of the villages that the army had destroyed some years back, and to which the surviving villagers were now slowly returning, a helicopter flew by in the distance. Some minutes later, we saw a helicopter again. Whether it was the same helicopter or another was impossible to tell. But the solidarity worker jumped to the conclusion that there were scores of helicopters deployed in the region, supplied by his own government. He was yet another expert at getting behind appearances; for him, as for a psychoanalyst, nothing was what it seemed. When children played, for example, it was because deep down they were so wretched. All the same, there was no disguising his slight disappointment in Guatemala.

'They seem happy enough,' he said, referring to Guatemalans. 'Everything seems peaceful and normal. You see them smiling and laughing . . .'

In his disappointment there was just a hint of disapproval. The people were showing insufficient solidarity with the solidarity workers. The least they could have done to make the long journey south worthwhile was to *look* miserable.

A journalist was overheard asking to go to the worst model village there was. She wanted to go that same afternoon for she was leaving the next day. In the event, there was no one to take her.

'Never mind,' she said, deciding to sunbathe instead. 'I know what they're like already.'

Would her report be any less trivial than this item about Guatemala that appeared in a Canadian newspaper?

KILLER TOADS ATTACK TOWN

In a real-life drama more horrifying than the worst nightmare imagineable, a horde of huge and hungry toads went on a rampage in a remote Central American village, leaving a trail of bloodshed and destruction . . . The entire village of Sohalo, north of Antigua, was razed in the unprecedented and spine-chilling incident.

According to the story, hundreds of 'beserk 3 lb toads' charged through the village hurling themselves at walls and blinding babies with their poisonous skins. Has not Guatemala misfortunes enough without journalists to invent yet more?

Another time we went up to the Ixil Triangle with a young North American civil engineer who was going to help design a piping system to bring water to one of the villages. He seemed perfectly sensible and I was surprised to discover that he believed implicitly in the healing power of crystals. I wondered how it was possible for a man to go through a long and rigorous training, and for it not to affect the way he approached other subjects. The engineer had a problem with his marriage that was half the reason he came to Central America. He had read a book about the occult knowledge and wisdom of Mayan diviners, and decided to consult one of them about his problems. To this end, he went to Momostenango, a town said to have 300 such diviners (one in ten of all the men there). He found one without difficulty, who told him there was hope of reconciliation with his wife, but of course it required a large 'gift' to him, the diviner, and a follow-up visit with another such gift. These the engineer gladly gave him, and now he 'felt good about' his marriage. Of course, he was not able to disclose what the diviner had done, as disclosure would have vitiated it. My curiosity being aroused, I drove to Momostenango myself to consult one of the wise men. I didn't have a problem, so I resolved to make one up. I had the name of a particular magician to visit and asked the way to his house. But every man I asked was a magician too, and offered his help. In the end, I left Momostenango without consulting anyone because I couldn't think of a plausible problem, a lie I could tell without flinching, so perhaps the old Mayan magic worked after all.

Another of the visitors to the Ixil Triangle was a young man who had kitted himself out as though for the North Africa campaign, or rather as an actor in a film about the North Africa campaign. He let it be known he had seen a thing or two in his time and was always on the alert. Having served in the US Navy in Vietnam, he had been trained to sense aggression among those around him, and it was to his heightened awareness of danger, he said, that he owed his survival. He sensed evil as certain moths sensed pheromones, in one part per hundred billion, but somehow he never sensed that people were laughing at him.

He returned from the model village of Acul as bristling with experiences as a paranoid schizophrenic. Nothing had actually happened to him there and he had spoken to no one, but he detected menace hovering over the place like a cloud.

Acul is in a lost valley of paradisiacal beauty, in a glorious stadium of mountains. But only the whitewashed adobe church remains of the old village, which was scattered on the mountainsides. Now it is concentrated into a grid of brown wooden houses, in streets with names like *Avenida del Ejército*, and *Avenida de la Libertad* (Avenue of the Army, and Avenue of Liberty). Just before you reach Acul is a white farmhouse, set back in a field in which cattle graze. Here lives a ninety-six-year-old Italian, his memory unimpaired, his eyes still bright. He left Italy in 1913 to avoid conscription, and went to live in the United States. He hinted at political activities that made it advisable for him to leave. He bought the farm at Acul in 1938, and told stories of a visit by the dictator Ubico. When he, the owner of the farm, was eighty-eight years old, the guerrillas came and burnt it down. The arrival of the army, he said, saved his life. He lost all his possessions, all the objects to which long memories were attached. Now his house has been rebuilt but it remains bare: for who starts accumulating posessions to treasure at the age of eighty-eight?

The main complaint in Acul was the distance peasants now lived from their lands. Agricultural work was quite back-breaking enough without a daily trek to and from the fields. I had heard the same complaint in Tanzania where, at the whim of Julius Nyerere, Tanzanian peasants had been herded by force into consolidated villages and subjected to much closer political supervision than they had ever known before. Every event was, in theory, known to the Party representative and spy, and freedom of movement severely curtailed. Yet the very internationalists who found such a policy reprehensible or worse in Guatemala – where at least there had been a civil war to excuse it – had sung the praises of Nyerere for more than a decade.

For myself, I found the model villages unattractive, but I saw none of the barbed wire fences by which they were reportedly surrounded. In one village, I was drawn to the school by the sound of small children reciting lessons. There were two classrooms barely separated from each other by a partition; on the walls were children's paintings of birds and flowers and mountains, with none of the helicopters and guns and corpses which filled such pictures a few years ago, and which appeared in Amnesty International's reports. On the desks were books, paper and crayons. The children of this village were well-dressed and healthy; their laughter blew in gales through the school. These young Indians, both boys and girls, were learning to read, and were being taught to do so in both Ixil and Spanish. They were in the charge of two teachers who clearly loved them. I left the school with a spring in my step, never having felt more optimistic about the future of Guatemala.

Nearby was a carpentry workshop for older boys. It was well-equipped (funded from abroad) and useful furniture was made there. The teacher spoke *sotto voce* while his pupils pretended to continue their work. Yes, he said, it was true that until a year and a half ago the villagers could not leave the village without the written permission of the military. Things were better now: no permission was needed and for the moment there was peace.

'But I fear that it could all happen again,' he said, referring to the violence. 'And if it does, it will be worse than the first time.'

TWENTY-ONE

It is a slightly disconcerting experience in a country in which so many people have disappeared without trace to walk into a bookshop and find a book for sale which advertises itself as having sold more than 100,000 copies, and is entitled *Kidnapped by Extraterrestrials*.

To investigate more mundane kidnappings, I went near the end of my stay in Guatemala to the offices of *Grupo de Apoyo Mutual*, the Mutual Aid Group, or GAM. Its offices change location frequently for reasons of security; when I visited, they were in a bleak zone of Guatemala City where the wide streets were of dust and rubble, the houses flat and one-storey high, and the bars mere aids to the attainment of oblivion. Nothing grew there; it might have been a desert. But it was not the poorest part of the city by any means, and there were probably many who aspired to live there.

GAM is an organisation of people who have lost a close relative by abduction or murder, usually by the death squads or security forces. In some cases, the bodies are never found. GAM demands that all such crimes are elucidated and the perpetrators punished. It argues, with a cogency difficult to deny, that until this happens the rule of law in Guatemala will have no guarantee.

It is not, however, an organisation that has found universal favour in the country. The first two leaders were themselves murdered, and threats have been received ever since. When GAM is accused of demagoguery, the flesh of its leaders must creep. As I pulled up to GAM's offices, I was aware that the surrounding streets were nearly deserted and devoid of traffic, and that my arrival would have been obvious to any observer. Were the offices under surveillance? A man at a door in the house opposite watched me carefully. Whether he was a bored local gossip or a government agent (or both) I had no way of knowing. When I left the offices, he was still there. I checked in my rear-view mirror to see if I was followed, and, finding that I was not, I was surprised to discover that my relief was tinged by disappointment.

I knocked on the office door, which was made of iron. It was opened cautiously by a man in his fifties, dressed in the ill-fitting suit of a minor bureaucrat. He asked me to take a seat in the front room where a secretary sat at a desk. On the walls were posters demanding human rights and an end to unemployment. The man who opened the door to me was a member of GAM; his son, a student, had been abducted four years previously and had never been heard of again. The father had tried everything: interviews with the army and police commanders; writs of *habeas corpus*; he had even obtained an audience with the then president, General Mejía Victores. He was always told the same thing, that the matter was being looked into, there was no news for the present but as soon as something was known he would be informed. His face betrayed the hollowness of prolonged despair. He knew, of course, that his son was dead, but the absence of definite information allowed him just that glimmer of irrational, false hope that prevented him from mourning and hence from recovering. When you meet such a man, the statistics of death and disappearance take on a new meaning.

While we were talking, the telephone rang. The secretary took a cyclostyled form and began to ask questions. Where was the victim last seen? At what time? Who was he with? Were the abductors armed? How many abductors were there? What was the registration number of their vehicle? Her manner was practised.

A new disappearance was being reported to GAM. An agronomy student who had returned from foreign exile a year ago (he had been a student activist) had been abducted from a bus stop by a group of heavily armed men that very morning, in full view of many witnesses. In such cases – there was at least one every day, said the father with the missing son – GAM alerted the foreign and domestic press, informed the Guatemalan Procurator of Human Rights and the President of the Republic, sought writs of *habeas corpus*, and gave whatever assistance it could to the victim's family. It had been successful in very few cases, if any at all, but what choice was there but to continue the efforts? And this case was not one of GAM's few successes: the mutilated corpse of the missing student was found next day by the roadside some miles from where he was abducted.

The vice-president of GAM, Isabel de Castañon, arrived. She was a teacher whose husband had been abducted and murdered; she still taught, and worked for GAM after classes. She was short, with raven-black hair and attractive, vivacious dark eyes that shone with purpose, but not humourlessly. Her movements were fiercely energetic, her speech fluent, forceful and very much to the point. No one could have mistaken her small stature for insignificance. She was a formidable person, in the best possible way.

Her arrival coincided with that of two delegations from the United States, from St Louis and Colorado. Among them were a couple of nuns in mufti who were, however, still recognisably nuns. The delegations were on a human rights tour of Central America, next stop El Salvador. I admit that such delegations do much good, that in all probability they forestall even worse violations than already occur, but I cannot help remarking that they are generally composed of somewhat unattractive people. They dress drably, they do not smile, generally they are thin, and their lips are bloodless.

I had a strange feeling that I had seen these delegations somewhere before, as in a way I had. For I had visited the archives of the Nazarene Church Mission, which contained photographs of missionaries from the early years of this century. There they were with the same pinched expressions, the same lips stretched bloodless with disapproval, the same consciousness of doing good. The women in particular had not changed.

While I had waited for the arrival of the vice-president, I had read the quarterly bulletins of GAM for the last year, and counted up the murders in Guatemala (not all of them, surely, political). When the American delegation sat down, preparing to tut-tut and shake their heads with that sense of outrage that gives the same warm glow inside as a whisky on a winter's evening, I longed to disturb their complacency by announcing to them that if during the last thirty years Guatemala had suffered the present murder rate of Washington DC, about 30,000 more Guatemalans would have died by violence: but in that thirty years, Guatemala had fought a full-scale civil war. I said nothing, however, because I did not want to upset the proceedings.

Isabel de Castañon spoke to us, and her words were a clarion call to justice. There was no self-indulgence in what she said, no simulation or straining after indignation. It was tragic experience that gave her words force. With each new case of disappearance, her personal memories were reawakened and strengthened her resolve. She thanked everyone present for their interest and support, and said it was vital for GAM's work. She was witheringly scornful of President Cerezo's prevarications over human rights and his cowardly failure to punish the wrongdoers. But, somewhat surprisingly, she said that what was needed above all in Guatemala was an awareness among the people of the value of human rights. It was not fear alone that prevented them from supporting GAM: it was indifference also. The problem was not only one of a handful of evil men, but also one of immemorial attitudes to life that were still prevalent. Few people in Guatemala cared about other people's rights until personal tragedy struck. That was why foreign pressure was so important; it was the only protection Guatemalans had. As for herself, when she said she would never abandon the struggle for justice, she made it clear that she had long overcome any inhibitions caused by fear. Such steadfastness is beyond all praise.

The next day, I had an appointment with a captain in the public relations department of the army. His office was on the sixth floor of the Military Institute of Social Security. In the same building is the computer centre of the Bank of the Army, a bank that one suspects has achieved its rapid expansion not exclusively by shrewd commercial activity. I arrived a few minutes early and took the opportunity to look round the nearby National Palace, the grandest building in the city, built on the orders and to the taste of Ubico. (It is the argument of all apologists for this dictator that the best buildings in the capital were constructed during his rule, and have survived several earthquakes.) The National Palace is of green stone, in Italian Renaissance style with a few Hollywood elements thrown in. The principal reception hall is an elaborate throne room where the President of Guatemala receives the credentials of ambassadors. Throughout the palace are murals depicting historical scenes, or rather, scenes that are supposedly historical. They were painted when history was still unproblematical, full of glory and not yet a tale of uninterrupted woe. The handsome Spaniards defeated the valiant, gentlemanly Indians in fair contest. It was all rather like a cricket match, with the winners taking the land for the next four hundred and fifty years.

The palace is the nerve centre of the government, with the office of the presidency and several ministries, each with its knot of petitioners outside, ready to present their requests to the eternal prevaricators within. On the flat roof of the palace, among the electronic communications equipment, are a couple of machine gun nests. In the tiled corridors below civil servants assemble in little groups to discuss matters of ultimate national importance. In the banqueting hall I found a series of stained-glass windows, each with a figure hypostasising virtues such as *Labor, Libertas, Iustitia, Probitas, Concordia*, etc. Unfortunately, all but one had been destroyed by the blast of a car bomb outside the palace some years before. They had never been repaired and all that remained of *Progressus* was his feet.

I met the captain. I had expected someone bluff and cordial in a slightly menacing way; on the contrary, he was slight and wore black-rimmed spectacles; he was nervous rather than hail-fellow-well-met, and had the appearance of a studious intellectual. At school he would have been a member of the chess club, and probably the target of bullies. All the time I was with him, I wondered how he had survived the *Escuela Politécnica;* he must have been tougher than he looked. Did he know about, was he responsible for, the atrocities committed by his army?

On his desk was the latest report by Amnesty International. I asked him what he thought of it. Did he think, as many officers did, that Amnesty was a communist front organisation dedicated to the overthrow of western civilisation? He replied that he had not yet read the report, but did not discount the possibility that it contained some truth. In any war, he said, there were excesses, soldiers who went wild or lost their nerve. Excesses did not seem to me quite the word for the destruction of so many villages, for so many killings. They had been, rather, part of a deliberate policy to drain the sea in which the guerrillas were the fish, as General Ríos Montt put it, alluding to Mao Tse-tung. In doing so, many innocent people had died. One's attitude to the war, therefore, depended on the answers one gave to two questions:

1. Was the *status quo* worth preserving?
2. Was what the guerrillas fought for worthwhile?

My answer to both these questions is no. A plague, then, on both your houses: except that a choice between them has been made inevitable, because the guerrillas will not give up until they have power (one does not fight ten years in the jungle for the chance to lose the next elections) and there is no prospect of the army defeating them completely. My admiration therefore is all the greater for those Guatemalans who, in practical ways, try to relieve the suffering the war has caused, knowing that their work is but the staunching of a bleeding wound.

The captain, to prove to me that what was written about the army was one-sided, produced from his drawer a series of horrifying photographs of the mutilated bodies of soldiers. They were captured and tortured by the EGP, he said; some had had their tongues cut

out, others had been burned, others had the letters 'EGP' slashed
into their flesh. He showed me pictures of a village in which the EGP
had killed twenty inhabitants; their corpses were strewn in the road.
My hand trembled as I held these horrible pictures. Of course they
proved nothing beyond the fact that an atrocity had taken place: a
corpse with the letters EGP carved into it could have been produced
as easily by the army as by the EGP itself. I asked whether the army
had published these photographs and disseminated them widely.

'We do not have many resources,' he replied. 'And no one would
believe us. The world's press is not on our side.'

Was this self-pity, paranoia or the truth? In my opinion, there was
enough truth in what he said to keep the fires of paranoia burning.

I bade the captain goodbye. I had formed the impression he did
not quite believe in what he was doing. Part of the work of his
department was to post the roadsides of Guatemala with absurd
hoardings picturing soldiers in combat dress, charging towards the
traveller or posing in an otherwise aggressive manner, above slogans
such as, 'An Army Always Ready'. Yes, but ready for what? How
could such posters fail to have the effect opposite to that intended?

Where better to escape the tensions of a civil war than a
bookshop? Bookish people, whatever their faults, are generally
gentle, or at least not given to violence. The *Librería Marquense* is
one of the best in the city, and the owner, Don Gustavo, is probably
the largest second-hand bookseller in the country. One morning, he
took time off work to tell me the story of his life. I had feared that he
might find my questions intrusive, but my fears were groundless. A
man of extreme modesty, it had never occurred to Don Gustavo that
his life was of interest to others, and he was delighted to discover this
was not so.

We drove to a café in the Tenth Zone, along the Avenida de la
Reforma, where stands the United States embassy, the mirrored-
glass headquarters of the Banco del Café, and the Guatemalan offices
of giant international corporations. Among the offices nestle
boutiques, discotheques and restaurants patronised by the rich. Our
café was the least pretentious in the district, where we could talk
quietly and without interruption.

Don Gustavo grew up in a village near San Marcos (hence the
Marquense of the *Librería Marquense*), the third of nine children of
poor peasants. At the age of six he remembered thinking that babies
were brought by aeroplanes that occasionally flew over the village.
He rode in a motor vehicle for the first time when he was eight and

swore to himself that he would work hard to own a car himself.
Every day he was sent out with other children to look after pigs in a
field, but one day, while the children were playing football as usual,
one of the pigs strayed and returned home, so that Gustavo's father
knew that his son was failing in his duty. Thereafter he was sent to
work in the fields, which was much harder work and which he hated.

He went to school only for a very short time, and was teased there
because his clothes were so ragged. His father could not afford to
buy him either textbooks or exercise books. Until he left school aged
twelve, he had never owned a pair of shoes. To own some shoes was
then his greatest ambition: he was one of only two children in the
school without them. But his father did not have the three *quetzales*
they cost (in those days, the *quetzale* equalled the dollar). The
purchase of his first pair of shoes was therefore one of the greatest
days of his life.

Throughout his childhood, he had to collect the night-soil. He
was often beaten to make him work harder. His elder brother was
not beaten, even though he worked much less – the oldest son was
regarded as someone special by the family. It was unjust, and the
young Gustavo knew it; but now he harboured no bitterness, and
felt only sorrow that his father had been forced by poverty to behave
in this way.

Every Sunday, Gustavo received one or two centavos, with which
he could buy one or two oranges. When he was thirteen, a rich
family from San Marcos with a workshop in Guatemala City needed
a house servant and general factotum. The job was offered to his
elder brother, but he did not want to leave the village for the city, so
Gustavo was sent instead. He slept on the floor of a corridor, or on a
table, and was always hungry. The family fed him only a few beans
and tortillas; Don Gustavo related with a shame he still felt that he
started to sneak food whenever he was able. And he told me
something that shook me deeply: he was fed from the same plate as
the family's dog.

For the first six months, he was not paid at all; for the next six and
a half years fifteen *quetzales* a month. After seven years, his pay was
increased to thirty *quetzales* a month, of which he sent twenty home.
By then, he was a full-time mechanic in the family's workshop. He
worked from six in the morning to ten or eleven at night. On
Sundays he was allowed some free time, but had to return to the
workshop by seven in the evening.

Don Gustavo agreed that the family had exploited him, yet he was grateful to them also. They were evangelicals, and allowed no smoking, drinking or swearing. They instilled in him the virtue of hard work. Many young men who came to Guatemala City from the countryside fell into bad ways, and they had prevented that.

His release from the family's control was in the manner of a fairy story. Every month a Chinaman called Francisco Lo, who was the owner of the workshop building, used to call to collect the rent. Several times he noticed that Gustavo was left alone in charge of the family business, and eventually asked him about his conditions of employment. Mr Lo asked Gustavo to come and work for him. At first, Gustavo refused, saying he could not let down his present employers, but Mr Lo prevailed, promising shorter hours, time for Gustavo to educate himself, and wages of seventy *quetzales* a month. He told Gustavo to be at his shop at six o'clock the next Monday morning.

This was by way of a test of Gustavo's reliability. There was no public transport so early in the morning, and Mr Lo's shop was two hours away on foot. Setting out at four o'clock, before dawn, Gustavo arrived on time, to Mr Lo's surprise and pleasure. He gave Gustavo a proper room, where he could hide from the wrath of his former employers when they searched for him.

Francisco Lo opened a bank account for Gustavo and told him to go to night school after work, from six until ten. He encouraged him to sell textbooks to his fellow students, some of whom were fifty years old and taking elementary education for the first time. At his first attempt he sold ten, making a profit of twenty per cent. Next Mr Lo lent him money to buy fifty textbooks, and then a hunded.

Mr Lo set up a *librería* in the shop next to his and made Gustavo the manager. In the first two months, he earned 125 *quetzales* a month, then 200. When he was put on commission he earned 400. Two years later, Mr Lo told him to consider himself half-owner of the shop, with a half-share of the profits. In three months he earnt 6000 *quetzales*.

By then, Gustavo was taking a commercial course at night school. A friend at the school told him not to be stupid, everyone knew that Chinamen were swindlers, and therefore he should steal from the till while he could. After all, the Chinaman would never know. But Gustavo told Mr Lo what the student had said; Mr Lo took him to his back room, where the safe was, and gave him the keys, saying that he should take whatever he needed whenever he needed it.

Gustavo then got married, and Francisco Lo gave him as a

wedding present all his share of the profits in the *librería* since it started, which he had been putting aside for precisely this event.

Shortly afterwards, Mr Lo's troubles began. He felt a pain in his jaw where twenty years before he had had an operation for the removal of a cancer. The pain worsened and he was unable to work. His own business declined. The recurrence of the cancer was declared inoperable and he retired to his house some fifty kilometres from the city. On 4 February 1976, this house was destroyed by an earthquake. He, his wife and his six children miraculously escaped but now he was nearly a ruined man, racked by great pain. In 1978, Don Gustavo drove him every other day in a 1954 Austin from the village to the Cancer Institute for palliative treatment. Soon Mr Lo could no longer eat and he had to be admitted to hospital. In October 1978, aged sixty-five, he told Don Gustavo that he was going to die. The doctor, mistaking Gustavo for Mr Lo's son, said, 'Your father has little time left'.

Mr Lo's wife was expecting another baby. On his deathbed, Mr Lo said to Don Gustavo *'Voy a suplicar un gran favor'* ('I am going to ask a big favour'). He told Gustavo that all his money was gone, having spent it all on treatment and living these last few years. He asked Gustavo to build a house for his family and to look after them until they were old enough to look after themselves. On 12 November 1978 he died. His son was born a month later.

Don Gustavo began to build the house the following year. He had to stop for a time because of lack of funds, but by the end of 1980 the house was built. Francisco Lo's eldest son, also called Francisco, had grown up, and now ran a successful business of his own. Don Gustavo's help was no longer needed.

It was in the early 1980s that Don Gustavo expanded into second-hand books. Professors and teachers at San Carlos University were fleeing for their lives or being killed in increasing numbers. One way and another, their book collections went up for sale, and Don Gustavo, with no feeling of glee, bought them. He became a collector on his own account, anxious that the books should not all be dispersed. Life in Guatemala was now better than it had been. In his bookshop he showed me items that a few years ago it would have been dangerous, possibly fatal, to display. In those days, soldiers came into his shop and subjected his shelves to military-style lit. crit.

Don Gustavo spoke as a man unembittered by his experience of life, who spoke ill of no man. His only regret was that, having retained the habit of working from morning till night, he had seen less of his children than he would have wished. His ambitions were to learn an Indian language (though he looked wholly Indian, he spoke only Spanish), to endow libraries in those Guatemalan towns without them (he had started with San Marcos), and to study the history of his country.

How had a man born in poverty and who had been made to eat from the same plate as a dog conceived a love for books and learning? What was the secret of his serenity?

'My life has convinced me,' he said, 'that if you do good, good will be returned to you; but if you do evil, evil will be returned to you.'

And everyone who knows Don Gustavo knows that he lives by this belief.

TWENTY-TWO

For anyone who has lived in Guatemala, other countries, by contrast, are lacking in savour. The problem confronting the people who want to promote a prosperous tourist industry is how to take out this over-strong flavour so that only the safely picturesque remains.
Norman Lewis, *The Volcanoes Above Us*.

I had spent eight months in Guatemala, and it was time to leave. The longer I stayed, the less certain was I that I understood the country I had chosen to write about; I left before the increasing intricacy of what I found there sapped my confidence altogether. Indeed, I began to wonder what it meant to understand a country. Did it mean to have a nodding acquaintance with all its social classes, to have interviewed its president, to know its past, to predict its future? Suppose a Guatemalan were to write a book about England after a stay of only seven months: should I not laugh at his errors, were I not angered by the presumption of his enterprise?

In Guatemala, the lives and beliefs of half the population remain opaque and mysterious to the other half, let alone to complete outsiders. The Indians are enclosed in an hermetic world of their own, and the visitor to Guatemala is condemned to see them entirely from the exterior, in a Technicolor but silent movie. Nevertheless, the visitor's sympathy is now entirely with the Indian, though his sympathy is that of intellectual fashion rather than of genuine understanding, a reflection of the general loss of confidence in the superiority of western civilisation (a word that now always appears in inverted commas in writing about Guatemala). Seventy years ago the fashion was for progress – roads, railways, sanitation, industry, and the export of bananas. Now the fashion is for Mayan cosmology, the simple life, and hand-woven textiles. Neither fashion was, or is, entirely honest.

Before I went to Guatemala, I never realized the great wisdom of the words inscribed over the entrance to the Academy in ancient Athens: know thyself. It seemed to me that many visitors (I am not talking about simple tourists) deceived themselves as to their own motives and emotions. They used Guatemala as a kind of psychotherapy, but not to achieve self-knowledge; rather, the country was for them a Disneyland of horror, where the attraction was not delight but moral outrage. Problems at home – with marriages, with crime on the streets, with the meaninglessness that material comfort brings – were insoluble, but here in Guatemala, at least, it was possible to be on the side of the angels.

Guatemala was the wish-fulfilment of the strangest of dreams: a country where everything that existed was utterly bad, yet where a capacity for infinite good awaited liberation by violence. It was not sufficient that the country had just lived through a horrifying civil war: every fact, every statistic, had to be adduced to prove that nothing had ever changed for the better. Otherwise the dream lay shattered, and Guatemala was as other countries are, a realm of dilemma and uncertainty.

In *Guatemala: Eternal Spring, Eternal Tyranny*, Jean-Marie Simon says that forty per cent of Guatemalan children die before the age of five. There can be little doubt of the impression with which she wishes to leave the reader, for she gives the figure not once but twice; it is no misprint. Alas, she fails to notice that it has the mathematical consequence, if the figure she herself gives for Guatemalan life expectancy is correct, that the average age at death of the sixty per cent of Guatemalans fortunate enough to survive childhood must be at least eighty-six. I have seen her figure for childhood deaths given elsewhere: in Ikle's book, for example, about the involvement of the CIA in the plot to overthrow the Arbenz government. But there it referred to conditions before 1944. Jean-Marie Simon wants us to believe, as she herself wants to believe, that nothing has changed for the better in four and a half decades.

In this, she is at one with the great majority of Guatemalan intellectuals. They, too, need to believe that all is for the worst in this, the worst of all possible worlds. In numerous recent works by members of the Guatemalan intelligentsia, I do not recall a single reference to progress: progress that is writ as large upon the country as the continued existence of daunting problems. Nowhere, for instance, have I seen it mentioned that in the last thirty years the life expectancy of Guatemalans has risen by a third, or that the proportion of Guatemalans entering higher education has risen three times in twenty years. Yet these are facts in precisely the same way that stastistics of hunger and deprivation are facts.

Of course, Guatemala is not the only country in which present problems loom larger than past progress; historical miseries never console for contemporary woes. And it is not only in Guatemala that intellectuals seek problems as Pooh Bear sought honey. Yet there is a peculiar, determined quality to this denial of progress by both foreign and Guatemalan intellectuals that throws light on the existential void in modern life that is felt in the rest of the world as much as in Guatemala.

Most people seek meaning and certainty in their lives, especially when they are young (and most Guatemalans *are* young). Once upon a time, religion would have sufficed: when empirical enquiry was despised, revelation provided truth, and divine providence explained the existence of evil when technical capacity to change the world was very limited. But if the answers provided by religion do not any longer command assent among intellectuals, the questions do not thereby go away. A meaning to existence that transcends the petty flux of daily experience is still ardently desired.

Where better to find this meaning than in social doctrines? The church itself, ever less certain of its dogmas, turns increasingly to politics and sociology. And what more attractive doctrine could there be than one which assures young intellectuals that upon them rests the salvation of their country? Here is meaning, purpose, certainty and self-importance all in one.

The acknowledgement that some improvement has taken place in Guatemala over the last four decades would threaten the foundations of the new faith. This is because such improvement has not been brought about by good government: for everyone is agreed there has been no good government in Guatemala. The question then arises – horrible, from the intellectual's point of view – of whether progress is not possible without the activities of intellectuals to initiate and guide it. Questions even more subversive of the new faith present themselves: does not the humble teacher or vaccinator of children (both of whom I have seen at work in the remotest Guatemalan villages), or even the repairer of punctured tyres, contribute more to the welfare of humanity than the writer of revolutionary verses? And if progress has in fact occurred, largely as the result of the irresistible spread throughout the world of technical civilisation, is it not at least as much the duty of the intellectual to prevent deterioration as to promote improvement? Naturally, it is much easier for the intellectual not to think of these things, for him simply not to recognise that any progress has occurred. That way he has no existential void still to face: a void as unbearable as the sun to look at for very long.

This is not a problem that assails traditional Catholics, whose faith is staunch and whose ceremonies are splendid. During *Semana Santa* in Antigua, hundreds of thousands of people gather to watch the processions. On the night before Good Friday, Antigueños decorate their cobbled streets with flowers and coloured sawdust, working them into exquisite but ephemeral patterns to be crushed underfoot as the processions pass. Their meticulous labour is half religious devotion, half municipal pride. They guard their creations with tender solicitude, keeping the flowers fresh and the sawdust from blowing away with a gentle spray of water, until the processions approach through swirling clouds of incense. First come the bronze-complexioned Romano-Indian centurions with papier-mâché breastplates and helmets surmounted by plumes that are obviously the heads of household brooms dyed red. Then come censer-bearers, adding to the odour of sanctity with fresh clouds of incense from censers that they swing lugubriously on long chains, and penitents in purple satin habits and white gloves, eighty of whom take it in turns to carry the several tons of statuary on wooden platforms, swaying from side to side as they go. On these platforms, angels weep as Christ carries the Cross on His knees. Behind them follow the clergy, gorgeously clad according to rank, protected from such sun as filters through the incense by silken canopies held over them by young boys. And finally come the brass bands, playing funeral music and dead marches that wrench the heart despite – or because of – their discordance.

Early in the morning of Good Friday, before dawn, two thieves are selected at the local prison. They are dressed in the costume of Roman plebeians and light wooden crucifixes are attached to their backs. They spend the rest of the day following one of the processions, most of the time with their arms spread across the crucifixess, but with breaks from time to time for a rest, a chat and even a cigarette. At two in the afternoon, they are publicly pardoned on the steps of the cathedral and set at liberty.

On this Good Friday, a more villainous pair of thieves could scarcely have been imagined, a pair to delight Lombroso, the Italian physiognomist who thought criminals were detectable by their facial features and expressions alone. The thieves in the holy procession were short and wiry; they had long stubble on their chins; a few rotten pegs for teeth in the black hole of their mouths; low, sloping foreheads; eyes too close together and cunning grins. I should not have placed much faith in their abjuration of wrongdoing.

It would be easy, of course, to mock the ceremony of forgiveness on the cathedral steps. How were the thieves who were pardoned chosen from among the others? Surely corruption must have been involved. And what could the ceremony have done to stem the rising tide of crime in Guatemala? Nothing. As for the Easter processions, were they not a commercial opportunity for the ladies who sold pork crackling, tortillas, ice creams and religious trinkets from scores of little stalls behind the crowds that lined the streets? Of the hundreds of purple-robed penitents, how many would not sin again on the very next day?

But Man, besides being a natural backslider, is a ceremonial animal; all societies have their symbols, even those that live by social doctrines claiming to be wholly rational. For myself, though not religious, I prefer sacred ceremony to profane, and not only for aesthetic reasons: for by acknowledging something greater than himself, Man accepts limits to his own power, at least in theory. The symbolic reenactment of universal forgiveness, hypocritical as it may be, is preferable in my eyes to the celebration of political power or military triumph.

In Guatemala, one learns to mistrust lovers of humanity. Too often, their conception of love is Nechaev's: 'to love the people is to drive it into a hail of bullets.' Hatred of the rich is a stronger emotion than sympathy for the poor; and often this hatred is self-hatred. The leader of the Organisation of the People in Arms, for example, is the son of Guatemala's only Nobel Prize winner, Miguel Angel Asturias. The New Jerusalem will not be builded here.

Nor anywhere else. The bravest and most noble are not those who take up arms, but those who are decent despite everything; who improve what it is in their power to improve, but do not imagine themselves to be saviours. In their humble struggle is true heroism.

INDEX

Acatenango, 6, 24
Acul, 229–30
Agua, 6–7, 11, 24
Alvarado, Pedro de, 32, 61
Angel Asturias, Miguel, 66–7, 246
Antigua, 5, 7, 10–12, 20–21, 57–8, 135, 151, 156, 208, 244–5
Arana, Colonel, 205
Arbenz, President Jacobo, 18, 34, 149, 205, 206, 243
Arévalo, President Juan Jose, 14–15, 16, 34, 102
Atitlán, 151
Ayerdis, Julio César, 117

Barrios, General Rufino, 17, 33, 63, 66, 102, 137, 167
Batista, 102
Bauer, Lord, 44
Belize, 193, 203
Bill, 123
Blake, Nick, 177–9
Blake, Sam, 178
Bogota, 50
Borge, Comandante Tomás, 129–30
Bradlaugh, Charles, 61
Brady, Mr and Mrs, 24–7
Burma, 121
Bush, President, 177, 178

Caal, Pop, 12–13
Cabezas, Omar, 115–16
Cabrera, Estrada, 14–32
Cambranes, J. C., 35–6
Carlos, 101–4, 107–10
Carmen, 221–4
Carter, President, 193
Casas, Fray Bartoleme de las, 24, 227
Castañon, Isabel de, 233–5
Castillo Armas, President, 18, 34, 149, 204, 206
Castro, Fidel, 90, 102
Catano, Quirio, 69
Catarina, Doña, 184

Cerezo Arevalo, Marco Vinicio, 212, 217, 234
Cerro de Oro, 172
Chacaya, 172
Chajul, 149, 199
Chalatenango, 91–4, 97, 98–9
Chel, 196
Chiquimula, 66–7
Chuil, 59–60
Cindy, 118–22, 126
Coatepeque, 217
Coban, 221
Colegio Americano, 47–50
Colville, Lord, 57
Comalpa, 204
Contras, 107, 111, 115, 126, 132
Cortés, Hernan, 32, 105
Costa Rica, 108, 109, 115
Cuba, 101, 117, 123, 148

Dalton, Roque, 83
Darío, Ruben, 215–16
De la Rue and Co, Thomas, 104
Diaz C., Dr Fernando J., 67
Diaz Muller, Mauricio, 117
Duarte Napoléon, José, 84
Dulce Nombre de María, 98
Dulles, John Foster, 34

El Salvador, 66, 74, 78–100, 102
Engles, 137
Enrique Arenas, Don, 176–7, 181–2, 183, 199–201, 204, 209
Escuela Politécnica, 135–40, 149, 194, 236
Escuintla, 142
Esquipulas, 66, 68–73, 74, 111
Estelí, 111–15
Evans-Pritchard, Ambrose, 158

Fanon, 137
Federico, Don, 218–20
Finca el Manzano, 217, 219–20
Finca la Perla, 176, 177, 181–5, 188–202, 204, 205, 209

Finca San Francisco, 61, 134
Flores, 92, 93, 95–8, 224
Ford, Henry, 83
Francisco Marroquín University, 43–6
Fuego, 6, 24
Fuentes, Ýdigoras, 18
Fuentes y Guzmán, Antonio, 7, 12

Garcia Bauer, Carlos, 192
García family, 20–2
George (the English physiologist), 174
George (the German artist), 154–6
Girón, Father Andrés, 211–17
Granada, 111
Grosz, Georg, 153
Guatemala City, 50–6, 121, 135, 148, 150, 160, 169, 171, 232
Guevara, Che, 137, 207–8
Gulf of Fonesca, 104–5
Gustavo, Don, 237–41
Guzmán Bockler, Carlos, 13

Havana, 101, 102
Hegel, 41, 192
Hernández Martínez, General Maximiliano, 83, 97
Himmler, Heinrich, 181
Hitler, Adolf, 83
Honduras, 101–6, 132
Huehuetanango, 211
Huxley, Aldous, 5, 151, 225

Ikle, 243
Ilom, 176, 199
Isabel, Doña, 13, 18–19
Ixcán, 176, 193, 199, 209
Ixil Triangle, 177, 225, 227, 228, 229

Jaime, 74–7
Jirón, H., José Benito, 117

La Estrella, 187
Lake Atitlán, 151, 154
Lake Managua, 119
Lanzas, Oswaldo, 117
Lenin, 137
León, 111, 115–17
Lewis, Norman, 53, 242
Lo, Francisco, 239–40
Locke, 41
London, 50
Lucas García, General Benedicto, 141, 146–50

Lucas García, General Romeo, 49, 141, 146
Luis, 185–6, 191, 198
Luis Arenas, Don, 176, 180, 183, 197, 199–210

Madrid, Miguel de la, 49
Managua, 107, 109, 110, 111, 114, 115, 119–31
Manuel Arévalo, Juan, 141, 205
Mao, 137, 236
Mark, 50–6
Marnham, Patrick, 59, 61
Martínez Pelaez, Severo, 7, 35, 203
Marx, 137
Maslow, Jonathan, 11–12, 59
Matagalpa, 132
Merton, Thomas, 212
Metapán, 74–9
Miami, 130
Mólina, Father Uriel, 124–6
Momostenango, 229
Mozambique, 103, 113, 121

Nebaj, 177, 184, 188, 189, 196, 200, 202
Nechaev, 246
Neruda, Pablo, 8–9
New Orleans, 146
New York, 51
Nicaragua, 3, 101, 104, 107
Nueva Concepción, 212–13, 214, 217
Nyerere, Julius, 230

Oazaca, 71

Panajachel, 151–3, 157, 158
Panama Canal, 5
Paraguay, 103
Páramos Chiquitos, 225, 226
Paraxtut, 59–61
Paris, 50
Patzun, 151
Payeras, Mario, 176, 180, 197, 199
Pedro de Bethancour *see* Pedro, Hermano
Pedro, Hermano, 21–4
Perera, Victor, 59, 160
Perez, Señora, 219
Petén, 221, 222
Petén Itza, 224

Quiché, 146

Ramírez, Sergio, 215

Rasch, Dr Otto, 140
Reagan, Nancy, 159
Reagan, Ronald, 49, 200
Rene Castillo, Otto, 39–40
Ríos Montt, General Efraín, 137, 141–6, 161, 216, 236
Romero, Archbishop, 101
Romero, Jose Jimenez, 164
Roosevelt, Theodore, 215
Rother, Father Stanley, 158, 160
Rubi P., Francisco, 117

Salama, 67–8
San Andrés Ixtapa, 167–8
Sandalistas, 118
Sandinistas, 107, 115, 116, 119, 123, 124
Sandino, General, 119–20
Sandoval Alarcón, Mario, 141
San Juan Sacatepequez, 136
San Lucas Tolimán, 161, 162
San Miguel, 99–100
San Pablo, 160
San Pedro, 151
San Pedro de la Laguna, 159–62
San Salvador, 79, 80–91, 99, 103, 121
Santa Delfina, 184, 199, 200
Santa Rosa de Lima, 100
Santiago Atitlán, 158–62, 164–76
Santiago de los Caballeros de Guatemala *see* Antigua
Sayaxché, 221, 222, 223, 224
Shawcross, Mike, 58–62, 177, 181–8, 225–7
Simon, Jean-Marie, 47, 131, 152, 193, 243

Skinner-Klee, Don Jorge, 202–7
Sohalo, 228
Sololá, 165–6
Somoto, 110–11
Somoza, 111, 112, 115, 119, 123, 124
Spielberg, Stephen, 70
Steve, 118–22, 126
Swaggart, Jimmy, 189

Tanzania, 121, 230
Tikal, 224–5
Tiquisate, 211, 212, 213
Todos Santos, 61
Tolimán, 151, 169
Trujillo, 206
Turcios Lima, 201
Tzalbal, 227

Ubico, General Jorge, 15, 16–18, 33, 37, 42, 97, 150, 230, 235
Ungo, Guillermo 84,
University of San Carlos, 37–43, 48, 51, 240

Vessey, Father, 159–63, 164, 165, 166
Victores, General Mejia, 57, 233
Victoria, Doña, 185, 189

Warhol, Andy, 92
Wheelock, Jaime, 124
Wyld Ospina, Carlos, 102

Zacapa, 66
Zamora, Dr Ruben, 82, 84, 85

Y C^u
C

I

M E X

Usumacinta

M

16°N

G U A T E

Chixoy

▲ *3396*
▲ *3993* • Nebaj
Cobá

• Huehuetenango

P A C I F I C

▲ *4210*
• Totonicapán

Quezaltenango •
Sololá • • Tecpán
• Chimaltenango
Gua
◉

▲ *3596*
Antigua •

• Retalhuleu
Mazatenango •
▲ *3752*

O C E A N
• Escuintla

N
• Chiquimulilla

Guazacapáno

Scale 1:3,055,000

Miles 0 10 20 30 40 50 100 150

Kilometres 0 50 100 200

Spot heights in metres